Courthouse Democracy and Minority Rights

Courthouse Democracy and Minority Rights

Same-Sex Marriage in the States

ROBERT J. HUME

OXFORD
UNIVERSITY PRESS

OXFORD
UNIVERSITY PRESS

Oxford University Press is a department of the University of Oxford. It furthers the University's objective of excellence in research, scholarship, and education by publishing worldwide.

Oxford   New York
Auckland   Cape Town   Dar es Salaam   Hong Kong   Karachi   Kuala Lumpur   Madrid
Melbourne   Mexico City   Nairobi   New Delhi   Shanghai   Taipei   Toronto

With offices in
Argentina   Austria   Brazil   Chile   Czech Republic   France   Greece   Guatemala   Hungary
Italy   Japan   Poland   Portugal   Singapore   South Korea   Switzerland   Thailand
Turkey   Ukraine   Vietnam

Oxford is a registered trade mark of Oxford University Press in the UK and certain other countries.

Published in the United States of America by
Oxford University Press
198 Madison Avenue, New York, NY 10016

Library of Congress Cataloging-in-Publication Data
Hume, Robert J.
  Courthouse democracy and minority rights : same-sex marriage in the states/
  Robert J. Hume.
    pages cm
  Includes bibliographical references and index.
  ISBN 978-0-19-998217-2 (hardback)
1. Same-sex marriage—Law and legislation—United States—States. 2. Political questions and judicial power—United States—States. 3. Constitutional law—United States—States. I. Title.
  KF539.H86 2013
  346.7301'68—dc23

                                                                    2012043763

Note to Readers
This publication is designed to provide accurate and authoritative information in regard to the subject matter covered. It is based upon sources believed to be accurate and reliable and is intended to be current as of the time it was written. It is sold with the understanding that the publisher is not engaged in rendering legal, accounting, or other professional services. If legal advice or other expert assistance is required, the services of a competent professional person should be sought. Also, to confirm that the information has not been affected or changed by recent developments, traditional legal research techniques should be used, including checking primary sources where appropriate.

(Based on the Declaration of Principles jointly adopted by a Committee of the American Bar Association and a Committee of Publishers and Associations.)

"It should come as no surprise that judges are most at risk when they uphold the rights of politically unpopular minorities against the wishes of the majority."

—The Honorable Marsha Ternus,
Former Chief Justice, Iowa Supreme Court

CONTENTS

Preface   ix
Table and Figures   xi

PART I   ◼ **INTRODUCTION**   1

CHAPTER 1. Promises, Promises   3

CHAPTER 2. Understanding the Impact of State Supreme Courts   25

PART II   ◼ **THE LEGAL CONTEXT**   55

CHAPTER 3. Early Same-Sex Marriage Decisions   57

CHAPTER 4. Massachusetts and Beyond   76

PART III   ◼ **AN ANALYSIS OF STATE
JUDICIAL IMPACT**   97

CHAPTER 5. Policy Initiation: The Diffusion of Same-Sex Marriage
Cases across the States   99

CHAPTER 6. Policy Legitimation: Evaluating the Capacity of State
Courts to Change Public Opinion   142

CHAPTER 7. Policy Endurance: The Enactment of State
Constitutional Amendments Prohibiting Same-Sex
Marriage   165

CHAPTER 8. The Promise of State Courts   188

Bibliography   199
Table of Authorities   211
Index   213

PREFACE

Works of this scope incur many debts. It should go without saying that there would be no book if same-sex couples had not pressed the cause of marriage equality in state supreme courts over the past two decades. These pioneers—along with the LGBT public interest groups that coordinated their efforts, such as Lambda Legal and the Gay & Lesbian Advocates & Defenders (GLAD)—made possible a sea change in state marriage law, reforms that were virtually unthinkable as recently as the early 1990s. Of no less significance were the efforts of judges in states such as Hawaii, Vermont, Massachusetts, California, Connecticut, and Iowa, who withstood withering public criticism, and sometimes the loss of their jobs, for standing up for equal rights.

I began working on this book in the spring of 2009, when I was on leave from the political science department at Fordham University, thanks to the award of a faculty fellowship from the university. The previous year had been a period of remarkable highs and lows for supporters of marriage equality, with court victories in California and Connecticut followed quickly by the passage in California of Proposition 8. Then, during the semester when I was on leave, the Iowa Supreme Court surprised the nation with its own decision favoring marriage equality. The time seemed right to begin studying the origins and consequences of these decisions, to make sense of whether and how the impact of state supreme courts differed from the impact of landmark U.S. Supreme Court decisions from the past. As it turned out, the spring of 2009 also proved to be a turning point for same-sex marriage reform efforts, as the focus shifted from state courts to state legislatures and the federal courts, making it a particularly appropriate time to reflect on what the contribution of state courts had been to the movement.

Numerous colleagues assisted me over the next few years in developing the final manuscript. Perhaps most generous were the colleagues within my own department. Jeff Cohen, who suggested the title, gave comments on several early draft chapters. He also, together with Rich Fleisher and Costas Panagopoulos, collaborated with me on the 2008 Cooperative Congressional Election Study (CCES), which forms the backbone of Chapter 6. Fordham's participation in the 2008 CCES was made possible by a special grant from Nancy Busch, the Dean of the Graduate School of Arts & Sciences and the Chief Research Officer/Associate Vice President for Academic Affairs. Melissa Labonte, from the political science department, suggested the descriptive typology that appears in Chapter 5. Other faculty members in the department provided feedback on a draft of Chapter 7 at a brown bag presentation in the fall of 2010. I also received research assistance from Andrew Steffan and Richard Trotter.

Outside of the University, special thanks are extended to Stephen Ansolabehere and the other organizers of CCES, as well as Stephen Wasby, who commented on an early draft. I also appreciated comments that I received on chapters at various academic conferences. An early version of Chapter 6 was presented at the 2009 Annual Meeting of the American Political Science Association (APSA), where Kevin McGuire provided feedback. Portions of that same chapter were presented at APSA in 2010, where Lisa Holmes and Chris Bonneau gave comments, and at the 2012 Annual Meeting of the Midwest Political Science association, where I received feedback from Greg Goelzhauser. I presented Chapter 5 at the Midwest conference in 2011, where the discussants were Mark McKenzie and Robert Robinson. I thank all of my colleagues at these conferences for their comments.

Portions of two chapters have been published in academic journals. Parts of Chapter 6 were published as *State Courts and Policy Legitimation: An Experimental Study of the Ability of State Courts to Change Opinion*, 42 Publius 211 (2012), under the editorial direction of Carol Weissert. A version of Chapter 7 appeared as *Comparing Institutional and Policy Explanations for the Adoption of State Constitutional Amendments: The Case of Same-Sex Marriage*, 39 Am. Pol. Res. 1097 (2011), edited by James Gimpel.[1] I would like to thank the editors and the anonymous reviewers at these journals for their help in developing the manuscript.

I would also like to thank editor Tony Lim at Oxford University Press for all of his help with getting this book into print, as well as Katy Linsky, Jennifer Gong, and David Lipp, who provided administrative assistance.

Last, but not least, I benefit every day from the love and patience of my wife, Shannon, and my children, Megan and Sean. I could not have completed this book without their willingness to give me the space that I need to write and reflect. I dedicate this book to them.

TABLES AND FIGURES

Figure 1.1   Stages of Judicial Policy Development   18

Table 2.1   Methods of Initial Selection and Retention of High Court Judges   40

Table 2.2   Overview of Procedures for Amending State Constitutions   45

Table 5.1   State Supreme Court Decisions Concerning Same-Sex Marriage, 1971–2009   101

Table 5.2   Median High Court Ideology   106

Table 5.3   Method of Retention and Professionalism of State High Courts   111

Table 5.4   The Inclusion of an Equal Rights Amendment   115

Table 5.5   Constitution Age   119

Table 5.6   Mean Citizen Support for Same-Sex Marriage   123

Table 5.7   State Institutional Ideology   125

Table 5.8   Percentage of Citizens Who Are Evangelical   128

Table 5.9   Percentage of Households That Are Same-Sex   131

Table 5.10   A Descriptive Typology of Same-Sex Marriage Decisions   134

Table 5.11   Cloglog Model of Same-Sex Marriage Decisions, 1993–2009   136

Table 6.1   Public Attitudes about Same-Sex Marriages and the Recognition of Same-Sex Marriages from Other States, October 2008   144

Table 6.2   "Who do you trust more to deal with the issue of... [gay marriage/abortion/the death penalty], your state legislature, or your state court?" General Results   151

Table 6.3   "Who do you trust more to deal with the issue of... [gay marriage/abortion/the death penalty], your state legislature, or your state court?" Breakdown by Judicial Retention Method   152

Table 6.4   Probit Model of Public Trust in State Courts to Decide Morality Policy Issues   154

Table 6.5   "If the [state legislature/governor/judges in your state] legalized
               same-sex marriage, would you support the decision?" General
               Results   157

Table 6.6   "If the [state legislature/governor/judges in your state] legalized
               same-sex marriage, would you support the decision?" Breakdown
               by Judicial Retention Method   158

Table 6.7   Probit Model of Public Support for the Legalization of Same-Sex
               Marriage   160

Figure 6.1   Z-Statistics of Election Interaction Effects   162

Table 7.1   Dates of Initial Consideration and Adoption of State Constitutional
               Amendments Prohibiting Same-Sex Marriage, 1990–2008 (with
               Date of Statutory Prohibition)   167

Table 7.2   Summary of State Constitutional Amendments, by Amendment
               Procedure   170

Table 7.3   Event History Analysis of the Enactment of State Constitutional
               Amendments Prohibiting Same-Sex Marriage, 1997–2008
               (Logistic Regression Coefficients, Standard Errors in
               Parentheses)   181

Table 8.1   Factors Influencing Judicial Policy Development   188

Figure 8.1   Public Support for Civil Unions (and Same-Sex Marriage),
               2003–2009   194

INTRODUCTION

CHAPTER 1

Promises, Promises

There were two major state supreme court decisions on same-sex marriage in 2008, similar in their holdings but strikingly different in their impacts on state policy. First in California and then in Connecticut, state supreme court justices ruled that the legislatures were violating their state constitutions by refusing to permit same-sex couples to marry.[1] In both states, the justices promised full marriage equality to same-sex couples, ruling that the legislatures could not create alternative institutions such as civil unions or domestic partnerships. Either decision could have had a major impact on state marriage policy, but in the end only the Connecticut decision lived up to its promise. Before the year was out, same-sex couples in Connecticut were receiving marriage licenses, whereas the decision from California was overturned by a state ballot initiative.

The responses to these cases illustrate how variable the impact of state supreme courts can be. They also present a puzzle: Why was the decision from Connecticut accepted and the California decision rejected? The question matters because state supreme courts were the government institutions driving same-sex marriage policy, not just in California and Connecticut, but in other states such as Hawaii, Massachusetts, and Iowa.[2] The impact of these decisions varied considerably, however, with some cases resulting in full marriage equality for same-sex couples and others resulting in a public backlash and the passage of state constitutional amendments overturning the decisions. Some decisions also had indirect consequences for same-sex marriage policies in other states, prompting the passage of state constitutional amendments and statutes limiting marriage to opposite-sex couples.

Despite this activity, we know very little about why the responses to the same-sex marriage decisions have been so variable or, more generally, when state supreme

---

[1] For the California litigation, see *In re* Marriage Cases, 43 Cal. 4th 757 (2008); for Connecticut, see Kerrigan v. Comm'r of Public Health, 289 Conn. 135 (2008).

[2] For the Hawaii Supreme Court's decision, see Baehr v. Lewin, 852 P.2d 44 (Haw. 1993); for Massachusetts, see Goodridge v. Dep't of Public Health, 798 N.E.2d 941 (Mass. 2003) and the Opinion of the Justices to the Senate, 802 N.E.2d 565 (Mass. 2004); for the Iowa decision, see Varnum v. Brien, 763 N.W.2d 862 (Iowa 2009).

courts are more likely to have a lasting impact on government policy. We also know very little about whether the capacity of state courts to influence government policy is distinct from that of federal courts or other state institutions, such as legislatures and governors. Because state supreme courts outpaced federal courts and legislatures at the state and federal level in their willingness to act on behalf of same-sex couples, understanding the impact of state supreme courts has become very important. Is the impact of judges constant across states, or do differences among the courts or among the states in which these courts are located determine whether decisions result in policy change?

This book examines the conditions under which state supreme courts are more likely to have an enduring impact on government policy. By impact, I mean the capacity of state supreme court justices to move formal policy, as well as public opinion, closer to the justices' revealed positions on particular issues. I consider, for example, why some state supreme court decisions have prompted the passage of constitutional amendments while others have become lasting policy. I also consider why some state court decisions have engendered a favorable response from the public while other decisions have resulted in a backlash. When considering the answers to these types of questions, I am interested in knowing how judges influence policy in their own states and the nation at large.

It is important to emphasize that the focus of this book is on state courts and not the U.S. Supreme Court. Much of the most important research on the impact of court decisions has focused on the Supreme Court,[3] which makes sense given that the Supreme Court has often been at the forefront of civil rights issues, responsible for landmark decisions on race and women's rights such as *Brown v. Board of Education* and *Roe v. Wade*.[4] In the area of same-sex marriage policy, however, the initiative has been taken not by the federal judiciary, but by state courts. The Supreme Court has handed down a few rulings in favor of gay rights, most notably *Lawrence v. Texas*, in which the justices struck down state antisodomy laws.[5] However, it is state courts that took the lead on the issue of same-sex marriage, interpreting state constitutions to provide marriage equality for same-sex couples.

The thesis of my book is that state supreme courts differ from the U.S. Supreme Court and from one another in ways that influence their impact on government policies. Differences in the institutional design of state courts, in state constitutional systems, and in the political and cultural environments in which state judges reside

---

[3] See BRADLEY C. CANON & CHARLES A. JOHNSON, JUDICIAL POLICIES: IMPLEMENTATION AND IMPACT (2nd ed. 1999); Michael J. Klarman, *How Brown Changed Race Relations: The Backlash Thesis*, 81 J. AM. HIST. 118 (1994) [hereinafter Klarman, *How Brown Changed Race Relations*]; GERALD N. ROSENBERG, THE HOLLOW HOPE: CAN COURTS BRING ABOUT SOCIAL CHANGE? (2nd ed. 2008); STEPHEN L. WASBY, THE IMPACT OF THE UNITED STATES SUPREME COURT: SOME PERSPECTIVES (1970).

[4] Brown v. Board of Education, 347 U.S. 483 (1954); Roe v. Wade, 410 U.S. 113 (1973).

[5] Lawrence v. Texas, 539 U.S. 558 (2003).

all account for variations in judicial impact. The thesis is intuitive, yet leading impact studies have neither fully considered how the impact of state supreme courts is likely to differ from the impact of federal courts, nor have they paid much attention to the institutional contexts in which state judges operate.[6] The oversight is surprising because the literature on state courts has demonstrated that certain characteristics, unique to state courts, can explain variations in the behavior of state supreme court justices[7] as well as the public's confidence in them.[8]

A logical extension of this literature is to investigate the effects of institutional variations on judicial impact. Specifically, I focus on how the democratization of state courts and state constitutional systems has shaped the impact of judges, particularly their capacity to advance minority rights. Over the past two centuries, during a time when the basic structure of the federal judicial system remained unchanged, state judiciaries underwent a process of democratic transformation. In many states, courts became more responsive to the public through judicial elections, while state constitutions came to reflect popular values through initiative amendment procedures.[9] The purpose of these reforms was to make state judicial systems less insular,

---

[6] Two of the most prominent scholars to have studied the impact of the same-sex marriage decisions are Michael Klarman and Gerald Rosenberg. *See* Michael J. Klarman, Brown *and* Lawrence (*and* Goodridge), 104 MICH. L. REV. 431 (2005); MICHAEL J. KLARMAN, FROM THE CLOSET TO THE ALTAR: COURTS, BACKLASH, AND THE STRUGGLE FOR SAME-SEX MARRIAGE (2012); ROSENBERG, *supra* note 3.

[7] Much of the research on how institutional characteristics have shaped the behavior of state supreme court justices has been done by Paul Brace and Melinda Gann Hall. *See* Paul Brace & Melinda Gann Hall, *Integrated Models of Judicial Dissent*, 55 J. POL. 914 (1993); Paul Brace & Melinda Gann Hall, *The Interplay of Preferences, Case Facts, Context, and Rules in the Politics of Judicial Choice*, 59 J. POL. 1206 (1997); Paul Brace & Melinda Gann Hall, *Neo-Institutionalism and Dissent in State Supreme Courts*, 52 J. POL. 54 (1990); Paul Brace & Melinda Gann Hall, *Studying Courts Comparatively: The View from the American States*, 48 POL. RES. Q. 5 (1995) [hereinafter Brace & Hall, *Studying Courts Comparatively*]; Melinda Gann Hall, *Constituent Influence in State Supreme Courts: Conceptual Notes and a Case Study*, 49 J. POL. 1117 (1987) [hereinafter Hall, *Constituent Influence in State Supreme Courts*]; Melinda Gann Hall, *Electoral Politics and Strategic Voting in State Supreme Courts*, 54 J. POL. 427 (1992) [hereinafter Hall, *Electoral Politics and Strategic Voting*]; Melinda Gann Hall & Paul Brace, *Order in the Courts: A Neo-Institutional Approach to Judicial Consensus*, 42 W. POL. Q. 391 (1989).

[8] For research on how institutional characteristics shape public confidence in courts, see Sara C. Benesh, *Understanding Public Confidence in American Courts*, 68 J. POL. 697 (2006); Sara C. Benesh & Susan E. Howell, *Confidence in the Courts: A Comparison of Users and Non-Users*, 19 BEHAV. SCI. & L. 199 (2001); Damon M. Cann & Jeff Yates, *Homegrown Institutional Legitimacy: Assessing Citizens' Diffuse Support for State Courts*, 36 AM. POL. RES. 297 (2008); TOM R. TYLER, WHY PEOPLE OBEY THE LAW (1990); James P. Wenzel, Shaun Bowler & David J. Lanoue, *The Sources of Public Confidence in State Courts: Experience and Institutions*, 31 AM. POL. RES. 191 (2003).

[9] For a brief history of judicial selection in the states, see Larry C. Berkson, Rachel Caufield & Malia Reddick, *Judicial Selection in the United States: A Special Report*, AMERICAN JUDICATURE SOCIETY (2004), www.ajs.org/selection/docs/Berkson.pdf. Berkson, Caufield, and Reddick observe that "as early as 1812 Georgia amended its constitution to provide that judges of inferior courts be popularly elected. In 1816, Indiana entered the Union with a constitution that provided for the election of associate judges

ensuring that state constitutional law reflected majoritarian values instead of those of legal and political elites.[10]

However, an unintended consequence of these reforms has been to make state judicial systems less capable of performing one of their traditional democratic functions: safeguarding minority rights. The ease with which many state judges can be removed from office, and the facility with which many state constitutions can be amended, has crippled the capacity of judges to stand against popular majorities, particularly on salient morality policies. When levels of democratization are high, state courts have been able to engage in virtually none of the policy leadership exhibited by the U.S. Supreme Court on issues such as race, sex, and school prayer.[11] Though many Supreme Court decisions have been deeply opposed—particularly *Roe v. Wade*—there is little threat that the decisions will be overturned by political actors outside of the Court, or that the justices will lose their jobs because of the decisions.[12]

The limitations of state courts as instruments of social change have gone largely undocumented, I suspect, because traditionally state courts have not performed this function. Although there have been exceptions, notably the California Supreme Court's landmark decision in *Perez v. Sharp* prohibiting the state's ban on interracial marriage,[13] in the past most major civil rights litigation has focused on the federal courts. During the Warren and early Burger Court years of the 1950s, 1960s, and

---

of the circuit court. Sixteen years later, Mississippi became the first state in which all judges were popularly elected. Michigan held elections for trial judges in 1836." *Id.* at 1.

[10] Kermit L. Hall observes that judicial elections were also designed to enhance the power of judges by giving them a democratic base of support. He writes: "pragmatic judicial reformers believed that the democratic goal of popular accountability and the professional goal of an able, powerful judiciary were reciprocal and reinforcing.... Popular elections... promised to make judicial review more credible; a popular base of power provided judges a democratic means of countering legislative power." Kermit L. Hall, *Progressive Reform and the Decline of Democratic Accountability: The Popular Election of State Supreme Court Judges, 1850–1920,* 9 Am. B. Found. Res. J. 345, 348 (1984).

[11] The cases in which the U.S. Supreme Court has exercised policy leadership in morality policy controversies are too numerous to count. Major landmark decisions concerning race discrimination include Brown v. Board of Education, 347 U.S. 483 (1954) (mandating an end to compulsory school segregation), Gomillion v. Lightfoot, 364 U.S. 339 (1960) (concerning racial gerrymandering), and Grutter v. Bollinger, 539 U.S. 306 (2003) (upholding the University of Michigan Law School's affirmative action program). Cases advancing women's rights include Griswold v. Connecticut, 381 U.S. 479 (1965) (striking down a state contraception law), Roe v. Wade, 410 U.S. 113 (1973) (concerning state abortion laws), and United States v. Virginia, 518 U.S. 515 (1996) (involving single-sex education). Leading religion cases include Engel v. Vitale, 370 U.S. 421 (1962) (addressing school prayer) and Church of Lukumi Babalu Aye v. City of Hialeah, 508 U.S. 520 (1993) (striking down an ordinance prohibiting ritual animal sacrifice).

[12] Indeed, the few occasions when *Roe v. Wade* has been in jeopardy have been when the justices themselves have reconsidered the decision. See Planned Parenthood of Southeastern Pennsylvania v. Casey, 505 U.S. 833 (1992); and Webster v. Reproductive Health Servs., 492 U.S. 490 (1989).

[13] Perez v. Sharp, 32 Cal.2d 711 (1948).

1970s, liberal majorities on the U.S. Supreme Court proved willing to vindicate liberal civil rights claims on issues ranging from racial segregation to abortion policy to religious freedom.

As the U.S. Supreme Court became more conservative in the 1980s and 1990s, however, liberal interest groups increasingly found it more attractive to litigate in the states. With federal judges less willing to vindicate civil rights claims, liberal interest groups anticipated that they could at least achieve regional victories in state courts, where liberal majorities still persisted in some jurisdictions and where judges were becoming increasingly open to using their own state constitutions to expand the floor of federal rights.[14] It is not surprising, then, that same-sex marriage litigation originated in liberal states such as Hawaii, Massachusetts, and Vermont. Reform groups soon discovered, however, that the decisions of state courts fared less well than those of their federal counterparts. Where landmark civil rights decisions of the U.S. Supreme Court have come to have a lasting impact on government policy, the influence of state court decisions has been more variable, and in some instances quite limited.

I maintain that the democratization of state judicial institutions has been largely responsible for these differences in judicial impact. Through an intensive examination of the issue of same-sex marriage, I show that "courthouse democracy" has consistently impeded efforts by gay rights advocates to transform state marriage laws. Two institutional features have been particularly burdensome to these groups. First, citizens have been more likely to curb state court activity on the marriage issue when initiative amendment procedures have been available to them. Initiative amendment procedures permit citizens to propose constitutional amendments directly through a petition drive, often without requiring the approval of the state legislature. Proposition 8, in California, is perhaps the most famous initiative amendment that was designed to overturn a court decision favoring marriage equality, but in fact citizens across the country have approved similar measures to overturn or preempt state court activity on this issue.

Second, judicial elections have enabled citizens to hold judges accountable for unpopular decisions. Supreme court justices in Iowa learned this lesson the hard way when three members of the state's high court were voted out of office in 2010 shortly after requiring full marriage equality in *Varnum v. Brien*.[15] Electoral incentives have made judges risk averse, reluctant to make decisions that they think the

[14] The most prominent advocate of this strategy was U.S. Supreme Court justice William Brennan, who remarked: "State constitutions, too, are a font of individual liberties, their protections often extending beyond those required by the Supreme Court's interpretations of federal law. The legal revolution which has brought federal law to the fore must not be allowed to inhibit the independent protective force of state law—for without it, the full relation of our liberties cannot be guaranteed." William J. Brennan, Jr., *State Constitutions and the Protection of Individual Rights*, 90 HARV. L. REV. 489, 491 (1977).

[15] Varnum v. Brien, 763 N.W.2d 862 (Iowa 2009).

public will oppose, particularly on high-profile issues.[16] In fact, same-sex marriage litigation has rarely been filed in states that use contested judicial elections, no doubt because reform groups understand that accountability mechanisms make it unlikely that judges will vindicate the groups' claims.[17] Iowa uses uncontested retention elections for state supreme court justices, but even the absence of opposition candidates did not stop the public from voicing its displeasure and voting the justices out.

I argue that one cannot begin to assess the impact of state courts without considering how the democratization of state courts and state constitutional systems has fundamentally shaped the capacity of state judges to act as reform agents. With state supreme court justices taking the initiative on prominent civil rights issues such as same-sex marriage, it is necessary to develop models of judicial impact that are appropriate for state courts and that take their unique institutional features into account. Such factors as the method of judicial selection, the language of state constitutional texts, and the procedures for amending state constitutions all have the potential to influence judicial impact, as do variations in the cultural and political environments in which judges find themselves. By systematically examining how these factors have shaped judicial impact, we can arrive at a better understanding of when state courts are more likely to influence government policy. We can also make sense of why the reactions to the same-sex marriage decisions in California and Connecticut were so different.

The California and Connecticut Decisions

At first it was surprising that the state supreme court decisions in California and Connecticut generated such different responses, because on the surface the similarities between the two decisions seemed to outweigh the differences. Both state supreme courts were evaluating legislative frameworks that were already generous to same-sex couples. Connecticut in 2005 had enacted a law establishing that parties to a civil union "shall have all the same benefits, protections and responsibilities under law…as are granted to spouses in a marriage."[18] Similarly, the California legislature in 2003 had approved a law guaranteeing registered domestic partners the same "rights, protections, and benefits…as are granted to and imposed upon spouses."[19] The question before the courts in Connecticut and California was

---

[16] See, e.g., Hall, Constituent Influence in State Supreme Courts, supra note 7; and Hall, Electoral Politics and Strategic Voting, supra note 7.

[17] Only two state supreme courts retained through contested elections have been asked to consider legalizing same-sex marriage, Minnesota and Washington. Baker v. Nelson, 191 N.W.2d 185 (Minn. 1971); Anderson v. King Cnty., 138 P.3d 963 (Wash. 2006). Both courts are retained with nonpartisan elections, and in neither case did the justices require marriage equality.

[18] An Act Concerning Civil Unions, Public Act No. 05–10 (Conn. 2005).

[19] California Domestic Partner Rights and Responsibilities Act, AB 205 (Cal. 2003).

whether the state legislature could assign a name other than marriage to committed relationships between same-sex couples.

The rulings in California and Connecticut were both different from same-sex marriage decisions in other states, such as Hawaii and Vermont, in which state legislatures did not, at the time of the litigation, provide same-sex couples with the same rights and benefits as married couples. The only other state supreme court to have considered whether legislatures could reserve the title of marriage for opposite-sex couples was in Massachusetts, in the landmark *Opinion of the Justices to the Senate*.[20] That case was the follow up to *Goodridge v. Department of Public Health*, in which the Supreme Judicial Court held that the state could not deny same-sex couples the benefits of marriage.[21] Subsequently, the legislature asked for an advisory opinion clarifying whether civil unions were acceptable alternatives. In the *Opinion to the Justices*, the Supreme Judicial Court said no, that same-sex couples must be permitted to marry.

The high courts in California and Connecticut reached the same conclusion as the Massachusetts court did in the *Opinion of the Justices*. The state legislatures could not create alternatives to marriage for same-sex partners, even if same-sex couples received all of the same rights and benefits as married couples. Connecticut's use of civil unions as a substitute was impermissible under its state constitution, as was California's establishment of domestic partnerships. It did not make a difference to the justices in either state that these arrangements had been created to improve the conditions of gays and lesbians instead of to disadvantage them. By excluding same-sex couples from the institution of marriage, the legislatures were assigning them second-class status.

The supreme courts in Connecticut and California offered substantially similar reasons for their decisions. Both courts ruled that existing marriage laws violated their states' equal protection clauses and that sexual orientation was entitled to heightened protection under these clauses.[22] The courts disagreed over the level of protection that sexual orientation should receive. In California, sexual orientation was identified as a suspect class that was entitled to strict scrutiny, which was the highest level of protection under the state constitution, while in Connecticut it was identified as a quasi-suspect class, entitled to somewhat less protection. But in both states the bottom line was the same: The legislature could not prevent same-sex couples from marrying, even to preserve the traditional definition of

---

[20] Opinion of the Justices to the Senate, 802 N.E.2d 565 (Mass. 2004).

[21] Goodridge v. Dep't of Public Health, 798 N.E.2d 941 (Mass. 2003).

[22] CONN. CONST. art. I, § 20 ("No person shall be denied the equal protection of the law nor be subjected to segregation or discrimination in the exercise or enjoyment of his civil or political rights because of religion, race, color, ancestry or national origin."); CAL. CONST. art I, § 7 ("A person may not be . . . denied equal protection of the laws").

marriage. The couples' interest in equality outweighed the competing state interest in maintaining the status quo.

Despite the similarities of their holdings, the same-sex marriage decisions from California and Connecticut followed very different trajectories after they were released. In California, same-sex marriages took place for a period of about six months following the California Supreme Court's decision in *In re Marriage Cases*,[23] but the following November, California voters approved Proposition 8, amending the state's constitution to read: "Only marriage between a man and a woman is valid or recognized in California."[24] That same day, voters in Connecticut reached a very different conclusion, refusing to authorize a special constitutional convention that would have allowed lawmakers in the state to overrule the Connecticut Supreme Court's decision in *Kerrigan v. Commissioner of Public Health*.[25] Same-sex marriages began in Connecticut a month after the state supreme court's decision and were still continuing as of this writing. By the end of 2008, same-sex marriage in Connecticut had been maintained by its citizens, while the California decision had been repudiated.

Reactions to other state supreme court decisions outside of California and Connecticut have been just as variable. Besides the Connecticut Supreme Court, state supreme courts that have so far been successful at securing full marriage equality for same-sex couples have been in Massachusetts and Iowa, where the justices also rejected alternative institutions for same-sex couples, such as civil unions and domestic partnerships. As in Connecticut, the actual implementation of Iowa's same-sex marriage decision was smooth. When the first same-sex marriages were conducted in Iowa in April 2009, the same month that the Iowa Supreme Court issued its decision in *Varnum v. Brien*,[26] hardly any protesters turned out, even though a majority of citizens in the state expressed their disapproval of same-sex marriage.[27] Iowans instead took their disapproval out on the judges themselves:

---

[23] *In re* Marriage Cases, 43 Cal.4th 757 (2008).

[24] Proposition 8 added a new section, section 7.5, to Article I of the California Constitution.

[25] Kerrigan v. Commissioner of Public Health, 289 Conn. 135 (2008). The issue was on the ballot in Connecticut because the Connecticut Constitution provides that every twenty years, voters will be asked, "Shall there be a Constitutional Convention to amend or revise the Constitution of the State?" CONN. CONST. art. XIII, § 2. By chance, the question was before the voters a month after *Kerrigan*. Because supporters and opponents of same-sex marriage treated the ballot initiative as a referendum on same-sex marriage, the vote against the convention was interpreted as a vote in support of *Kerrigan*. *See* Christopher Keating, *A Powerful Question for Voters; Should State Constitution Be Opened Up for Change?; On the Ballot*, HARTFORD COURANT, Oct. 18, 2008, at A1.

[26] Varnum v. Brien, 763 N.W.2d 862 (Iowa 2009).

[27] Monica Davey, *A Quiet Day in Iowa as the State Begins Allowing Same-Sex Couples to Marry*, N.Y. TIMES, Apr. 28, 2009, at A12; Amy Lorentzen, *In Iowa, Same-Sex Couples Rush to Tie the Knot*, WASH. POST, Apr. 28, 2009, at A4.

three of the justices who had ruled in favor of marriage equality lost their seats in the next retention election.

The Supreme Judicial Court of Massachusetts created more of a sensation five years earlier when it became the first state supreme court in the nation to require its state legislature to permit same-sex couples to marry. *Goodridge v. Department of Public Health*, together with its companion case the *Opinion of the Justices to the Senate*, prompted vigorous demonstrations and debate from individuals on both sides of the same-sex marriage issue and at least two attempts to enact constitutional amendments to overturn the decision.[28] However, these challenges were not successful in disrupting the celebration of marriages, which began in Massachusetts in May 2004.

Other same-sex marriage decisions have had less of an impact. In Hawaii, for example, voters in 1998 approved a constitutional amendment overturning the state supreme court's decision in *Baehr v. Lewin*, which had ruled that the state's denial of marriage licenses to same-sex couples qualified as sex discrimination under the state's equal protection clause.[29] The same day, voters in Alaska approved a constitutional amendment to overturn the decision of a state trial court judge, who had ruled in *Brause v. Bureau of Vital Statistics* that Alaska's prohibition of same-sex marriage was in tension with the privacy and equal protection clauses of the state constitution.[30] Even though their holdings and reasoning were substantially similar to the decisions from Massachusetts, Connecticut, and Iowa, the judges in Alaska and Hawaii did not succeed in transforming state marriage policy the way that the judges in these other states did.

Of course, the decisions in Hawaii and Alaska might still have influenced same-sex marriage policy in other ways. The decisions might have inspired supporters of same-sex marriage to mobilize in favor of marriage equality or to litigate in other jurisdictions.[31] The decisions might also have made state legislators across the country more willing to consider establishing civil unions or domestic partnerships for same-sex couples as alternatives to same-sex marriage. Keck notes that "the Hawaii decision immediately changed domestic partnership policies from radical, cutting-edge proposals to moderate compromises."[32] In the short-term, however,

---

[28] For the first attempt at an amendment in Massachusetts, see Raphael Lewis, *After Vote, Both Sides in Debate Energized*, Bos. GLOBE, Sept. 15, 2005, at A1; and Emelie Rutherford, *Lawmakers Nix Measure to Prohibit Gay Marriage*, Bos. HERALD, Sept. 15, 2005, at 16. For the second attempt, see Pam Belluck, *Same-Sex Marriage Vote Advances in Massachusetts*, N.Y. TIMES, Jan. 3, 2007, at A12; and Frank Phillips & Lisa Wangsness, *Same-Sex Marriage Ban Advances; Lawmakers OK Item for Ballot, but Hurdle Remains*, Bos. GLOBE, Jan. 3, 2007, at A1.

[29] Baehr v. Lewin, 852 P.2d 44 (Haw. 1993).

[30] Brause v. Bureau of Vital Statistics, No. 3AN-95-6562 (Alaska Super. Ct. Feb. 27, 1998).

[31] Thomas Keck, *Beyond Backlash: Assessing the Impact of Judicial Decisions on LGBT Rights*, 43 LAW & SOC'Y REV. 151 (2009).

[32] *Id.* at 158–59.

the Alaska and Hawaii decisions did not result in any same-sex marriages in these two states. Worse, the decisions seemed to have created a backlash against the movement, as reflected by the passage of state constitutional amendments in these states and in twenty-nine others.[33]

In California and Connecticut, at least from studying the text of the two opinions, it was not immediately clear why the same-sex marriage decisions generated such different responses. From the opinions alone, one would have expected California's decision to have elicited the more sympathetic response because, on paper at least, it is the more carefully reasoned of the two. A problem both courts faced was that there were no previous decisions from either tribunal on the subject of same-sex marriage or even on the question of whether sexual orientation should receive heightened protections under the states' equal protection clauses. These were cases of first impression.[34] With no prior case law on the subject and nothing in the texts of their constitutions to provide clear guidance, the courts in Connecticut and California needed to explain why their state constitutions nevertheless prevented the legislatures from establishing civil unions or domestic partnerships as alternatives to marriage. Otherwise the justices risked being accused of judicial activism, putting their policy preferences ahead of the rule of law.

The California Supreme Court took the more cautious approach, justifying its decision by extending the logic of California precedents. Because there were no previous California decisions that were precisely on the subject of same-sex marriage, the court turned to other marriage discrimination cases. Twenty years before the U.S. Supreme Court struck down state miscegenation laws in *Loving v. Virginia*,[35] the California Supreme Court in *Perez v. Sharp* became the first state supreme court since Reconstruction to rule that a ban on interracial marriage violated the right to marry.[36] In the majority opinion, the *Perez* court characterized the marriage right broadly, as "the right to join in marriage with the person of one's choice."[37]

In its same-sex marriage opinion, the California Supreme Court cited the expansive language of *Perez*, as well as subsequent California decisions affirming the right to marry, as justification for permitting gay couples to wed. "As these and many other California decisions make clear," Chief Justice Ronald M. George wrote, "the right to marry represents the right of an individual to establish a legally recognized family with the person of one's choice, and, as such, is of fundamental

---

[33] Klarman, Brown *and* Lawrence (*and* Goodridge), *supra* note 6; Klarman, FROM THE CLOSET TO THE ALTAR, *supra* note 6; and ROSENBERG, *supra* note 3.

[34] A lower court in California had previously invalidated policies discriminating against gays and lesbians but did not identify sexual orientation as a suspect classification. See *Citizens for Responsible Behavior v. Superior Court*, 1 Cal. App. 4th 1013 (1991). The court used a rational basis test, which requires only that the state provide a legitimate justification for its classification.

[35] Loving v. Virginia, 388 U.S. 1 (1967).

[36] Perez v. Sharp, 32 Cal. 2d 711 (1948).

[37] *Id.* at 716.

significance both to society and to the individual."[38] The court explained that this right to marry was guaranteed "to *all* individuals and couples, without regard to their sexual orientation."[39] Drawing upon principles that were embedded in its own precedents, the Court explained that the marriage right was broad enough to include same-sex couples.

The California Supreme Court observed that the state legislature's actions in recent years affirmed that attitudes about gay people had changed and that Californians had come to accept committed same-sex unions as no different from marriage. "There can be no question," Chief Justice George wrote, "but that, in recent decades, there has been a fundamental and dramatic transformation in this state's understanding and legal treatment of gay individuals and gay couples."[40] The opinion cited a string of legislative acts, beginning in 1999, when the state legislature first recognized domestic partnerships, as evidence of the shift in perspective. "This state's current policies," Chief Justice George continued, "recognize...that gay individuals are fully capable of entering into the kind of loving and enduring committed relationship that may serve as the foundation of a family and of responsibly caring for and raising children."[41]

The California Supreme Court relied primarily on its own precedents and other resources from within the state to establish the next point, that sexual orientation was entitled to heightened protection under the state equal protection clause. Previous California decisions had established the criteria that judges should use for identifying "suspect classifications" that are subject to "strict scrutiny," the most exacting standard of review under the state Equal Protection Clause. In *Sail'er Inn v. Kirby*, a case involving sex discrimination, the court had explained that among the criteria the justices would consider when identifying suspect classes were whether members of the class were identified by an "immutable trait," whether the characteristic "bears no relation to ability to perform or contribute to society," and whether there is a "stigma of inferiority and second class citizenship" associated with the group.[42]

Using these same criteria, the California Supreme Court in its same-sex marriage opinion argued that sexual orientation was a suspect class. Although the justices were unprepared to state that sexual orientation was an immutable characteristic based on the record before them, they did believe that sexual orientation satisfied the other two criteria of *Sail'er Inn*. Past California decisions suggested

---

[38] *In re* Marriage Cases, 43 Cal. 4th 757, 814–15 (2008). The California Supreme Court cited *Elden v. Sheldon*, 46 Cal. 3d 267 (1988); *Williams v. Garcetti*, 5 Cal. 4th 561 (1993); and *Warfield v. Peninsula Golf & Country Club*, 10 Cal. 4th 594 (1995).

[39] *Marriage Cases*, 43 Cal. 4th at 820.

[40] *Id.* at 821.

[41] *Id.* at 821–22.

[42] Sail'er Inn v. Kirby, 5 Cal.3d 1, 18–19 (1971).

that sexual orientation bore no relationship to a person's ability to contribute to society,[43] and that gay people suffered a stigma of inferiority and second-class citizenship.[44]

Whether or not one agrees with how the California Supreme Court applied its precedents, the justices at least grounded their opinion squarely within California law. The opinion takes care to identify the principles underlying precedents such as *Perez* and *Sail'er Inn* and to explain why these same principles also required permitting same-sex couples to marry. Critics of the California Supreme Court's decision might disagree about the manner in which the justices applied these principles, but they are unlikely to suggest that the justices were selectively choosing authorities. Each of the Court's conclusions was rooted in established California precedents. The justices did not depend on standards from other federal or state courts to reach their judgment.

The Connecticut Supreme Court, in contrast, based much of its opinion on precedents from outside the state. The move was necessary, the majority opinion explained, because "we previously have not articulated the specific criteria to be considered in determining whether recognition as a quasi-suspect class is warranted."[45] Instead of developing a test of its own, however, the Connecticut Supreme Court adopted the U.S. Supreme Court's criteria for quasi-suspect classes, as developed in *City of Cleburne v. Cleburne Living Center* and other cases.[46] These criteria included whether "the group has suffered a history of invidious discrimination," whether "the characteristics that distinguish the group's members bear no relation to their ability to perform or contribute to society," whether "the characteristic that defines the members of the class as a discrete group is immutable or otherwise not within their control," and whether the group is "a minority or politically powerless."[47]

Applying these standards, the Connecticut Supreme Court concluded that sexual orientation was entitled to quasi-suspect status under the state constitution. The majority noted that there had been a long history in the state of discrimination based on sexual orientation, that the classification bore no relation to the ability of individuals to contribute to society, and that the discrimination was based on a characteristic that would not change. The Court was also satisfied that the LGBT community as a whole was politically powerless, because gay marriage advocates had achieved only limited victories in a few states. Much of this discussion was based on authorities from outside the state, including federal and state court precedents,

---

[43] Gay Law Students Ass'n v. Pacific Telephone & Telegraph Co., 24 Cal. 3d 458 (1979).

[44] People v. Garcia, 77 Cal. App. 4th 1269 (2000).

[45] Kerrigan v. Comm'r of Public Health, 289 Conn. 135, 165 (2008).

[46] City of Cleburne v. Cleburne Living Center, 473 U.S. 432 (1985).

[47] *Kerrigan*, 289 Conn. at 165–66.

psychological and public opinion research,[48] and commentators such as Ronald Dworkin, Richard Posner, and David Satcher.[49]

It is not unusual for state supreme courts to look to other states or federal courts, including the U.S. Supreme Court, for guidance when interpreting their own constitutions. The problem with the majority opinion in *Kerrigan* was that it did not clarify the criteria that the justices were using to determine which precedents from outside the state were authoritative. The *Kerrigan* majority simply asserted that it was using the U.S. Supreme Court's standards for identifying suspect classifications to interpret Connecticut law. "Because of the evident correlation between the indicia of suspectness identified by the United States Supreme Court and the issue of whether a class that has been singled out by the state for unequal treatment is entitled to heightened protection under the federal constitution," Justice Richard Palmer wrote for the majority, "we conclude that those factors also are pertinent to the determination of whether a group comprises a quasi-suspect class for purposes of the state constitution."[50]

As members of the state's highest court, the justices in *Kerrigan* of course had the authority to decide that their state constitution meant whatever they thought it did, but a more persuasive opinion would have established why the principles they established were grounded in Connecticut law. Instead, the selection of precedents seemed ad hoc, chosen to support the result that the justices wanted to reach. This tendency was most apparent when the justices turned to other state and federal precedents to defend their application of the U.S. Supreme Court's criteria for identifying quasi-suspect classes. As the majority opinion conceded, most state and federal courts that have considered whether sexual orientation is a suspect or quasi-suspect class have determined that it is not. The U.S. Supreme Court had not declared that sexual orientation was afforded special scrutiny under the federal Equal Protection Clause, instead using the less exacting rational basis test to review sexual orientation classification in cases such as *Romer v. Evans*.[51] By not clarifying why Connecticut law compelled a more generous standard of review, the majority opinion placed itself in the awkward position of using federal law to defend a conclusion that most other courts, looking at the same precedents, had rejected.

The *Kerrigan* majority responded to this dilemma by asserting that the majority of judges who had ruled on the protected status of gay persons had applied the

[48] Kaiser Family Foundation, Inside Out: A Report on the Experiences of Lesbians, Gays and Bisexuals in America and the Public's View on Issues and Policies Related to Sexual Orientation (2001).

[49] Ronald Dworkin, *Three Questions for America*, N.Y. Rev. Books, Sept. 21, 2006, at 28; Richard Posner, Sex and Reason (1992); David Satcher, The Surgeon General's Call to Action to Promote Sexual Health and Responsible Sexual Behavior (2001).

[50] *Kerrigan*, 289 Conn. at 167.

[51] Romer v. Evans, 517 U.S. 620 (1996).

Supreme Court's precedents incorrectly. The majority cited as persuasive just two other state court opinions: the dissent in *Hernandez v. Robles*, from New York's highest court,[52] and the majority opinion from *In re Marriage Cases* from California.[53] Other courts had premised their analyses on what the justices characterized as unsound interpretations of federal precedents. "We conclude," Justice Palmer wrote, "that the state court cases that have determined that gay persons do not constitute a quasi-suspect class, like the federal cases described in this part of the opinion, employed a flawed analysis, and, therefore, they do not constitute persuasive authority."[54]

It is open to question, however, whether the U.S. Supreme Court at the time would have accepted the Connecticut Supreme Court's interpretation of federal precedents. As mentioned above, the U.S. Supreme Court in *Romer v. Evans* used only a rational basis test to evaluate whether classifications based on sexual orientation were permissible. The other major gay rights case, *Lawrence v. Texas*, expanded gay rights under the Due Process Clause, but had little to say about equal protection, and made a point of noting that the decision, which invalidated state sodomy laws, had nothing to do with marriage.[55] Concurring in the judgment in *Lawrence*, Justice O'Connor would have favored an Equal Protection Clause analysis but did not believe that it was necessary to establish sexual orientation as a suspect classification.[56] It is not clear, then, that the decisions in *Romer* and *Lawrence* suggested the Supreme Court was prepared, at least at the time, to recognize sexual orientation as a suspect or even a quasi-suspect class.

By premising its decision on interpretations of federal law that were not endorsed by a majority of state or federal courts, including the Supreme Court, the Connecticut Supreme Court in *Kerrigan* unnecessarily opened itself up to criticism. The reasoning might have been more convincing if, like the California Supreme Court, the *Kerrigan* majority had based its decision squarely in state law, showing how its ruling was grounded in its own constitutional text, precedents, and tradition. If relevant state precedents were unavailable and the justices wished to consult federal law in an advisory capacity, then the justices at least could have clarified the criteria they were using in selecting federal precedents. That way the reasoning would have appeared less ad hoc.

In the end, of course, it was the California decision and not *Kerrigan* that was repudiated by voters. More likely than not, most of the public and many of the policy makers in California and Connecticut did not even bother to read the opinions, so it did not end up mattering how the justices actually defended their judgments.

[52] Hernandez v. Robles, 855 N.E. 2d 1 (N.Y. 2006).
[53] *In re* Marriage Cases, 43 Cal. 4th 757 (2008).
[54] *Kerrigan*, 289 Conn. at 240–41.
[55] Lawrence v. Texas, 539 U.S. 558 (2003).
[56] *Id.*, at 579 (O'Connor, J., concurring).

The question this book seeks to understand is what drives these variations in judicial impact if the actual legal merits of the justices' arguments seem to have little to do with it. What makes decisions such as California's less enduring than decisions from states such as Connecticut? Why do some state courts seem to be more capable of acting as reform agents, standing against majorities and vindicating minority rights?

Understanding the Impact of State Supreme Courts

My suggestion is that the impact of state courts varies depending on the contexts in which judges are operating. State judges are not similarly situated to each other, and the differences among them affect their capacities to influence policy. Institutional variations among state courts and state constitutional systems, as well as differences in the political and cultural environments in which judges are located, all have the potential to shape the judges' impact. Some judges might find, for example, that their state constitutions provide little textual support for decisions that favor same-sex marriage. Other judges might find that the text is supportive, but that the public refuses to accept any decisions favoring marriage equality. Elected judges might be particularly vulnerable to public opinion because the judges risk losing their seats in the next election cycle when they issue decisions that the public dislikes, particularly in salient cases. Still other judges might find that the constitutional amendment procedures in their states are so accessible that the public can easily overturn court decisions favoring marriage equality.

Because the focus of this book is on the behavior and impact of state judges, I devote less attention to public interest lawyers and other gay rights advocates, whose activities have been well documented elsewhere.[57] LGBT public interest groups have, of course, played a central role in advancing gay civil rights. Without their efforts, and the efforts of the individual litigants who filed suit in the years before the same-sex marriage movement became organized, there would be no litigation and no opportunity for state judges to influence marriage policy. Although I acknowledge the significant contributions of these groups, my interest here is primarily on the impact that state supreme courts have had on the issue. This emphasis is appropriate because state judges have themselves been significant policy leaders on the issue of same-sex marriage, and there is reason for concluding that the impact

---

[57] *See* ELLEN ANN ANDERSEN, OUT OF THE CLOSET & INTO THE COURTS: LEGAL OPPORTUNITY STRUCTURE AND GAY RIGHTS LITIGATION (2005); PATRICIA A. CAIN, RAINBOW RIGHTS: THE ROLE OF LAWYERS AND COURTS IN THE LESBIAN AND GAY CIVIL RIGHTS MOVEMENT (2000); David J. Garrow, *Toward a More Perfect Union*, N.Y. TIMES MAG., May 9, 2004, at 52; DANIEL R. PINELLO, AMERICA'S STRUGGLE FOR SAME-SEX MARRIAGE (2006); MARC STEIN, RETHINKING THE GAY AND LESBIAN MOVEMENT (2012); EVAN WOLFSON, WHY MARRIAGE MATTERS: AMERICA, EQUALITY, AND GAY PEOPLE'S RIGHT TO MARRY (2004).

of judges has been distinct from the efforts of LGBT interest groups. LGBT litigants did not win every case, despite their strategic choice of venues, nor did every victory actually produce desired social change. As the different responses to the California and Connecticut decisions indicate, even when LGBT groups have managed to find judges who were sympathetic to their claims, the judges have not always been capable of providing them with the relief they sought. It is therefore appropriate, and necessary, to study the impact of state judges as a distinct matter.

I have already previewed my argument that I believe that it is the democratization of state courts and state constitutional systems that has been primarily responsible for observed differences in the impact of state judges. In the next chapter, I describe in greater detail the types of institutional and environmental differences that I think are the most likely to be influential. Over the course of the book, I examine how these factors have shaped the impact of judges in a variety of different contexts. As an overview, in Figure 1.1 I describe three stages that I believe are fundamental to judicial policy development. These stages are not unique to state courts—federal judicial policies go through a similar process of development—but they are a useful way to begin thinking about how state courts differ from federal courts and from one another in their impact on government policies such as same-sex marriage. I maintain that in each stage described in Figure 1.1, institutional features of state courts have the potential to affect their impact.

In the first stage, the *initiation* stage, a court must be *willing* to innovate in the relevant area of policy. That is, in the area of same-sex marriage policy, state judges must be *willing* to rule in favor of its legalization. To some extent, this condition is rather straightforward—quite obviously, judges can have no impact on government policy if they are unwilling to make a decision in the first place. However, state judges vary tremendously in their willingness to act, and the reluctance of some judges may be attributable not just to their sincere policy preferences but to institutional constraints. For example, it is well documented that elected judges are less likely to cross the public on salient issues, such as the death penalty.[58] Elected judges risk their careers when they make decisions that the public does not support,

Initiation	→	**Legitimation**	→	**Endurance**
a court must be *willing* to innovate (e.g., to legalize same-sex marriage)		a decision must be accepted by relevant policy communities (e.g., the public)		a decision must not be trumped by other policies (e.g., constitutional amendments)

Figure 1.1 Stages of Judicial Policy Development

[58] See Brace & Hall, *Integrated Models of Judicial Dissent, supra* note 7; Brace & Hall, *The Interplay of Preferences, Case Facts, Context, and Rules in the Politics of Judicial Choice, supra* note 7; Brace & Hall, *Neo-Institutionalism and Dissent in State Supreme Courts, supra* note 7; Brace & Hall, *Studying Courts Comparatively, supra* note 7; Hall, *Constituent Influence in State Supreme Courts, supra* note 7; Hall, *Electoral Politics and Strategic Voting, supra* note 7; Hall & Brace, *supra* note 7.

because they can be voted out of office in the next election. Perhaps for this reason, it is unsurprising that most of the judges who have ruled in favor of same-sex marriage have been relatively insulated from these types of popular reprisals.

Another institutional characteristic that has the potential to influence policy initiation is the degree of high court professionalization. State supreme courts differ in their capacities to generate and evaluate information.[59] Courts vary in their ability to attract high quality candidates, in the size of judicial staffs, and in the amount of control they have over their dockets, among other attributes. Research has found that professionalization improves the odds that state supreme court justices will intervene in disputes involving disadvantaged parties and side with these parties on the merits.[60] It is quite possible, then, that supporters of same-sex marriage will find that they are less likely to win pro-marriage rulings in states with less professionalized courts.

In the second stage, the *legitimation* stage, state court decisions must be accepted by the most relevant policy communities.[61] Depending on the policy, these communities might include interpreting populations, such as other judges; implementing populations, such as state administrators; and consumer populations, such as the public.[62] When it comes to morality policies such as same-sex marriage, the reaction of the public is likely to be of primary importance. Research on morality policies has demonstrated that public opinion is central to their development, because the public is more likely to be interested in them than in other, more routine policies.[63]

[59] *See* Burton M. Atkins & Henry R. Glick, *Formal Judicial Recruitment and State Supreme Court Decisions*, 2 AM. POL. Q. 427 (1974); Paul Brace & Melinda Gann Hall, *"Haves" versus "Have Nots" in State Supreme Courts: Allocating Docket Space and Wins in Power Asymmetric Cases*, 35 LAW & SOC'Y REV. 393 (2001); HENRY R. GLICK & KENNETH N. VINES, STATE COURT SYSTEMS (1973); Peverill Squire, *Measuring the Professionalization of State Courts of Last Resort*, 8 ST. POL. & POL'Y Q. 223 (2008).

[60] Brace & Hall, *supra* note 59.

[61] One might dispute the ordering of the three stages, arguing for example that policy legitimation is necessary before judges will agree to initiate policy. I agree that the stages are fluid, and the order I present is not intended to be overly rigid. For the purposes of this study, I have found the ordering of the stages to be logical because it permits me to study the initial court decision (initiation) followed by the short-term response (legitimation) and the long-term response (endurance).

[62] I derive this terminology primarily from CANON & JOHNSON, *supra* note 3.

[63] *See* Donald P. Haider-Markel & Kenneth J. Meier, *The Politics of Gay and Lesbian Rights: Expanding the Scope of the Conflict*, 58 J. POL. 332 (2001); William T. Gormley, Jr., *Regulatory Issue Networks in a Federal System*, 18 POLITY 595 (1986); Sung-Do Hwang & Virginia Gray, *External Limits and Internal Determinants of State Public Policy*, 44 W. POL. Q. 277 (1991); Theodore J. Lowi, *American Business, Public Policy, Case-Studies, and Political Theory*, 16 WORLD POL. 677 (1964); Theodore J. Lowi, *Four Systems of Policy, Politics, and Choice*, 32 PUB. ADMIN. REV. 298 (1972); Theodore J. Lowi, *Forward: New Dimensions in Policy and Politics, in* SOCIAL REGULATORY POLICY: MORAL CONTROVERSIES IN AMERICAN POLITICS (Raymond Tatlovich & Byron W. Daynes eds., 1988); Christopher Z. Mooney & Mei-Hsien Lee, *Legislative Morality in the American States: The Case of Pre-Roe Abortion Regulation Reform*, 39 AM. J. POL. SCI. 599 (1995).

On issues such as same-sex marriage, the public is likely to pressure elected officials to defy or evade unpopular court decisions. In systems with direct democracy, citizens can take action against the decisions themselves.

It seems reasonable to expect public reactions to state court decisions to be shaped by institutional conditions. We know from research on state public opinion that citizens have attitudes about state courts and that institutional design choices affect these attitudes. For example, a number of studies have shown that judicial selection methods influence general levels of public confidence in courts.[64] It is possible that these design choices also affect the willingness of the public to accept decisions from certain types of judicial tribunals. Because appointed judges enjoy greater independence from routine political activity, the public might be more willing to trust that the judges are engaged in principled decision making. If, in contrast, elected judges appear to be less principled, the public might be less trusting in them and less willing to support their judgments.

Another type of institutional factor that has the potential to influence policy legitimation is the design of state constitutions. State supreme court justices do not have the same legal resources available to them to justify their decisions. Although Americans are probably the most familiar with the U.S. Constitution, each state has its own constitution and its own unique precedents and traditions concerning the interpretation of its constitution. I suspect that these textual and interpretive differences influence the capacity of state supreme court judges to rule in favor of same-sex couples. Depending on what state constitutions say and how state constitutions have been interpreted by other judges in these states in the past, some judges might find that they have fewer legal resources to establish the legitimacy of pro-marriage rulings.

For example, one way that state constitutional systems differ from one another is in their levels of protection against sex discrimination. A number of states, including Hawaii, have equal rights amendments (ERAs) in their constitutions specifically barring discrimination on the basis of sex.[65] This language is important because it can provide a foundation for state supreme court justices to invalidate state laws prohibiting same-sex marriage as a form of sex discrimination. The Hawaii Supreme Court used this logic in *Baehr v. Lewin*, ruling that when a state prohibits individuals from marrying the partners of their choice because of their sex, it qualifies as sex discrimination.[66] Even when state judges have not relied specifically on ERAs in their own marriage rulings, the presence of an ERA might help to establish that a state constitutional system is broadly protective of civil rights. Without this foundation,

---

[64] *See* Benesh, *supra* note 8; Cann & Yates, *supra* note 8; Wenzel et al., *supra* note 8.

[65] *See* HAW. CONST. art. I, § 5 ("no person shall…be denied the enjoyment of…civil rights or be discriminated against in the exercise thereof because of race, religion, sex, or ancestry").

[66] Baehr v. Lewin, 852 P.2d 44, 59 (Haw. 1993).

judges in less-permissive systems might find that their same-sex marriage decisions have less legitimacy.

In the final stage, the *endurance* stage, state court decisions must survive without being trumped by other state policies. When court decisions involve the interpretation of state statutes, a superseding policy might simply be another piece of legislation. For the same-sex marriage decisions, however, which involve the interpretation of state constitutions, the primary obstacle to policy endurance has been the passage of state constitutional amendments. When states choose to amend their constitutions to limit marriage to the union of one man and one woman, they necessarily overturn decisions, such as California's, which favored marriage equality. These amendments also prevent state courts from ruling in favor of same-sex marriage in the future.

Among the institutional differences that are likely to influence policy endurance are differences in state constitutional amendment procedures, which vary considerably from state to state. In many states the procedures for amending state constitutions are considerably simpler than they are at the federal level. In California, for example, which permits initiative amendments, a constitutional amendment can be proposed by a small minority of citizens and then approved by a simple majority of citizens voting in a general election. Policy endurance is therefore much harder to achieve in states such as California than it is at the federal level or in states such as Connecticut that do not permit initiative amendments. Rigorous amendment procedures help to give judicial policies greater chances of having enduring legacies.

Along with these institutional variations, environmental differences among the states are also likely to influence the three stages of judicial policy development that I have identified. The political and cultural environments within states are crucial to judicial impact because they determine how receptive citizens and elected officials are likely to be to judicial policies. Depending on the demographic composition of the citizenry, the political climate, and the activity of interest groups, judges might find that the environment is simply too unsympathetic to a decision favoring marriage equality. Judges from more liberal states, with a friendlier interest group presence, will have a greater capacity to issue pro-marriage decisions that gain acceptance and endure.

Plan for the Book

The remainder of this book explores how institutional and environmental conditions have influenced the impact of state supreme court justices on same-sex marriage policy, focusing on each of the three stages of judicial policy development that I described in Figure 1.1. I argue that in order to understand the impact of state supreme courts on same-sex marriage policy or on any salient morality policy, one must be attentive to the institutional, cultural, and political contexts in which justices operate. Understanding how institutions shape the impact of judges is not merely academic. Across the states, there have been vigorous debates about methods of judicial selection and retention, the procedures for amending state constitutions, and the language of state constitutional texts.[67] My research informs these debates by exploring the consequences of these institutional design choices for judicial policy development.

Chapter 2 develops my theory of state supreme court impact. At the center of the theory is my expectation that institutional and environmental differences among the states can account for why the reactions to same-sex marriage decisions have been so divergent. Institutional variations are important, I explain, because they establish the constraints under which state judges operate as well as the resources that judges possess to help them overcome these constraints. For example, unlike federal judges, most state judges lack the institutional protection of life tenure, making them more vulnerable to political reprisals for unpopular decisions. It is also considerably easier to amend many state constitutions than it is to amend the federal constitution, giving the constitutional decisions of state judges less staying power. I discuss how these and other institutional and environmental differences among the states make it harder for judges in some states to have a meaningful impact on salient morality policies such as same-sex marriage.

In Chapters 3 and 4, I trace the history of state supreme court activity on the issue of same-sex marriage from the 1970s through the Iowa Supreme Court's decision in 2009. Chapter 3 focuses on the earliest same-sex marriage decisions, including the landmark decisions from Hawaii and Vermont, while Chapter 4 describes the *Goodridge* decision from Massachusetts and subsequent rulings in the years

---

[67] *See* Lynn A. Baker, *Governing by Initiative: Constitutional Change and Direct Democracy*, 66 U. Colo. L. Rev. 143 (1995); Luke Bierman, *Judicial Independence: Beyond Merit Selection*, 29 Fordham Urb. L.J. 851 (2002); Chris W. Bonneau & Melinda Gann Hall, In Defense of Judicial Elections (2009); Meryl J. Chertoff, *At Home and Abroad: Trends in Judicial Selection in the States*, 42 McGeorge L. Rev. 47 (2010); Frank B. Cross, *Thoughts on Goldilocks and Judicial Independence*, 64 Ohio St. L.J. 195 (2003); Jason J. Czarnezki, *A Call for Change: Improving Judicial Selection Methods*, 89 Marq. L. Rev. 169 (2005); Marie A. Failinger, *Can a Good Judge Be a Good Politician? Judicial Elections from a Virtue Ethics Approach*, 70 Mo. L. Rev. 433 (2005); Stephen M. Griffin, *Trust in Government and Direct Democracy*, 11 U. Pa. J. Const. L. 551 (2009); Elizabeth A. Larkin, *Judicial Selection Methods: Judicial Independence and Popular Democracy*, 79 Denv. U. L. Rev. 65 (2001); Kaitlyn Redfield-Ortiz, *Government by the People for the People? Representative Democracy, Direct Democracy, and the Unfinished Struggle for Gay Civil Rights*, 43 Ariz. St. L.J. 1367 (2011); Richard B. Saphire & Paul Moke, *The Ideologies of Judicial Selection: Empiricism and the Transformation of the Judicial Selection Debate*, 39 U. Tol. L. Rev. 551 (2008); G. Alan Tarr, *Balancing the Will of the Public with the Need for Judicial Independence and Accountability: Do Retention Elections Work?*, 74 Mo. L. Rev. 605 (2009); Peter D. Webster, *Selection and Retention of Judges: Is There One "Best" Method?*, 23 Fla. St. U. L. Rev. 1 (1995); James Andrew Winn, Jr. & Eli Paul Mazur, *Judicial Diversity: Where Independence and Accountability Meet*, 67 Alb. L. Rev. 775 (2004); Steven Zeidman, *To Elect or Not to Elect: A Case Study of Judicial Selection in New York City. 1977–2002*, 37 U. Mich. J.L. Reform (2004).

following. The history reveals just how variable judges have been in their willingness to act as policy initiators in same-sex marriage policy. Supporters of same-sex marriage gained little traction in courts in the 1970s, but by the 1990s judges in states such as Hawaii and Alaska began interpreting their constitutions to require marriage equality for same-sex couples. Even then, however, judges who were asked to decide the question responded with various levels of commitment to marriage equality. Judges in Massachusetts, Connecticut, and Iowa required full marriage equality, but judges in other states such as Vermont and New Jersey permitted civil unions as substitutes. Still other judges in states such as New York, Maryland, and Washington refused to interpret their constitutions so expansively, leaving it to state legislatures to determine what, if any, benefits same-sex couples would receive.

In the rest of the book, I analyze the impact of state courts on same-sex marriage policy, dividing the analysis into three chapters corresponding to the three stages of judicial policy development that I outlined above. In Chapter 5, I focus on *policy initiation*, describing general characteristics of the state supreme courts that voted yes on the marriage question and developing a descriptive typology of these tribunals. I also use event history analysis to model the timing and sequence of state supreme court decisions favoring marriage equality. I find that, to some extent, variation in judicial policy initiation is explained by interest group activity: LGBT interest groups have been strategic in their selection of states in which to pursue a litigation strategy, litigating primarily in states with favorable institutional and environmental conditions. However, the variation in state court policy initiation cannot be attributed entirely to forum shopping by supporters of same-sex marriage. Among those states in which judges were asked to consider the marriage question, judicial policy initiation has varied based on institutional conditions. Appointed judges have been more likely than other judges to rule in favor of same-sex marriage. I also find that judges have been more likely to rule in favor of marriage equality when they have prestigious reputations.

Chapter 6 focuses on *policy legitimation*, with particular emphasis placed on the capacity of state courts to build public support for government policies. Using a combination of existing and original survey research, I investigate whether institutional differences among state supreme courts, particularly differences in methods of judicial selection, influence whether the public is likely to support decisions favoring same-sex marriage. I find that, as a general matter, state supreme courts are no more effective than other institutions at increasing public support for same-sex marriage, but that methods of judicial selection do help to account for when judges are more effective at building public support. Specifically, I find that the public is more likely to trust appointed judges to deal with the issue of same-sex marriage, and that the public is less likely to support court decisions legalizing same-sex marriage that are attributed to elected judges.

The subject of Chapter 7 is *policy endurance*, evaluating the long-term impact of state courts by studying the enactment of state constitutional amendments restricting marriage to the union of one man and one woman. Some of these amendments overturned specific state supreme court decisions, while others prevented state supreme courts from ruling in favor of marriage equality in the future. In both circumstances, I expect institutional differences among state supreme courts and state constitutional systems to account for when amendments have been more likely to pass. I find that states with professionalized courts, which have a greater tendency to vote in favor of disadvantaged parties,[68] have been more likely to have been targeted by amendments. I also find that states that permit citizens to propose constitutional amendments using initiative amendment procedures have tended to approve amendments.

In the final chapter, I summarize the major findings of the book and reflect on their normative implications. I also consider whether, in the final analysis, it was good strategy for supporters of same-sex marriage to turn to state courts as instruments of social change. Although the legacy of the same-sex marriage decisions has been mixed, and critics such as Rosenberg are correct to point out the limitations of judicial intervention,[69] ultimately I am persuaded that state courts have advanced the cause of gay civil rights. The public policy environment has transformed dramatically since state supreme courts first ruled in favor of same-sex marriage in the early 1990s, and the prospects for comprehensive marriage reform are much more promising because of their intervention. However, these advances have occurred in spite of, and not because of, the democratization of state courts and state constitutional systems. In the issue area of same-sex marriage, the judges who have proved the most capable of producing meaningful social change have resided in states that have provided judges with the institutional resources they need to stand against popular opinion.

---

[68] Brace & Hall, *supra* note 59.
[69] ROSENBERG, *supra* note 3.

CHAPTER 2

Understanding the Impact of State Supreme Courts

When judges first began to rule in favor of marriage equality in the early 1990s, the most striking feature of this activity was that it was conducted by state judges. In the popular imagination, it is the U.S. Supreme Court that is often thought of as the nation's foremost guarantor of constitutional rights. This perception is reinforced by landmark U.S. Supreme Court decisions in the areas of civil rights, abortion, school prayer, and free speech, among other issue areas. On the issue of same-sex marriage, however, the U.S. Supreme Court in the 1990s and early 2000s was merely a silent observer, with the justices issuing no opinions relating to the landmark state court decisions from this period.

The silence was understandable. Same-sex marriage litigation did not, at the time, present federal questions that were appropriate for the justices to review. The avoidance of federal courts also reflected a deliberate strategy by LGBT litigants, who were wary of a U.S. Supreme Court that was considerably more conservative in the 1990s than in decades earlier, when Earl Warren was chief justice. "I can't think of a less sympathetic prospect," said Mary Bonauto of the Gay & Lesbian Advocates & Defenders (GLAD), who oversaw the litigation in Vermont, Massachusetts, and Connecticut. "I would like the opportunity for states to wrestle with this before we have to go into federal court."[1] These perceptions were backed by empirical evidence. Pinello reports that, during the 1980s and 1990s, "state courts interpreting state constitutions were far more receptive to lesbian and gay rights claims than either court system was in applying the federal constitution."[2] For these reasons, in the twenty years after *Baehr v. Lewin*,[3] judicial battles over same-sex marriage occurred primarily in the states, with the most important landmark decisions authored by state supreme court justices.

---

[1] Garrow, *supra* Chapter 1, note 57; *see also* Andersen *supra* Chapter 1, note 57.
[2] DANIEL R. PINELLO, GAY RIGHTS AND AMERICAN LAW 110 (2003).
[3] Baehr v. Lewin, 852 P.2d 44 (Haw. 1993).

In this chapter, I theorize about the conditions under which state supreme court justices are more likely to influence salient government policies such as same-sex marriage. The chapter begins by summarizing what we know about the impact of courts, based primarily on research that has been conducted on the U.S. Supreme Court. I then discuss how reactions to state supreme court decisions are likely to be different. Put briefly, my argument is that context matters. The institutional design of state courts, the structure of state constitutional systems, and the political and cultural environments in which state judges operate all have the potential to influence their impact. Context matters because it defines the conditions under which state court decisions are made and received. It establishes the constraints under which judges operate as well as the resources that judges possess to overcome these constraints. Depending on how state supreme court justices are selected and retained, how state constitutions are written, and how receptive the public is to public policy innovations, many judges might find that they are less capable of making significant policy change.

The theory of state supreme court impact that I present in this chapter owes much to the neo-institutional approach to the study of state supreme courts that was developed by Brace and Hall.[4] These scholars did not directly address the issue of judicial impact, but in a series of studies they demonstrated that the behavior of state supreme court justices varies depending on their institutional contexts. Among the most important determinants of judicial behavior that they identified were methods of judicial selection and retention. Brace and Hall showed that when judges are retained through contested elections, they are more likely to vote responsively to constituent preferences, especially when cases involve salient issues such as the death penalty.[5]

My approach extends this theory by maintaining that another way that institutions matter is by influencing the impact of state supreme courts. Specifically, I argue that institutional design choices have two main types of consequences for judicial impact. First, institutions matter because they establish the rules of the game, defining the constraints under which judges operate. For example, when judges are attempting to influence policy, it matters how difficult it is to amend their state constitutions. If constitutional amendment procedures are burdensome,

---

[4] *See* Brace & Hall, *Integrated Models of Judicial Dissent*, *supra* Chapter 1, note 7; Brace & Hall, *The Interplay of Preferences, Case Facts, Context, and Rules in the Politics of Judicial Choice, supra* Chapter 1, note 7; Brace & Hall, *Neo-Institutionalism and Dissent in State Supreme Courts, supra* Chapter 1, note 7; Brace & Hall, *Studying Courts Comparatively, supra* Chapter 1, note 7; Hall, *Constituent Influence in State Supreme Courts, supra* Chapter 1, note 7; Hall, *Electoral Politics and Strategic Voting in State Supreme Courts, supra* Chapter 1, note 7; Hall & Brace, *supra* Chapter 1, note 7.

[5] *See, e.g.,* Brace & Hall, *The Interplay of Preferences, Case Facts, Context, and Rules in the Politics of Judicial Choice, supra* Chapter 1, note 7, at 1206 ("Personal preferences notwithstanding, individual justices' support for the death penalty is affected by competitive electoral conditions and institutional arrangements that create linkages with the political environment.").

judges will have more potential for influence because their constitutional rulings on issues such as same-sex marriage cannot be easily overturned. Also important is whether judges are held directly accountable to the voting public for unpopular decisions. Elected judges, who have diminished independence, might be less willing to press for unpopular reforms because they will feel pressured to vote in ways that the public supports.

A second, related way that institutions matter is by defining the resources that are available to judges to establish the legitimacy of their holdings. Depending on how state constitutions are written, some judges might find that they have more favorable texts, such as equal rights amendments, which they can use to justify pro-marriage rulings. Alternatively, certain judges might find that, in the absence of such text, they have well-established precedents or constitutional traditions that support their judgments. To the extent that the legitimacy of state court decisions depends on how well judges defend their policy choices, these types of variations in constitutional resources might influence how well court decisions on issues such as same-sex marriage are received.

In both respects, the democratization of state courts and state constitutional systems has made it more difficult for judges to reform state marriage laws. The direct participation of citizens in the selection of judges and the drafting of constitutional language has created environments in which judges have less cover to take principled stands against majority preferences. Using initiative amendment procedures, citizens can ensure that the language of their state constitutions reflects their values. Judges in initiative states will consequently have a harder time justifying pro-marriage decisions because their constitutions will contain fewer textual hooks to support them. Indeed, judges in many states have contended with constitutional language specifically forbidding them to legalize same-sex marriage, the result of constitutional amendments that were approved since 1998. Many of these states also use judicial elections, so citizens can remove from office judges who try to stand against them. Judges therefore have found that they have both fewer textual resources available to them to justify pro-marriage decisions as well as greater costs incurred when they do.

Democratization also has the potential to transform how citizens think about judges, causing citizens to view judges less as principled interpreters of legal texts and more like other career politicians, such as legislators and governors. As I discuss below, there is evidence to suggest that citizens have less confidence in elected judges and that citizens are less likely to trust elected judges to deal with morality policies such as same-sex marriage as compared to judges in appointment and merit systems. A consequence of these attitudes is that elected judges may be less capable of building public support for their decisions. Elected judges cannot as easily persuade the public that, when they do take a stand for minority rights, they are doing so on the basis of constitutional principles.

In the rest of the chapter I go into more detail about my theory, examining the factors that limit the impact of all judges, state and federal, and exploring how institutional and environmental variations among the states can strengthen or weaken the capacity of state judges to overcome these constraints on their power. By investigating how institutional and environmental differences among the states have influenced same-sex marriage policy, we can have a better understanding of why the reactions to the same-sex marriage cases have been so variable and, more generally, why judges appear to have such different capacities to influence salient government policies.

Constraints on Judicial Power

From the outset it should be noted that there are good reasons for supposing that courts in general are constrained institutions, subject to significant limitations on their capacity to bring about meaningful social change. Much of the literature on judicial impact has focused on the U.S. Supreme Court.[6] However, there are good reasons for supposing that many of the constraints described in this literature also limit the power of state judges. Like the U.S. Supreme Court, state supreme courts are reactive institutions, and for the most part the judges have only limited control over the implementation of their decisions.

The difference, as I discuss below, is that many state supreme courts lack the institutional resources that they need to overcome these formal constraints on their power or even to weather temporary storms of public discontent with their decisions. There is a resilience to U.S. Supreme Court decisions that forces the public and policy elites to contend with them, even when the decisions are highly unpopular. Moreover, the U.S. Supreme Court possesses a reserve of public confidence that can assist the Court in the implementation of controversial decisions. When state supreme courts are structured in ways that undermine public confidence in their capacity to make principled decisions, or when their constitutional decisions have fewer institutional safeguards to protect them, state supreme court justices will have a diminished capacity to overcome the constraints on their power.

Claims about the institutional weaknesses of courts are long-standing. Alexander Hamilton, who was among the leading supporters of the Constitution at the time of its ratification, described the federal judiciary in *Federalist* No. 78 as the "least dangerous" branch because it has "neither force nor will but merely judgment."[7] Without Congress's power of the purse or the president's power of the sword, the Supreme Court must rely on its written word, backed by its institutional legitimacy

---

[6] CANON & JOHNSON, *supra* Chapter 1, note 3; Robert A. Dahl, *Decision-Making in a Democracy: The Supreme Court as a National Policy-Maker*, 6 J. PUB. L. 279 (1957); Klarman, *How Brown Changed Race Relations*, *supra* Chapter 1, note 3; ROSENBERG, *supra* Chapter 1, note 3; WASBY, *supra* Chapter 1, note 3.

[7] THE FEDERALIST NO. 78, at 77 (Alexander Hamilton) (Clinton Rossiter ed., 1961).

and the public's trust, to influence government policy. Hamilton assumed that these resources would be incapable of competing with the resources that were available to the other branches.

In an influential article written much later, Dahl questioned whether Supreme Court justices were even interested in vindicating minority rights most of the time.[8] More often than not, Dahl suggested, the justices were likely to be members of the majority coalition. "Except for short-lived transitional periods when the old alliance is disintegrating and the new one is struggling to take control of political institutions, the Supreme Court is inevitably part of the dominant national alliance," Dahl wrote. "As an element in the political leadership of the dominant alliance, the Court of course supports the major policies of the alliance."[9] Dahl observed that most presidents get to appoint about two new justices over the course of a term, which ensures that over time the composition of the Supreme Court will reflect majoritarian values.

Dahl also believed that the Supreme Court was unlikely to be very successful when the justices acted against majority will. "By itself, the Court is almost powerless to affect the course of national policy," he wrote. "In the absence of substantial agreement within the alliance, an attempt by the Court to make national policy is likely to lead to disaster, as the *Dred Scott* decision and the early New Deal cases demonstrate."[10] During periods in which the majority coalition is unstable or undergoing a transition, Supreme Court justices might have a greater capacity to influence national policy, but Dahl believed that the justices were likely to be more successful at playing their more natural role, conferring legitimacy on the policies of the majority coalition.

Dahl's description of the U.S. Supreme Court as an inherently constrained institution received considerable empirical and theoretical elaboration in Rosenberg's seminal work, *The Hollow Hope*.[11] In the first edition of the book, published in 1991, Rosenberg evaluated the capacity of the U.S. Supreme Court to produce social change; primarily he did so by studying the influence of two landmark cases, *Brown v. Board of Education* and *Roe v. Wade*.[12] The Supreme Court is credited in *Brown* with bringing about an end to segregation in the public schools, whereas *Roe* is said to have liberalized national abortion policy. Both cases have been heralded as landmark victories for reform groups.

However, Rosenberg demonstrates that neither case actually produced the changes that reform groups sought. The impotence of the Supreme Court in the years after *Brown* is especially striking. Ten years after the justices ruled that segregation had no place in the public schools, less than 1 percent of black school children in the South were attending public schools with whites.[13] Meaningful social

---

[8] Dahl, *supra* note 6.

[9] *Id.* at 293.

[10] *Id.*

[11] Rosenberg, *supra* Chapter 1, note 3.

[12] Brown v. Board of Education, 347 U.S. 483 (1954); Roe v. Wade, 410 U.S. 113 (1973).

[13] Rosenberg, supra Chapter 1, note 3, at 49–54.

change occurred only after Congress enacted the 1964 Civil Rights Act, and the Department of Health, Education, and Welfare threatened to cut off federal funds to school districts that refused to integrate. By itself, *Brown* had virtually no impact on integration rates.

Rosenberg also maintains that the importance of *Roe v. Wade* in establishing abortion rights has been overstated. Although *Roe* did strike down abortion laws in forty-six states in addition to the District of Columbia, the justices did not single-handedly transform abortion policy. Public support for abortion rights had begun to increase in the years prior to *Roe*, and in fact a number of states had already liberalized their abortion laws by the time of the decision. Rosenberg finds that between 1966 and 1985 the largest increase in the number of legal abortions occurred in 1969–1971, several years prior to *Roe*.[14] The Supreme Court might have helped to validate these trends and facilitate their expansion, but the justices did not initiate them. The Supreme Court was acting consistently with an emerging pro-choice movement that was already gaining traction in states such as Alaska, Hawaii, New York, and Washington. Many other states were in the process of revising their laws but were preempted by *Roe*.

Rosenberg's analysis of the impact of *Brown* and *Roe* supports his hypothesis that litigation is a hollow hope, that reform groups are unlikely to bring about social change by taking their grievances to court. According to Rosenberg, the Supreme Court is an inherently constrained institution, confined by three structural limitations on its power. The first constraint is the limited nature of rights. Rosenberg explains that for Supreme Court justices to act on behalf of disadvantaged groups, they must establish a new right or expand the application of an existing one. Either approach requires the justices to ground their actions in a plausible interpretation of the Constitution or another legal authority. "Judicial discretion is bound by the beliefs and norms of this legal culture," Rosenberg writes, "and decisions that stray too far from them are likely to be reversed and severely criticized."[15] Even when the justices are sympathetic to disadvantaged groups and wish to rule in their favor, there may be only so much that they can do. The justices cannot create new constitutional rights out of whole cloth, not if they want their decisions to be accepted by other political actors and the legal community. Justices must achieve their policy goals within the existing legal framework.

A second constraint that Rosenberg describes is the lack of judicial independence. The Supreme Court operates in a system of checks and balances in which other government actors have resources to limit the effects of Supreme Court decisions that they dislike. Article V of the U.S. Constitution specifies procedures by which Congress and the states can amend the Constitution to overturn an unfavorable constitutional judgment by the Supreme Court.[16] Congress can also threaten

---

[14] *Id.* at 178–80.

[15] *Id.* at 11.

[16] U.S. CONST. art. V ("The Congress, whenever two thirds of both Houses shall deem it necessary, shall propose Amendments to this Constitution, or, on the Application of the Legislatures of two

to curb the power of the Supreme Court by changing the size of its membership, eliminating some of its appellate jurisdiction, or limiting the Supreme Court's budget.[17] In statutory cases, Congress can override the Supreme Court's interpretations of federal statutes simply by enacting new laws clarifying congressional intent.[18] These institutional checks and balances matter because they provide resources for the other branches to correct what they perceive to be excesses of judicial power. Although court-curbing measures are rarely employed at the federal level, the fact that they exist might be sufficient to discourage the justices from pushing their power too far beyond what other actors will accept.

Finally, and perhaps most important, Supreme Court justices lack formal implementation powers. "Court decisions, requiring people to act, are not self-executing," Rosenberg observes.[19] Unlike the president and Congress, Supreme Court justices who face resistance to their policies lack resources to compel other actors to follow them. The justices cannot, for example, deploy troops as the president can to secure compliance, or gain leverage using the financial incentives that Congress employs. The Supreme Court depends on other actors to interpret and implement their decisions consistently with their intentions. Yet, because these actors are likely to have their own attitudes about policies, they may not be willing to implement judicial decisions faithfully. When interpreting and implementing groups shirk their

thirds of the several States, shall call a Convention for proposing Amendments, which, in either Case, shall be valid to all Intents and Purposes, as Part of this Constitution, when ratified by the Legislatures of three fourths of the several States, or by Conventions in three fourths thereof, as the one or the other Mode of Ratification may be proposed by the Congress").

[17] Article III of the Constitution does not specify the size of the Supreme Court, and over time the number of justices has varied, from as few as six in 1789 to as many as ten in 1863. Perhaps the most famous controversy concerning the size of the Supreme Court occurred during the 1930s, when President Franklin Delano Roosevelt proposed adding up to six new justices to the Supreme Court for every justice who was over the age of seventy. Congress also has the power to restrict the appellate jurisdiction of the Supreme Court under the Exceptions Clause of Article III, section 2, as interpreted by Chief Justice John Marshall in *Marbury v. Madison*, 5 U.S. 137 (1803). Finally, the Supreme Court's budget must be approved by Congress, and it has become customary for two of the justices to attend a congressional hearing to comment on their expenditures. Congress can use the occasion to vent its frustrations with the justices about their decisions or other practices. *See* Linda Greenhouse, *Two Justices Indicate Supreme Court Is Unlikely to Televise Sessions*, N.Y. TIMES, Apr. 4, 2006, at A16.

[18] *But see* Richard L. Hasen, *End of the Dialogue? Political Polarization, the Supreme Court, and Congress*, S. CAL. L. REV. (forthcoming), at 4, *available at* SSRN: http://ssrn.com/abstract=2130190 ("In fact, in the last two decades the rate of Congressional overriding of Supreme Court statutory decisions has plummeted dramatically, from an average of 12 overrulings of Supreme Court cases in each two-year Congressional term during the 1975–1990 period to an average of 4.8 overrides for each term from 1991–2000 and to a mere 2.7 average number of overrides for each term from 2001–2002."); and Adam Liptak, *In Congress's Paralysis, a Mightier Supreme Court*, N.Y. TIMES, Aug. 21, 2012, at A10 ("An overlooked consequence of the current polarization and gridlock in Congress…has been a huge transfer of power to the Supreme Court. It almost always has the last word, even in decisions that theoretically invite a Congressional response.").

[19] ROSENBERG, *supra* Chapter 1, note 3, at 15.

responsibilities, the justices must wait for aggrieved parties to bring litigation to them so that they can issue new orders, perhaps more strongly worded than before. These new decisions are just as vulnerable to defiance or evasion by interpreting and implementing groups, leaving the justices once again in the position of having to clarify their intentions.

Rosenberg maintains that, in order to overcome the constraints on their power, Supreme Court justices must have the support of other actors outside of the judicial branch. However, this support is unlikely to be forthcoming when the justices do not have majorities on their side. In an issue area as controversial as same-sex marriage, in which there has been consistently strong public and elite opposition to extending the title of marriage to gay partnerships, the potential for courts to influence policy is likely to be diminished. "Courts may effectively produce significant social reform by providing leverage, or a shield, cover, or excuse, for persons crucial to implementation who are *willing to act*," Rosenberg writes.[20] Yet, unless a court decision is backed by other political actors, it is unlikely to bring about meaningful social change.

To some extent, these constraints on judicial power might be overstated. Federal judges can of course retain jurisdiction to ensure that their orders are being implemented.[21] The justices can also hold in contempt individuals or groups who refuse to put their orders into effect. These sanctions can be costly and are potentially embarrassing to government officials. Still, Rosenberg is most likely correct that the Supreme Court's formal powers are weaker than those of the other branches, particularly when decisions lack widespread support. For example, Rosenberg notes that in the aftermath of *Brown v. Board of Education*, meaningful desegregation did not occur until after the president and Congress became involved. In one of the most famous challenges to *Brown*—when the school system in Little Rock, Arkansas, refused to integrate—President Dwight D. Eisenhower had to deploy the military before the school system, under the direction of Governor Orval Faubus, would comply. If President Eisenhower had been unwilling to back the Supreme Court's order with military force, it is unclear what the justices could have done to ensure that the school district obeyed *Brown* and integrated.[22]

---

[20] *Id.* at 35.

[21] For example, in *Green v. County School Board of New Kent County*, 391 U.S. 430, 439 (1968), which concerned the implementation of *Brown*, Justice William Brennan indicated that the federal district court overseeing the case "should retain jurisdiction until it is clear that state-imposed segregation has been completely removed."

[22] Eisenhower's actions in Little Rock belied his ambivalence about the *Brown* decision. Although Eisenhower did not comment publicly on *Brown*, privately he is reported to have opposed it. ROSENBERG, *supra* Chapter 1, note 3, at 75–76. In his memoirs, Earl Warren revealed that while *Brown* was pending, the president lobbied him privately, stating, "These are not bad people. All they are concerned about is to see that their sweet little girls are not required to sit alongside some big overgrown Negroes." EARL WARREN, THE MEMOIRS OF EARL WARREN 291 (1977). *But see* DAVID A. NICHOLS, A MATTER OF JUSTICE: EISENHOWER AND THE BEGINNING OF THE CIVIL RIGHTS REVOLUTION (2007) (highlighting the numerous accomplishments of the Eisenhower administration in the area of civil rights).

In the second edition of *The Hollow Hope*, published in 2008, Rosenberg assesses the impact of state supreme courts on same-sex marriage. Although his focus is not on the institutional capacity of state courts, in a brief paragraph Rosenberg states that he does not think that the impact of state supreme courts is likely to be much different from that of the U.S. Supreme Court. Rosenberg observes that "there is no reason why the constraints and conditions that limit federal courts from producing significant social reform should not apply to state courts as well."[23] If anything, he believes that state court judges are likely to be more constrained because their decisions do not apply outside of their borders, state judges are often directly accountable to the public in states that hold judicial elections, and the public is less likely to be aware of state supreme court decisions than leading federal precedents. "This may make it easier for elected officials to ignore unpopular state-court decisions and make state courts wary of acting."[24]

Although Rosenberg does not devote much attention to how the influence of state supreme courts is likely to differ from that of the U.S. Supreme Court, he does describe public and elite reactions to several of the state supreme court decisions that favored marriage equality. The response, he finds, was mostly negative. Rosenberg argues that the primary effect of the marriage cases was to create a backlash, mobilizing opponents of marriage equality to support the passage of constitutional amendments prohibiting same-sex marriage, as well as other legislation.[25] Public opinion and media commentary in the aftermath of these decisions was also negative. Rosenberg finds that between 1996 and 2004 the number of negative media stories on same-sex marriage outnumbered positive stories, in one year by more than five to one.[26]

Rosenberg acknowledges that the same-sex marriage decisions had other, more positive effects as well. For example, the victories did result in marriages, giving at least some gay couples new rights and benefits that they otherwise would not have received. The decisions also helped to build mainstream support for civil unions, which seemed less radical to the public once the alternative was permitting same-sex couples to marry. However, Rosenberg maintains that overall the costs of the backlash outweighed the benefits for same-sex couples. "If the cause of same-sex marriage has taken a step forward," he writes, "it has also taken two steps back."[27] More broadly, the history of the same-sex marriage cases reinforces Rosenberg's conclusion that courts are not effective agents of social change. "The lesson here is a simple one," he emphasized, "those who rely on the courts absent significant public

[23] Rosenberg, *supra* Chapter 1, note 3, at 340.

[24] *Id.* at 340.

[25] For more on this backlash, see Klarman, Brown *and* Lawrence *(and* Goodridge*), supra* Chapter 1, note 6; and Klarman, From the Closet to the Altar, *supra* Chapter 1, note 6.

[26] Rosenberg, *supra* Chapter 1, note 3, at 391.

[27] *Id.* at 418.

and political support will fail to achieve meaningful social change, and may set their cause back."[28]

Rosenberg's account of judicial impact has received considerable scholarly attention, as well as its share of criticism.[29] Perhaps the most prominent critic is Michael W. McCann, who maintains that Rosenberg overstates his case, missing some of the less-tangible ways in which judges have influenced reform movements.[30] Particularly important is the potential for courts to legitimize unpopular policy alternatives. If the *Brown* decision did not bring about an immediate end to segregation, it still might have helped to validate the civil rights movement, encouraging further public support and laying the groundwork for future policy victories. Favorable court decisions might have also empowered supporters to stand up and fight for needed change. McCann observes that Rosenberg's own data show that enrollment in the NAACP increased significantly in the years following the *Brown* decision. The increase in registration rates might have been spurred by the Supreme Court's endorsement of civil rights causes in *Brown*.[31]

More broadly, McCann argues that Rosenberg overstates the weaknesses of the Supreme Court compared to the other branches. No institution of government is likely to have a meaningful impact on society without public or elite support. "My reading of scholarly literature, and the newspapers for that matter," McCann writes, "suggests an overwhelming consensus that executive and legislative institutions at all levels have trouble translating their will into effective social change."[32] The American constitutional system of separation of powers and checks and balances ensures that all national institutions will have difficulty making policy unilaterally.

---

[28] *Id.* at 419.

[29] *See* Michael W. McCann, *Reform Litigation on Trial*, 17 LAW & SOC. INQUIRY 715 (1992) (reviewing ROSENBERG, *supra* Chapter 1, note 3); MICHAEL W. MCCANN, RIGHTS AT WORK: PAY EQUITY REFORM AND THE POLITICS OF LEGAL MOBILIZATION (1994) [hereinafter MCCANN, RIGHTS AT WORK]; Michael W. McCann, *Causal versus Constitutive Explanations (or, On the Difficulty of Being so Positive …)*, 21 LAW & SOC. INQUIRY 457 (1996) [hereinafter McCann, *Causal versus Constitutive Explanations*]; Susan Lawrence, *Review*, 86 AM. POL. SCI. REV. 812 (1992) (reviewing ROSENBERG, *supra* Chapter 1, note 3); Jonathan Simon, *"The Long Walk Home" to Politics*, 26 LAW & SOC'Y REV. 923 (1992) (reviewing ROSENBERG, *supra* Chapter 1, note 3).

[30] McCann, *Reform Litigation on Trial, supra* note 29.

[31] Klarman discredits the possibility that *Brown* had this sort of legitimizing effect. *See* Klarman, *How* Brown *Changed Race Relations, supra* Chapter 1, note 3. He finds that, among Southern whites, *Brown* actually caused a blacklash against the movement, while whites in the North became sympathetic only after witnessing the violent repercussions of this backlash in the news media. Klarman also maintains that blacks did not need a Supreme Court decision to validate the civil rights movement for them. Far more important were the experiences of black soldiers returning home from serving in an integrated military in World War II who would not tolerate segregation at home. *But see* McCann, *Reform Litigation on Trial, supra* note 29, at 722, who cites oral history testimony that contradicts Klarman's contention that *Brown* had no legitimizing effect.

[32] McCann, *Reform Litigation on Trial, supra* note 29, at 727.

Meaningful social change almost always requires coordination and cooperation across branches. In subsequent work McCann elaborates on the futility of seeking specific causal explanations for complex social reforms.[33] "The problem," he writes, "is that linear, instrumental conceptions of causality are inadequate tools for explaining the dynamic, indeterminate, contingent, interactive processes of judgment, choice, and reasoned intentionality of people in action."[34] To blame a single institution for the fortunes of a reform movement is to grossly oversimplify how policies develop and societies change.

Ultimately, however, Rosenberg is right to observe that social reformers who try to use courts to produce social change are unlikely to be successful without winning the support of other government actors. Litigation, by itself, is unlikely to be the panacea that reform groups sometimes maintain that it is. Successful litigation strategies require coordinating with other institutions and preparing them to receive unpopular decisions. They also require knowing which courts to approach in the first place. Because state courts are so variable in their form and context, reform advocates must be sensitive to the particular constraints under which state judges operate and litigate in those states that have the greatest capacity to produce the desired outcomes.

Overcoming the Constraints on Judicial Power

The constraints on courts are powerful, but they are not insurmountable. The U.S. Supreme Court possesses institutional resources that permit it to be an effective policy leader in spite of the constraints that Rosenberg articulates. The problem for many state courts is that these advantages are not inherent to courts, but the product of institutional design choices that not all courts share. For example, one advantage that Supreme Court justices enjoy is a relatively high level of public support compared to other institutions.[35] At the time of the 2008 presidential election, for example, 41.9 percent of Americans said that they approved of the job that the Supreme Court was doing, compared to 29.0 percent who approved of President George W. Bush and 18.4 percent who approved of Congress.[36] The Supreme Court

[33] *See* McCann, Rights at Work, *supra* note 29; McCann, *Causal versus Constitutive Explanations*, *supra* note 29.

[34] McCann, *Causal versus Constitutive Explanations*, *supra* note 29, at 460.

[35] *See* Gregory A. Caldeira & James L. Gibson, *The Etiology of Public Support for the Supreme Court*, 36 Am. J. Pol. Sci. 635 (1992); Anke Grosskopf & Jeffrey J. Mondak, *Do Attitudes towards Specific Supreme Court Decisions Matter? The Impact of* Webster *and* Texas v. Johnson *on Public Confidence in the Supreme Court*, 51 Pol. Res. Q. 633 (1998); Walter F. Murphy & Joseph Tanenhaus, *Public Opinion and the United States Supreme Court*, 2 Law & Soc'y Rev. 357 (1968).

[36] Data are from the 2008 Cooperative Congressional Election Study, based on a national internet survey of 32,800 adults. For more information on the survey see Chapter 6.

enjoys such high approval ratings partly because the public holds mythic views of the Supreme Court, perceiving the justices as principled interpreters of the Constitution and defenders of rights. Research on legitimacy theory has found that this tendency to mythify the justices actually intensifies as knowledge about the Court increases and people become more educated about its intended function.[37]

Because confidence in the Supreme Court is so high, the public may be more inclined to support judicial policies that they would not accept from other institutions, such as the presidency and Congress. For example, it is hard to imagine any institution but the U.S. Supreme Court bringing about an end to the 2000 presidential election, as it did in *Bush v. Gore* with such authority and finality.[38] The justices endured criticism for this decision, but the ruling appears not to have had a negative long-term impact on levels of public support for the Court.[39] Moreover, the decision was obeyed without any serious effort by opponents to defy or evade it. Historically, this was not always the case. In the early days of the republic, there were serious questions about whether elected officials would follow Supreme Court decisions that they opposed. Such considerations led Chief Justice John Marshall to rule in favor of the Jefferson administration in *Marbury v. Madison*, despite disagreeing with President Jefferson on the merits of the case, because of the possibility of noncompliance by the president and, worse, sanctions against the Court.[40] A quarter century later, Marshall faced another standoff with a president in *Worcester v. Georgia*, when in response to his order requiring the Jackson administration to honor a treaty with the Cherokee nation, President Jackson is reported to have said, "John Marshall has made his decision, now let him enforce it."[41] The quotation is most likely apocryphal, but there is no doubt that Jackson refused to obey the Court.

Today, very few Supreme Court decisions are defied openly, even when they are unwelcome. Interest groups, elected officials, and other individuals who are

---

[37] Caldeira & Gibson, *supra* note 34; Gregory Casey, *The Supreme Court and Myth: An Empirical Investigation*, 8 LAW & SOC'Y REV. 385 (1974); JOHN R. HIBBING & ELIZABETH THEISS-MORSE, CONGRESS AS PUBLIC ENEMY: PUBLIC ATTITUDES TOWARD AMERICAN POLITICAL INSTITUTIONS (1995); James L. Gibson, Gregory A. Caldeira & Venessa A. Baird, *On the Legitimacy of National High Courts*, 92 AM. POL. SCI. REV. 343 (1998); Murphy & Tanenhaus, *supra* note 35; WALTER F. MURPHY, JOSEPH TANENHAUS & DANIEL KASTNER, PUBLIC EVALUATIONS OF CONSTITUTIONAL COURTS: ALTERNATIVE EXPLANATIONS (1973).

[38] Bush v. Gore, 531 U.S. 98 (2000).

[39] James L. Gibson, Gregory A. Caldeira & Lester K. Spence, *The Supreme Court and the U.S. Presidential Election of 2000: Wounds, Self-Inflicted or Otherwise?*, 58 BRIT. J. POL. SCI. 187 (2003). *But see* Grosskopf & Mondak, *supra* note 35, who found that attitudes about specific Supreme Court decisions such as *Webster v. Reproductive Health Services*, 492 U.S. 490 (1989), and *Texas v. Johnson*, 491 U.S. 397 (1989), can cause public confidence in the Supreme Court to decline.

[40] Marbury v. Madison, 5 U.S. 137 (1803).

[41] Worcester v. Georgia, 31 U.S. 515 (1832).

responsible for interpreting and implementing judicial decisions might try to over-turn Supreme Court precedents, evade them, or limit their effects, but these groups still generally conform to the letter of Supreme Court orders.[42] Government offi-cials who refuse to comply with Supreme Court decisions risk appearing to be flout-ing the rule of law. In this way, the justices are able to compensate, at least partially, for their lack of formal implementation powers. The institutional legitimacy of the U.S. Supreme Court is a source of power for the justices, making it costly for other actors to defy them.

It is open to question, however, whether state judges enjoy this same advantage. As I discuss below, there is research that suggests that public confidence in state courts is variable and that institutional explanations are at least partially responsible for this variation. Several studies have found that judicial elections reduce public confidence in state courts.[43] According to these studies, the problem with judicial elections is that they deprive judges of the appearance that they are principled decision makers who are above politics. The presence of money in campaigns is especially damaging to public confidence.[44]

A second advantage that U.S. Supreme Court justices enjoy over many state judges is that it is very difficult to overturn their constitutional decisions, requiring constitutional amendments that cannot be passed without extraordinary levels of coordination and consensus across the country. According to Article V of the U.S. Constitution, a constitutional amendment must be proposed by two-thirds of both houses of Congress or by a constitutional convention called for by two-thirds of the states. The final amendment must then be approved by three-quarters of the states for ratification.[45] This institutional reality gives even the most politically unpopu-lar U.S. Supreme Court decisions the potential to be game-changing. Although

---

[42] CANON & JOHNSON, *supra* Chapter 1, note 3. This deference also extends to decisions of the U.S. Courts of Appeals. *See* ROBERT J. HUME, HOW COURTS IMPACT FEDERAL ADMINISTRATIVE BEHAVIOR (2009) (on the deference afforded to the circuits by federal administrative agencies).

[43] See Benesh, *supra* Chapter 1, note 8, at 700 ("I expect that institutional features enhancing inde-pendence will contribute to confidence in state courts, while those promoting accountability will detract from it"); Cann & Yates, *supra* Chapter 1, note 8, at 309 ("Judicial election campaigns have yielded criticism from judges, journalists, and the public who argue that these election races are often unseemly and contribute to an erosion of the public's goodwill toward state courts and the public's perception of such courts as legitimate institutions. As these rancorous campaigns are most prevalent in states selecting judges via partisan elections…we hypothesize that citizens in states that use partisan elections (and perhaps nonpartisan election states as well) will have lower levels of diffuse support for their state courts"); and Wenzel et al., *supra* Chapter 1, note 8 at 196 ("partisan labels may cause voters to question the integrity of the bench").

[44] *See* James L. Gibson, *Challenges to the Impartiality of State Supreme Courts: Legitimacy Theory and "New-Style" Judicial Campaigns*, 102 AM. POL. SCI. REV. 59 (2008) [hereinafter Gibson, *Challenges to the Impartiality of State Supreme Courts*]; and James L. Gibson, *"New Style" Judicial Campaigns and the Legitimacy of State High Courts*, 71 J. POL. 1285 (2009).

[45] U.S. CONST. art. V.

Rosenberg is correct to acknowledge the limitations of *Brown* and *Roe*, the fact remains that these decisions were never overturned despite widespread criticism of both of them.

The constitutional decisions of state supreme courts are not necessarily so enduring, as the justices on the California Supreme Court discovered in 2008, when their decision legalizing same-sex marriage was quickly overturned by Proposition 8. As I discuss below, in states such as California citizens can propose constitutional amendments directly using initiative amendment procedures, which require the approval of only a simple majority of the voting public. Using these procedures, unhappy majorities can dispose of unpopular state supreme court decisions relatively quickly.

It is doubtful that a decision that has received the sort of persistent criticism that *Roe v. Wade* has endured would have lasted as long as it has if it were under California's initiative amendment system. Whether they like Supreme Court decisions or not, citizens understand that they must learn to live with these decisions until they can persuade the justices to change their minds. The resilience of U.S. Supreme Court decisions is an important institutional resource that gives the justices a degree of power that their peers on state tribunals often lack. Supreme Court justices know that, regardless of what the public thinks, their decisions will most likely remain on the books.

It should be clear by now that democratization, or rather the lack of it, is central to both of the institutional advantages that the U.S. Supreme Court enjoys over its peers in state tribunals. Variations in public confidence in state courts may be attributable, at least partially, to the fact that some judges are elected. The ease with which many state court decisions can be overturned is related to the availability of initiative amendment procedures. The more that the public participates in the selection of judges and the revision of state constitutions, the less capable judges are of standing against the public. Such accountability may be appropriate in a representative democracy, but the cost is that judges may be unable to act on behalf of minority rights.

Differences between Federal and State Courts

To this point I have written generally about the comparative advantages that federal courts enjoy over many state courts. Now I will explore these differences in detail. Although the institutional and environmental differences described in this chapter are not exhaustive, they give a good sense of the ways in which state courts differ from federal courts and from each other. They also illustrate the institutional advantages that federal judges enjoy that enable them to overcome the constraints on their power.

Because same-sex marriage is a morality policy, I premise my discussion on the assumption that public opinion is central to determining the amount of influence that judges will have. Consequently, the types of factors that I identify are those that the public is likely to be knowledgeable about and that might plausibly influence how the public responds to courts. It is probably necessary to modify the theory when applying it to other, less salient areas of policy, as I discuss in the final chapter. As a general matter, however, I do expect institutional and environmental variations among the states to condition the impact of courts, even if the particular factors that matter depend on the nature of the policy area and the public's level of engagement with the issue.

A. Selection and Retention

One important difference between state supreme courts and the U.S. Supreme Court is in how judges are selected and retained. Only a handful of states appoint their supreme court justices using the procedures employed for federal judges, with appointment by the executive and confirmation by the legislature. Instead many states use some form of election for state supreme court justices, although the procedures vary considerably, as shown in Table 2.1. Some states use partisan or nonpartisan elections for the initial selection of supreme court justices, who then serve for fixed terms before standing for reelection. Other states employ a merit selection system, in which judges are appointed by a governor after being nominated by a nonpartisan selection committee. Typically, judges in merit systems must win uncontested retention elections to keep their seats.

These variations in methods of judicial selection and retention have the potential to affect the impact of state supreme court decisions by influencing levels of judicial independence. On the whole, state supreme court justices in appointment systems enjoy greater independence from electoral and partisan pressures, whereas justices in election systems are more accountable.[46] Even nonpartisan and retention elections, which are designed to emphasize the qualifications of judicial candidates, reduce judicial independence by encouraging accountability.[47] This was their purpose. As Berkson et al. explain, judicial elections were used in the states as early as 1812 because "[p]eople resented the fact that property owners controlled the judiciary. They were determined to end this privilege of the upper class and to ensure

---

[46] *See* Benesh, *supra* Chapter 1, note 8; PHILIP L. DUBOIS, FROM BALLOT TO BENCH: JUDICIAL ELECTIONS AND THE QUEST FOR ACCOUNTABILITY (1980); Nicholas P. Lovrich Jr. & Charles H. Sheldon, *Voters in Contested, Nonpartisan Judicial Elections: A Responsible Electorate or a Problematic Public?*, 36 W. POL. Q. 241 (1983); and Webster, *supra* Chapter 1, note 67.

[47] *See* Melinda Gann Hall, *State Supreme Courts in American Democracy: Probing the Myths of Judicial Reform*, 95 AM. POL. SCI. REV. 315, 326 (2001) [hereinafter Hall, *State Supreme Courts in American Democracy*] ("Concerning independence, court reformers assert...that nonpartisan and retention elections will take politics out of the judicial selection process. Evidence now suggests that this is not the case. State-level patterns of partisan competition as well as competition unique to each contest penetrate retention and nonpartisan elections.").

Table 2.1 **Methods of Initial Selection and Retention of High Court Judges**

State	Initial Selection	Retention
Alabama	Partisan Election	Partisan Election
Alaska	Merit Selection	Retention Election
Arizona	Merit Selection	Retention Election
Arkansas	Nonpartisan Election	Nonpartisan Election
California	Gubernatorial Appointment	Retention Election
Colorado	Merit Selection	Retention Election
Connecticut	Merit Selection	Reappointment
Delaware	Merit Selection	Reappointment
Florida	Merit Selection	Retention Election
Georgia	Nonpartisan Election	Nonpartisan Election
Hawaii	Merit Selection	Reappointment
Idaho	Nonpartisan Election	Nonpartisan Election
Illinois	Partisan Election	Retention Election
Indiana	Merit Selection	Retention Election
Iowa	Merit Selection	Retention Election
Kansas	Merit Selection	Retention Election
Kentucky	Nonpartisan Election	Nonpartisan Election
Louisiana	Partisan Election	Partisan Election
Maine	Gubernatorial Appointment	Reappointment
Maryland	Merit Selection	Retention Election
Massachusetts	Merit Selection	Life Tenure
Michigan	Nonpartisan Election	Nonpartisan Election
Minnesota	Nonpartisan Election	Nonpartisan Election
Mississippi	Nonpartisan Election	Nonpartisan Election
Missouri	Merit Selection	Retention Election
Montana	Nonpartisan Election	Nonpartisan Election
Nebraska	Merit Selection	Retention Election
Nevada	Nonpartisan Election	Nonpartisan Election
New Hampshire	Merit Selection	Life Tenure
New Jersey	Gubernatorial Appointment	Reappointment
New Mexico	Partisan Election	Retention Election

State	Initial Selection	Retention
New York	Merit Selection	Reappointment
North Carolina	Nonpartisan Election	Nonpartisan Election
North Dakota	Nonpartisan Election	Nonpartisan Election
Ohio	Nonpartisan Election	Nonpartisan Election
Oklahoma	Merit Selection	Retention Election
Oregon	Nonpartisan Election	Nonpartisan Election
Pennsylvania	Partisan Election	Retention Election
Rhode Island	Merit Selection	Life Tenure
South Carolina	Legislative Appointment	Reappointment
South Dakota	Merit Selection	Retention Election
Tennessee	Merit Selection	Retention Election
Texas	Partisan Election	Partisan Election
Utah	Merit Selection	Retention Election
Vermont	Merit Selection	Reappointment
Virginia	Legislative Appointment	Reappointment
Washington	Nonpartisan Election	Nonpartisan Election
West Virginia	Partisan Election	Partisan Election
Wisconsin	Nonpartisan Election	Nonpartisan Election
Wyoming	Merit Selection	Retention Election

Source: American Judicature Society

the popular sovereignty."[48] Judicial elections have made judges more accountable to the public, and in this way have made state judicial systems more compatible with democratic values. The problem is that as their independence declines, state supreme court justices are less capable of issuing decisions that are at odds with public values. Compared to judges in appointment systems, judges who are directly accountable to the public may be less willing or less able to act without majority support.

One way that judicial elections can influence the impact of state supreme courts is by giving opponents of their decisions an opportunity to mobilize against the justices, adding to the numerous constraints under which judges already operate. As discussed above, even justices on the U.S. Supreme Court lack true independence because other branches have resources to blunt the impact of their decisions

---

[48] Berkson et al., *supra* Chapter 1, note 9, at 1.

using constitutional amendments and other court-curbing measures.[49] When state supreme court justices are elected directly by the public, they are likely to be even more constrained because they can be voted out of office for unpopular decisions and replaced with justices who pledge to interpret state constitutions more consistently with the public will.

A second potential influence of judicial elections is that they can affect whether the public is prepared to accept state supreme court decisions that they oppose. Because appointed judges are more insulated from political and electoral pressures, they benefit from a presumption that they decide cases differently from other policy makers, a presumption that elected judges may lack. As Webster explains, "the public's degree of respect for the judiciary bears a direct correlation to the belief that judges will decide cases fairly and impartially, in accordance with the 'rule of law'— that decisions will be reached based upon the facts and the applicable law, without regard to extraneous influences, whether in the form of special interest groups or popular opinion."[50] The public believes that U.S. Supreme Court justices, who are appointed to life terms, behave differently from other governmental actors. The public tends to ascribe to mythic views of the Supreme Court, that the justices are principled interpreters of the Constitution and defenders of constitutional rights.[51] Because Supreme Court justices are unelected and largely removed from politics, they are more likely to seem above politics, giving them freedom to act in controversial issue areas while retaining their legitimacy.

In states that use judicial elections, however, supreme court justices might seem less principled and less entitled to deference. Research suggests that overall public confidence in state courts varies with the selection system. Benesh, for example, found that public confidence in state supreme courts tends to be lower when states use partisan elections.[52] Other research has corroborated these results.[53] More

---

[49] ROSENBERG, *supra* Chapter 1, note 3, at 14 ("although Congress cannot directly reverse decisions based on constitutional interpretations, presumably untouched by the democratic process, it may be able to constrain them by threatening certain changes in the legal structure").

[50] Webster, *supra* Chapter 1, note 67, at 9.

[51] *See* Caldeira & Gibson, *supra* note 35; Casey, *supra* note 37; HIBBING & THEISS-MORSE, *supra* note 37; Gibson et al., *On the Legitimacy of National High Courts, supra* note 37; Murphy & Tanenhaus, *supra* note 35; MURPHY ET AL., *supra* note 37.

[52] Benesh, *supra* Chapter 1, note 8, at 704.

[53] *See* Cann & Yates, *supra* Chapter 1, note 8, at 313 ("State judicial selection dynamics have a profound effect on diffuse support of state courts. Citizens in states using partisan elections to select judges have lower levels of diffuse support than citizens in states that appoint their judges. This supports our hypothesis that competitive, politicized judicial elections vitiate citizen perceptions of the legitimacy of state courts"); and Wenzel et al., *supra* Chapter 1, note 8, at 200 ("partisan appointment systems are, as hypothesized, associated with a lower level of support for local courts"). *But see* Christine A. Kelleher & Jennifer Wolak, *Explaining Public Confidence in the Branches of State Government*, 60 POL. RES. Q. 60 (2007), at 715 (who found no statistically significant relationship between judicial elections and public confidence in state courts).

recently, Gibson found that elections, by themselves, enhance judicial legitimacy, but that certain features of "new style" judicial election campaigns are harmful to courts.[54] For example, Gibson found that campaign contributions hurt judicial legitimacy.[55] His findings are consistent with other research that suggests that campaign contributions undermine public confidence in courts by creating a perception of judicial impropriety.[56]

Bonneau and Hall dispute the finding by Benesh and others that judicial elections decrease public confidence in courts, observing that elections promote greater citizen participation and that voters consistently favor elections over other judicial selection alternatives.[57] The authors suggest that unobserved factors might explain the correlation between partisan elections and diminished public confidence.[58] Without denying this possibility, or the fact that there are positive benefits to judicial elections that the public might favor, it also seems reasonable to think that citizens will view the decisions of elected judges differently from those of their appointed colleagues. With the loss of their independence, elected judges are no longer likely to appear to be "above" politics, making it harder for them to maintain the impression that they are engaged in principled decision making. In this way, citizens might come to extend less deference to the decisions of elected judges, even if, on balance, they prefer to keep their judges accountable to them.

[54] *See* Chris W. Bonneau, *What Price Justice(s)? Understanding Campaign Spending in State Supreme Court Elections*, 5 St. Pol. & Pol'y Q. 107 (2005); Marie Hojnacki & Lawrence Baum, *Choosing Judicial Candidates: How Voters Explain Their Decisions*, 75 Judicature 300 (1992).

[55] *See* Gibson, *Challenges to the Impartiality of State Supreme Courts*, *supra* note 44, at 72 ("Those concerned about threats to the legitimacy of elected state courts would do well to turn their attention away from substantive policy pronouncements and focus instead on the corrosive effects of politicized campaigning, and especially campaign contributions from those having business before the bench"); and Gibson, *"New Style" Judicial Campaigns and the Legitimacy of State High Courts*, *supra* note 44, at 1298 ("When judges express their policy views during campaigns for elected judgeships, no harm is done to the institutional legitimacy of courts....At the same time, the current system of campaign contributions does appear to be injurious to courts").

[56] *See* Damon Cann, *Campaign Contributions and Judicial Behavior*, 23 Am. Rev. Pol. 261 (2002); and John R. Hibbing and Elizabeth Theiss-Morse, Stealth Democracy: Americans' Beliefs about How Government Should Work (2002).

[57] *See* Bonneau & Hall, *supra* Chapter 1, note 67, at 47; and Melinda Gann Hall & Chris W. Bonneau, *Mobilizing Interest: The Effects of Money on Citizen Participation in State Supreme Court Elections*, 52 Am. J. Pol. Sci. 457 (2008).

[58] Bonneau & Hall, *supra* Chapter 1, note 67, at 47 ("[W]e suggest that lower levels of confidence and diffuse support for courts in partisan states might be less related to judicial elections and more closely connected to factors in the broader political environment. Rather than judicial elections creating negative feelings about courts it seems just as likely that voters in some states start out being more negative toward government and, as a consequence, choose to elect judges rather than surrender this important power to political elites. Thus, partisan elections might well be the effect of negative feelings toward government rather than the cause.").

Altogether, these considerations suggest that methods of judicial selection and retention will influence the impact of state supreme courts. In particular, one might expect the public to be more likely to accept court decisions favoring same-sex marriage in states that promote judicial independence. This is not to say that the public will accept any decision from an appointed judge. However, compared to judges in election systems, appointed judges should be more likely to win the public's support because the public will be more likely to assume that the judges are engaging in principled decision making.

B. Constitutional Amendment Procedures

A second way that the state institutional context differs from the federal context is in the methods employed for amending state constitutions. Put simply, it is significantly easier to amend many state constitutions than it is to amend the U.S. Constitution, which gives constitutional judgments of the U.S. Supreme Court much greater staying power. Virtually all states permit their citizens to have at least some direct role in the adoption of amendments. An outline of these constitutional amendment procedures is provided in Table 2.2. In some states, citizens have the power to propose amendments to their state constitutions through initiative procedures, whereas in other states amendments are proposed by the legislature. In every state except Delaware, proposed amendments are then put before the citizens for a vote. Delaware does not let citizens vote directly on amendments, but amendments in Delaware must be approved by two-thirds majorities in two legislative sessions, with the second session occurring after a general election.[59]

States that permit citizens to propose amendments generally use one of two initiative procedures. In systems that use *direct initiatives*, amendments appear on the ballot once they have received enough signatures to qualify. The number of signatures is usually not high relative to the total state population, so the requirement is not too burdensome for groups that are organized. To get Proposition 8 on the ballot, for example, opponents of same-sex marriage in California needed to collect signatures equaling 8.0 percent of the voters who participated in the last gubernatorial election. On an issue as divisive as same-sex marriage, groups are unlikely to have much difficulty obtaining this many signatures. Once the signatures were collected, Proposition 8 needed the approval of a simple majority of California voters to go into effect.

Systems with *indirect initiatives* require proposed amendments also to be approved by the state legislature before they appear on the ballot.[60] Only two

---

[59] DEL. CONST. art. XVI, § 1.

[60] For initiative procedures, see THE INITIATIVE AND REFERENDUM INSTITUTE AT THE UNIVERSITY OF SOUTHERN CALIFORNIA, http://www.iandrinstitute.org.

Table 2.2 **Overview of Procedures for Amending State Constitutions**

State	Direct Initiative	Indirect Initiative	No Initiative	Anti-SSM Amendment	Amendment Also Bans Civil Unions
Alabama			X	X	X
Alaska			X	X	
Arizona	X			X	
Arkansas	X			X	X
California	X			X	
Colorado	X			X	
Connecticut			X		
Delaware			X		
Florida	X			X	X
Georgia			X	X	X
Hawaii			X	X	
Idaho			X	X	X
Illinois	X				
Indiana			X		
Iowa			X		
Kansas			X	X	X
Kentucky			X	X	X
Louisiana			X	X	X
Maine			X		
Maryland			X		
Massachusetts		X			
Michigan	X			X	X
Minnesota			X		
Mississippi		X		X	
Missouri	X			X	
Montana	X			X	
Nebraska	X			X	X
Nevada	X			X	
New Hampshire			X		

(Continued)

Table 2.2 (Continued)

State	Direct Initiative	Indirect Initiative	No Initiative	Anti-SSM Amendment	Amendment Also Bans Civil Unions
New Jersey			X		
New Mexico			X		
New York			X		
North Carolina			X	X	X
North Dakota	X			X	X
Ohio	X			X	X
Oklahoma	X			X	X
Oregon	X			X	
Pennsylvania			X		
Rhode Island			X		
South Carolina			X	X	X
South Dakota	X			X	X
Tennessee			X	X	
Texas			X	X	X
Utah			X	X	X
Vermont			X		
Virginia			X	X	X
Washington			X		
West Virginia			X		
Wisconsin			X	X	X
Wyoming			X		
Total	16	2	32	31	20

Sources: Initiative and Referendum Institute (for initiative amendment procedures)

states, Massachusetts and Mississippi, use indirect initiatives for state constitutional amendments, whereas the other sixteen states that permit initiatives use direct initiatives. In Massachusetts, citizens who would like to propose an amendment must collect signatures equivalent to 3.0 percent of the vote for the governor in the previous election. The proposed amendment must then be approved by 25 percent of the Massachusetts legislature, or fifty votes, in two successive sessions of the legislature before it can be put before the general public for a vote. Alternatively, the state legislature can propose its own amendment with the support of at least 50 percent of legislators convening in two successive sessions.

It is reasonable to think that these variations in state amendment procedures will influence the impact of judges. By increasing the ease with which the constitutional decisions of state supreme courts can be overturned, initiative amendment procedures increase the vulnerability of these decisions, reducing the capacity of state courts to have an enduring impact on government policy, particularly when their decisions run contrary to majoritarian preferences. Research suggests that political minorities, such as gay rights groups, are more likely to have their rights restricted in state constitutional systems that permit direct democracy.[61] Consistent with this research, Table 2.2 reports that of the eighteen states that currently permit voters to use initiatives to propose state constitutional amendments, sixteen (88.9 percent) have already amended their constitutions to forbid same-sex marriage. In contrast, just 46.9 percent of the states that have no initiative amendment procedures have enacted same-sex marriage amendments. The inclusion of state legislatures in the amendment process therefore seems to decrease the likelihood that constitutional amendments prohibiting same-sex marriage will pass.

In fact, a citizen initiative to overturn the Supreme Judicial Court of Massachusetts' 2003 *Goodridge* decision most likely would have made it onto the ballot in 2008 were it not for the intervention of the state legislature. Opponents of same-sex marriage collected the signatures they needed, but in 2007 the legislature did not produce the fifty votes that were necessary to put the amendment on the ballot. The failed vote came just a few months after the state legislature, in the previous session, had initially approved the amendment. If Massachusetts did not have such a demanding procedure, requiring a proposed amendment to be approved in two successive legislative sessions, the amendment more than likely would have been put to a public vote.

C. Judicial Federalism

Another important difference between state supreme courts and the U.S. Supreme Court is that state courts are not limited by the text or interpretive history of the U.S. Constitution. Each state has its own constitution and its own precedents that

---

[61] *See* Barbara S. Gamble, *Putting Civil Rights to a Popular Vote*, 42 Am. J. Pol. Sci. 1343 (1997); Donald P. Haider-Markel, Alana Querze & Kara Lindaman, *Lose, Win, or Draw? A Reexamination of Direct Democracy and Minority Rights*, 60 Pol. Res. Q. 304 (2007); Daniel Lewis, *Direct Democracy and Minority Rights: Same-Sex Marriage Bans in the U.S. States*, 92 Soc. Sci. Q. 364 (2011); Arthur Lupia, Yanna Krupnikov, Adam Seth Levine, Spencer Piston & Alexander Von Hagen-Jamar, *Why State Constitutions Differ in Their Treatment of Same-Sex Marriage*, 72 J. Pol. 1222 (2010); Gary Mucciaroni, Same-Sex, Different Politics: Success and Failure in the Struggles over Gay Rights (2008).

judges can use to justify case outcomes. Depending on what the text of a state constitution says and how that text has been interpreted in previous decisions, state supreme court justices might find that it is easier to have an impact on salient public policies such as same-sex marriage. If the language of a state constitution provides more generous rights protections than the federal constitution, a decision in favor of same-sex marriage might be viewed with greater legitimacy by citizens and lawmakers in the state.

Under principles of judicial federalism, state court judges are free to use their own constitutions to supplement federal rights, but they may not take away rights that are guaranteed by federal law. As Justice Richard N. Palmer observed in 2008 in the Connecticut same-sex marriage decision, "it is beyond debate that federal constitutional and statutory law establishes a *minimum* national standard for the exercise of individual rights and does not inhibit state governments from affording higher levels of protection for such rights."[62] So long as judges are clear that they are basing their decisions on state law, not federal law, and that their rulings do not apply outside the state, state courts may grant their citizens more generous protections than the U.S. Constitution provides.

The U.S. Supreme Court has recognized the practice of judicial federalism, and in *Michigan v. Long* established guidelines that state court judges must follow to make clear that their decisions rest on state law and not federal law.[63] Writing for the majority, Justice Sandra Day O'Connor announced that when a state supreme court invokes both federal and state law in its opinion, "then it need only make clear by a plain statement in its judgment or opinion that the federal cases are being used only for the purpose of guidance, and do not themselves compel the result that the court has reached."[64] If a state supreme court justice states clearly that the basis of the decision is state law, this plain statement will be enough to satisfy the U.S. Supreme Court that the state court has independent and adequate grounds for the decision. Otherwise the justices will assume that the decision is based on federal law and will assert jurisdiction.

Michigan v. Long was criticized by legal commentators at the time who were concerned that the ruling would enable Supreme Court justices to reach out and overturn state supreme court decisions that were not clearly grounded in state law.[65] Justice John Paul Stevens, dissenting in *Long*, would have preferred a more deferential standard than the U.S. Supreme Court endorsed. Instead of assuming that

---

[62] Kerrigan v. Comm'r of Public Health, 289 Conn. 135, 155 (2008) (referencing State v. Morales, 232 Conn. 707, 716 (1995)).

[63] Michigan v. Long, 463 U.S. 1032 (1983).

[64] *Id.* at 1041.

[65] *See* Gregory S. Bruch, Michigan v. Long: *Presumptive Federal Appellate Jurisdiction over State Cases Containing Ambiguous Grounds of Decision*, 69 Iowa L. Rev. 1081 (1984); Robert C. Wels, *Reconsidering the Constitutional Relationship between State and Federal Courts: A Critique of* Michigan v. Long, 59 Notre Dame L. Rev. 1118 (1984).

federal law was the basis of a decision in the absence of a plain statement, Stevens suggested taking the opposite approach: to assume that state law was the basis and to refuse to intercede. The appropriate role of the Court, Stevens argued, was to "vindicate federal rights" from encroachment by the states, not to make it harder for states to expand the federal floor.[66] The *Long* decision would make it easier for conservative justices to overturn state supreme court decisions they disliked, particularly liberal decisions that expanded the federal floor. As it turned out, however, judicial federalism has continued more or less unimpeded,[67] even though the Supreme Court is still committed to the plain statement rule.[68] When state supreme court justices wish to expand the floor of federal rights, they need only make clear in their opinions that their decisions are based on state law and do not apply outside the state. Otherwise, state supreme court justices are free to interpret their own state constitutions as they wish, using whatever interpretive or noninterpretive methods of constitutional interpretation that they feel are appropriate to justify their departures from federal law.

Interpretive approaches to judicial federalism emphasize textual differences between state and federal constitutions. For example, many state constitutions include language specifically protecting citizens against sex discrimination, language that the federal constitution does not contain. The Fourteenth Amendment to the U.S. Constitution is gender neutral, providing "persons" in the several states with equal protection and due process rights. The federal Equal Rights Amendment, which would have specifically provided for gender equality, was never ratified. However, twenty states have enacted equal rights amendments of their own.[69]

[66] Michigan v. Long, 463 U.S. at 1068 (Stevens, J., dissenting).

[67] *See* Patricia Fahlbusch & Daniel Gonzalez, Michigan v. Long: *The Inadequacies of Independent and Adequate State Grounds*, 42 U. Miami L. Rev. 159 (1987); and Ken Gormley, *The Silver Anniversary of New Judicial Federalism*, 66 Alb. L. Rev. 797 (2003).

[68] *See* Matthew G. Simon, *Revisiting* Michigan v. Long *after Twenty Years*, 66 Alb. L. Rev. 969 (2003). Simon examined every case in which the U.S. Supreme Court subsequently cited *Michigan v. Long*. Although the justices cited the decision in just twenty-three cases in twenty years, they made clear that they were committed to the principle. In fourteen cases, a state court included no plain statement and the Supreme Court asserted jurisdiction. In the other nine cases, the state court did include a plain statement, but the Supreme Court still asserted jurisdiction. In other cases, however, state supreme courts have managed to avoid review by the U.S. Supreme Court by including plain statements. *See, e.g.*, State v. Lynch, 796 P.2d 1150 (Okla. 1990) and Batch v. Town of Chapel Hill, 387 S.E.2d 655 (N.C. 1990).

[69] *See* Leslie W. Gladstone, Equal Rights Amendments: State Provisions (2004), *available at* http://www.policyarchive.org/handle/10207/bitstreams/3292.pdf. The twenty states with equal rights amendments are Alaska, California, Colorado, Connecticut, Florida, Hawaii, Illinois, Iowa, Louisiana, Maryland, Massachusetts, Montana, New Hampshire, New Mexico, Pennsylvania, Texas, Utah, Virginia, Washington, and Wyoming. New Jersey in 1947 amended its constitution to make the language gender neutral, but there is debate over whether this action qualifies as an ERA. *See* Robert F. Williams, *The New Jersey Equal Rights Amendment: A Documentary Sourcebook*, 16 Women's Rts. L. Rep. 69 (1994). Following Gladstone, I do not count the New Jersey amendment as an ERA.

For example, Maryland's Constitution was amended in 1972 to read, "Equality of rights under the law shall not be abridged or denied because of sex."[70] The Massachusetts Constitution similarly provides, in language that was adopted in 1976, that "Equality under the law shall not be denied or abridged because of *sex*, race, color, creed or national origin."[71]

These textual differences between state and federal constitutions can make it easier for state supreme court justices to write decisions in favor of same-sex marriage that will be accepted by the public and elected officials within their states. Certainly, this language has provided a legal foundation for judges to rule in favor of marriage equality. In Hawaii, for example, the judges in *Baehr v. Lewin* argued that the state was discriminating on the basis of sex when it refused to issue marriage licenses to same-sex couples.[72] The couples were being denied the right to marry solely because of the sex of their partners, which constituted unlawful sex discrimination under Article I, section 5, of the state constitution. Without this constitutional language to protect them, the justices in *Baehr v. Lewin* might have been more reluctant to act, as they would have had a harder time justifying why they though the decision was commanded by the state constitution. As it was, the reaction to *Baehr v. Lewin* was unfavorable, culminating in the passage in 1998 of a constitutional amendment that authorized the legislature to restrict marriage to opposite-sex couples.

Of course, it is no accident that some constitutional texts are more amenable to the expansion of civil rights than others. Judges in states such as Hawaii had favorable constitutional language available to them because the citizens in these states chose to include equal rights amendments in their constitutions. Citizens supported language that was consistent with their values, which in turn enabled the judges to liberalize state marriage laws. In systems of direct democracy, and particularly in systems in which citizens have initiative amendment procedures available to them, the connection between public attitudes and constitutional texts is likely to be closer than it is in other systems, in which the legislature plays a more dominant role in proposing amendments. In this way, direct democracy provides not only a way for the public to curb judicial power, but to determine which textual resources judges will have to work with in the first place.

A second approach to judicial federalism is noninterpretivism, which focuses on differences in state constitutional histories and traditions. Noninterpretivist approaches are necessary when the language of state and federal constitutions is identical but the interpretation of the language by state supreme courts has been different. It is also necessary when the state constitutional text is largely silent on the issue before the court. The state of Vermont, for example, does not have an equal rights amendment and does not specifically mention sex discrimination,

---

[70] MD. CONST., DEC. RTS., art. 46 (1972).
[71] MASS. CONST. part 1, art. 1 (1976) (emphasis added).
[72] Baehr v. Lewin, 852 P.2d 44 (Haw. 1993).

but in *Baker v. Vermont* the state supreme court observed that the interpretation of the state's Common Benefits Clause differed from the interpretation of the Equal Protection Clause of the federal Constitution.[73] State precedents interpreting the clause, rather than specific textual differences, justified extending the common benefits of marriage to same-sex and opposite-sex partners.

When noninterpretive approaches to judicial federalism are well grounded in state traditions and practices, they have the potential to enhance the legitimacy of state supreme court decisions. State judges might seem less activist if they can link their decisions in favor of same-sex couples to previous state court decisions or other practices within the state. In Vermont, for example, the majority opinion in *Baker* observed that the state legislature had already provided some benefits to same-sex couples, such as making it easier for same-sex couples to adopt.[74] These practices undermined the state's contention that denying same-sex couples the common benefits of marriage was necessary to preserve the link between procreation and child rearing. The link had already been broken by the behavior of the state legislature.

Establishing independent and adequate state grounds for a same-sex marriage decision might not be enough to shield state supreme court justices from criticism, but it does give them some cover for unpopular decisions. For this reason, judicial federalism might help to account for why some state supreme courts have had more of an influence on the same-sex marriage issue than others. Variations in the language and interpretive traditions of state constitutions might affect how a same-sex marriage decision is received by the public and other elected officials, and whether judges are even willing to act in the first place. Judges who have fewer resources within their state constitutions to serve as a foundation for their actions might simply choose to vote against marriage equality.

D. Environment

Just as state constitutions and methods of judicial selection vary from state to state, the social and political environments in which state judges operate are also variable and might influence their impact on controversial government policies. Unlike the U.S. Supreme Court, which presides over a large national constituency with considerable political and demographic variation, state supreme courts have narrower constituencies that can be more homogeneous and idiosyncratic. These environmental variations matter because they affect how receptive states are likely to be to decisions favoring marriage equality. A decision that fits the social and

---

[73] Baker v. Vermont, 744 A.2d 864 (Vt. 1999).
[74] *Id.* at 882.

political environment of one state might be a poor fit for another state, even when the judgments and opinions are identical.

The environment is also important because it shapes the attitudes of the justices who are deciding the same-sex marriage cases. Judges from socially and politically conservative states are more likely to be socially and politically conservative themselves and are probably less willing to write opinions that move marriage policy in a liberal direction. Courts might end up having a less dramatic impact on marriage laws in these states, not because the judges are institutionally constrained, but because their opinions reflect their own more conservative beliefs. For this reason, even appointed judges, who are more insulated than elected judges are from environmental pressures, might tend to make decisions that reflect the values of their constituents.

In particular, I expect three types of environmental differences to influence the impact of state judges on same-sex marriage policy. Perhaps the most important is the ideology of a state's citizenry. Because same-sex marriage is a morality policy, the potential impact of state judges on marriage policy is likely to be heavily conditioned by levels of public support.[75] We know that there is considerable variability in the general ideology of citizens from state to state,[76] as well as in their particular levels of support for same-sex marriage,[77] and these differences should lead to variability in judicial impact.

A second type of environmental difference that is likely to shape judicial impact is the ideology of a state's political institutions. State supreme court justices might find that they are more likely to have an impact on same-sex marriage policy in states that have liberal political institutions or in which the Democratic Party controls the state government. Even when the public opposes the legalization of same-sex marriage, liberal political institutions can serve to filter these sentiments, diffusing popular efforts to limit the effects of unpopular decisions or to curb judicial power.[78]

[75] See Haider-Markel & Meier, supra Chapter 1, note 63, at 333–34 ("The research literature finds that morality politics issues are highly salient with little need to acquire any information...to participate in the debate. Everyone is an expert on morality.... Citizens, therefore, are active and influential in morality politics with coalitions often mobilized around preexisting religious beliefs."); Mooney & Lee, supra Chapter 1, note 63, at 600 ("[M]orality issues tend to be more widely salient and lower in technical complexity than many economically based issues.... This means that not only can a wider range of people have a reasonably informed opinion on a morality policy, they may well care enough about that issue to let their voices be heard.").

[76] See William D. Berry, Evan J. Ringquist, Richard C. Fording & Russell L. Hanson, Measuring Citizen and Government Ideology in the American States, 1960–93, 42 Am. J. Pol. Sci. 327 (1998).

[77] See Jeffrey R. Lax & Justin Phillips, Gay Rights in the States: Public Opinion and Policy Responsiveness, 103 Am. Pol. Sci. Rev. 367 (2009).

[78] Indeed, James Madison envisioned just such a purpose for representative government, "to refine and enlarge the public views, by passing them through the medium of a chosen body of citizens, whose wisdom may best discern the true interest of their country, and whose patriotism and love of justice will be least likely to sacrifice it to temporary or partial considerations. Under such a regulation, it may

Finally, one might expect variations in the activity of interest groups to influence the impact of state supreme courts. Several studies have found that legislative prohibitions of same-sex marriage have been influenced by interest group activity, particularly the activities of LGBT public interest groups and the religious right.[79] When states have a politically active gay population that is willing to act on behalf of their rights, then state court decisions might have more of an impact. Conversely, when a state is populated with a large Evangelical population, or with other religious conservatives, the impact of state courts on marriage policy might be more muted. I examine the systematic influence of these and other environmental factors in subsequent chapters.

Conclusion

This chapter has considered the types of factors that have the potential to influence the impact of state supreme court justices on salient government policies. Among the ways that state judges differ from federal judges, and from one another, are in their methods of selection, their state constitutional texts and structures, and their political and cultural environments. These factors establish the constraints under which state judges operate as well as the resources that they have to overcome their constraints. Depending on whether judges have been elected or appointed, how flexible their state constitutions are, and whether their political and cultural environments support same-sex marriage, judges might find they have a reduced capacity to influence marriage policy.

The list of factors I have considered in this chapter is not intended to be exhaustive. Most likely other factors influence specific phenomena such as the behavior of judges, public support for state court decisions, and the passage of same-sex marriage amendments. The purpose of the discussion to this point has been to identify the types of factors that are the most likely to influence the impact of state supreme court justices across all three of the stages of judicial policy development that I identified in Chapter 1. The influence of other types of factors will be considered in subsequent chapters that are devoted to particular stages. Chapter 5 looks at *policy initiation*, examining when state judges have been more likely to rule in favor of same-sex marriage. Chapter 6 concerns *policy legitimation*, focusing on the conditions in which the public is more likely to support state supreme court decisions favoring

well happen that the public voice, pronounced by the representatives of the people, will be more consonant to the public good than if pronounced by the people themselves, convened for the purpose." THE FEDERALIST No. 10, at 82 (James Madison) (Clinton Rossiter ed., 1961).

[79] *See* Scott Barclay & Shauna Fisher, *The States and the Differing Impetus for Divergent Paths on Same-Sex Marriage, 1990–2001*, 31 POL'Y STUD. J. 331 (2003); and Donald P. Haider-Markel, *Policy Diffusion as a Geographic Expansion of the Scope of Political Conflict: Same-Sex Marriage Bans in the 1990s*, 1 ST. POL. & POL'Y Q. 5 (2001).

same-sex marriage. Chapter 7 focuses on *policy endurance*, identifying when states have enacted constitutional amendments that have overturned or preempted judicial activity on the marriage question. Before analyzing the impact of the same-sex marriage decisions, however, I spend the next two chapters detailing the history and content of these decisions.

THE LEGAL CONTEXT

CHAPTER 3

Early Same-Sex Marriage Decisions

The history of state judicial intervention in the area of same-sex marriage policy is extensive, encompassing the next two chapters. Although same-sex marriage launched onto the public agenda in 1993, when Hawaii ruled that the state's ban constituted sex discrimination under the state constitution, state supreme courts have actually been ruling on the issue since at least the 1970s, when the Minnesota Supreme Court ruled against same-sex couples in *Baker v. Nelson*.[1] These courts have been far from uniform in their approach to the marriage question. Despite headlines generated by high courts in Hawaii, Massachusetts, California, Connecticut, and Iowa, all of which required marriage equality, many state court decisions have been less favorable to same-sex couples.[2] State appellate judges refused to extend constitutional protections to couples in Arizona, Indiana, New York, Washington, Rhode Island, and Maryland.[3] Other states presented only partial victories to supporters of same-sex marriage, requiring legislatures in Vermont and New Jersey to create civil unions but not marriages.[4]

When considering the sort of impact that state supreme courts have had on same-sex marriage policy, it is important to recognize that state courts have been both helpful and harmful to LGBT interests. It is not as though state courts presented a consistently united front after Hawaii's landmark decision in 1993. Yet, it is also true that state judges were much more willing to rule in favor of marriage equality than either federal judges or state legislators were in the two decades after *Baehr v. Lewin*. It is state courts that took the initiative on same-sex marriage, and it is reactions to state

[1] Baker v. Nelson, 191 N.W.2d 185 (Minn. 1971).

[2] Baehr v. Lewin, 852 P.2d 44 (Haw. 1993); Goodridge v. Dep't of Public Health, 798 N.E.2d 941 (Mass. 2003); Opinion of the Justices to the Senate, 802 N.E.2d 565 (Mass. 2004); *In re* Marriage Cases, 43 Cal. 4th 757 (2008); Kerrigan v. Comm'r of Pub. Health, 289 Conn. 135 (2008); Varnum v. Brien, 763 N.W.2d 862 (Iowa 2009).

[3] Standhardt v. Superior Court, 77 P. 3d 451 (Ariz. App. 2003); Morrison v. Sadler, 821 N.E.2d 15 (Ind. Ct. App. 2005); Hernandez v. Robles, 855 N.E.2d 1 (N.Y. 2006); Anderson v. King Cnty., 138 P.3d 963 (Wash. 2006); Chambers v. Ormiston, 935 A.2d 956 (R.I. 2007); Conaway v. Deane, 932 A.2d 571 (Md. 2007).

[4] Baker v. Vermont, 744 A.2d 864 (Vt. 1999); Lewis v. Harris, 908 A.2d 196 (N.J. 2006).

court decisions that largely determined how the issue evolved during this period. Detailing the history of state court decisions in same-sex marriage policy provides an overview of the range of judicial responses to the marriage question and contextualizes the analysis of judicial impact that follows in the second half of the book.[5]

An Overview of Legal Challenges to Same-Sex Marriage Bans

Constitutional challenges to state prohibitions of same-sex marriage generally fall into one of two categories, regardless of whether the foundations of the challenges are federal or state constitutional law. Same-sex couples tend to argue either that a state's action has deprived them of a fundamental right, such as the right to marry, or that a state has denied them the equal protection of the laws. A combination of these arguments is also possible. Less commonly, supporters of same-sex marriage maintain that a state has unconstitutionally established religion or that it has denied them their freedom of speech.

The first type of legal challenge focuses on the fundamental rights of same-sex couples. In federal law, these rights are typically grounded in the Fourteenth Amendment's Due Process Clause, which provides that states cannot deprive citizens of their "life, liberty, or property without due process of law."[6] Most state constitutions also have clauses with similar language. For example, the Massachusetts constitution provides that "Each individual of the society has a right to be protected by it in the enjoyment of his life, liberty and property, according to standing laws."[7] The Connecticut Constitution reads, "No person shall...be deprived of life, liberty or property without due process of law."[8] Like much constitutional language, due process clauses are written in broad, ambiguous phrases, leaving it up to judges to determine what rights the clauses protect. Although judges disagree about how to give substantive meaning to due process clauses, a common approach was developed by Justice Benjamin Cardozo of the U.S. Supreme Court in *Palko v. Connecticut*.[9] Cardozo believed that one could identify fundamental rights by looking to the "traditions and conscience of our people," for those rights that "have been found to be

[5] This history looks only at litigation concerning same-sex marriage and not other related issues, such as adoption policies and antidiscrimination laws. For a more comprehensive overview of gay rights law, see WILLIAM N. ESKRIDGE, JR., GAYLAW: CHALLENGING THE APARTHEID OF THE CLOSET (1999); SUSAN GLUCK MEZEY, GAY FAMILIES AND THE COURTS: THE QUEST FOR EQUAL RIGHTS (2009); SUSAN GLUCK MEZEY, QUEERS IN COURT: GAY RIGHTS LAW AND PUBLIC POLICY (2007); MARK STRASSER, SAME-SEX UNIONS ACROSS THE UNITED STATES (2011).

[6] U.S. CONST. amend. XIV, § 1. The Fifth Amendment has a due process clause with identical language restricting the federal government. U.S.CONST. amend. V.

[7] MASS. CONST. part 1, art. 10.

[8] CONN. CONST. art. I, § 8.

[9] Palko v. Connecticut, 302 U.S. 319 (1937).

implicit in the concept of ordered liberty."[10] If certain rights are well established in the nation's traditions, they might be regarded as fundamental even if they are not specifically mentioned in the constitutional text.

Among the fundamental rights that judges have recognized in both federal and state constitutional law is the right to marry.[11] Most significantly for same-sex couples, the U.S. Supreme Court in *Loving v. Virginia* maintained that state laws barring interracial marriages violated the Fourteenth Amendment's Due Process Clause.[12] "The freedom to marry," Chief Justice Earl Warren observed, "has long been recognized as one of the vital personal rights essential to the orderly pursuit of happiness."[13] Building on *Loving* and analogous state court decisions,[14] supporters of same-sex marriage have argued that the fundamental right to marry cannot be denied to couples on the basis of sexual orientation, just as it cannot be denied on the basis of race. If state supreme court judges agree that same-sex marriage is a constitutionally protected fundamental right, then state legislatures would most likely have to demonstrate that they have a compelling interest for limiting that right, which can be difficult to establish.

Aside from making due process arguments, same-sex couples have maintained that statutes limiting marriage to opposite-sex couples deprive them of the equal protection of the laws. Federal equal protection challenges are also grounded in the Fourteenth Amendment.[15] Much like the Due Process Clause, the federal Equal Protection Clause has analogues in many state constitutions, some of which predate the Fourteenth Amendment. For example, Vermont has a common benefits clause that was included in its original 1777 Constitution.[16] Other state constitutions are more recent than the Fourteenth Amendment and more detailed. Hawaii's constitution provides that "no person shall...be denied the enjoyment of...civil rights or be discriminated against in the exercise thereof because of race, religion, sex, or ancestry."[17] The federal Constitution does not identify protected classes of citizens like the Hawaii Constitution does.

In federal constitutional law, most legislative classifications are subject to a rational basis test under the Equal Protection Clause. Legislation that makes distinctions among different classes of people must be rationally related to a legitimate government interest. However, certain types of governmental classifications are

---

[10] *Id.* at 325.

[11] *See* Meyer v. Nebraska, 262 U.S. 390 (1923); and Skinner v. Oklahoma, 316 U.S. 535 (1942).

[12] Loving v. Virginia, 388 U.S. 1 (1967).

[13] *Id.* at 12.

[14] *See* Perez v. Sharp, 32 Cal. 2d 711 (1948) (in which the California Supreme Court ended its state's ban on interracial marriage twenty years before the U.S. Supreme Court's decision in *Loving*).

[15] U.S. CONST. amend. XIV, § 1 ("No state shall... deny to any person within its jurisdiction the equal protection of the laws.").

[16] VT. CONST. ch. I, art. VII ("[t]hat government is, or ought to be, instituted for the common benefit, protection, and security of the people, nation, or community, and not for the particular emolument or advantage of any single person, family, or set of persons, who are a part only of that community.").

[17] HAW. CONST. art. I, § 5.

entitled to more exacting scrutiny. For example, the Supreme Court evaluates racial classifications using the standard of strict scrutiny, which requires states to have a compelling interest and for their legislation to be narrowly tailored to achieving that interest.[18] Gender classifications require an "exceedingly persuasive justification" under Supreme Court precedents.[19] The Supreme Court provides these special protections to suspect classes because of the history of discrimination against these groups, the immutability of group characteristics, and the political powerlessness of group members.

Many state supreme court justices use a similar framework to determine what their own equal protection clauses protect. Relying on these state equal protection clauses, as well as the language in the federal Constitution, supporters of same-sex marriage have argued that sexual orientation is entitled to heightened protections, just like race and gender. Alternatively, they have maintained that state bans on same-sex marriage do not satisfy the minimum requirements of a rational basis test. According to same-sex couples, the justifications that state legislators have provided for same-sex marriage bans, such as preserving the traditional definition of marriage, are not rational because they serve only to perpetuate a history of discrimination against gay people.

The remainder of this chapter discusses these constitutional arguments in greater detail, tracing efforts by supporters of same-sex marriage since the 1970s to use state courts to liberalize state marriage laws. I describe how judges responded to these requests and report what, if any, impact the decisions had on state marriage laws. The history shows that, in some respects, litigation reform efforts have been quite successful, achieving promising victories in states such as Hawaii and Alaska just twenty years after state courts in Minnesota and Kentucky dismissed similar claims. However, the impact of these victories has often been limited. Many of the legal decisions in favor of same-sex couples have been overturned, and the passage of constitutional amendments in other states has made it difficult for litigation strategies to gain traction.

State Court Decisions in the 1970s

The legal climate in the 1970s was not particularly favorable to same-sex marriage, but a few test cases emerged in the years following the 1969 Stonewall Riots and the start of the contemporary gay rights movement. Litigants might have been

---

[18] *See* Yick Wo v. Hopkins, 118 U.S. 356 (1886); Loving v. Virginia, 388 U.S. 1 (1967).

[19] United States v. Virginia, 518 U.S. 515 (1996). *See also* Craig v. Boren, 429 U.S. 190 (1976) (in which the Supreme Court established the intermediate scrutiny standard for sex-based classifications); and Frontiero v. Richardson, 411 U.S. 677 (1973) (in which Justice Brennan could not command a majority to apply strict scrutiny to sex-based classifications).

emboldened by the U.S. Supreme Court's decision in *Loving v. Virginia*, which struck down state bans on interracial marriage.[20] Same-sex couples might have also been inspired by the progress women's rights groups had achieved in cases such as *Griswold v. Connecticut*, which struck down a state contraception law.[21] By 1974, same-sex couples had asked at least three state appellate courts to evaluate the constitutionality of same-sex marriage bans.[22]

The first case, *Baker v. Nelson*, was the only one decided by a state supreme court.[23] Richard Baker and James McConnell applied for a marriage license in Hennepin County, Minnesota, but were refused by the county clerk, Gerald Nelson. Baker and McConnell observed that the state's marriage statutes did not expressly forbid same-sex unions. They also maintained that the same-sex marriage ban violated the federal Constitution, specifically the Fourteenth Amendment's Due Process and Equal Protection Clauses, the First Amendment's freedom of association, the Eighth Amendment's ban on cruel and unusual punishments, and the Ninth Amendment.

The Supreme Court of Minnesota dismissed these arguments. In a three-page opinion, Justice C. Donald Peterson ruled that the state's marriage statutes did not apply to same-sex couples because marriage was by definition the union of one man and one woman. To support this conclusion, Justice Peterson referred to two dictionaries.[24] A "sensible" interpretation of the state's marriage statutes, Justice Peterson believed, would limit the term *marriage* to its "common usage."[25] Justice Peterson did not think much of Baker and McConnell's constitutional arguments either, refusing to broaden the right to marry to include same-sex marriage. "The institution of marriage as a union of man and woman...is as old as the book of Genesis," he wrote. "This historic institution manifestly is more deeply founded than the asserted contemporary concept of marriage and societal interests for which petitioners contend. The due process clause of the Fourteenth Amendment is not a charter for restructuring it by judicial legislation."[26] The justices ruled that analogies to *Loving v. Virginia* were inapt. In *Loving*, the couples were not requesting a change

---

[20] *Loving*, 388 U.S. 1 (1967).

[21] Griswold v. Connecticut, 381 U.S. 479 (1965).

[22] A fourth decision on the subject of same-sex marriage was decided by a trial court in Queens County, New York. In Anonymous v. Anonymous, 67 Misc.2d 982 (N.Y. Sup. Ct. 1971), the plaintiff had married the defendant without realizing that his new wife was a man. Judge Albert H. Buschmann ruled that it was unnecessary to grant an annulment because the plaintiff had never married the defendant. "The marriage ceremony itself was a nullity," he wrote. "No legal relationship could be created by it." *Id.* at 984.

[23] Baker v. Nelson, 191 N.W.2d 185 (Minn. 1971).

[24] WEBSTER'S THIRD NEW INTERNATIONAL DICTIONARY 1384 (1966) ("the state of being united to a person of the opposite sex as husband or wife"); BLACK'S LAW DICTIONARY 1123 (4TH ED. 1968) ("Marriage...is the civil status, condition, or relation of one man and one woman united in law for life").

[25] *Baker*, 191 N.W.2d at 185.

[26] *Id.* at 186.

in the definition of marriage but were being denied the right to marry because of their race. "[I]n commonsense and in constitutional sense," Justice Peterson wrote, "there is a clear distinction between a marital restriction based merely upon race and one based upon the fundamental difference in sex."[27]

Supporters of same-sex marriage received an equally chilly reception from the Court of Appeals of Kentucky two years later in *Jones v. Hallahan*.[28] The facts of the case were mostly similar to *Baker*, only this time it was a lesbian couple that was denied a marriage license by a county clerk. As in *Baker*, the litigants raised a variety of federal constitutional challenges, arguing that the state's actions had denied them their right to marry. They also maintained that the state had infringed on their freedom of association and their free exercise of religion, and that the refusal of a marriage license constituted cruel and unusual punishment. The court dispensed with these arguments in just two pages. The right to marry did not apply to same-sex couples, the majority opinion concluded, because marriage was defined as the union of one man and one woman. "In substance," the court wrote, "the relationship proposed by the appellants does not authorize the issuance of a marriage license because what they propose is not a marriage."[29] Like the Minnesota Supreme Court in *Baker*, the court identified the "common usage" of the term *marriage* by looking in dictionaries.[30] The majority opinion also made passing reference to state custom, observing without much elaboration that "marriage has always been considered as the union of a man and a woman."[31]

If supporters of same-sex marriage had hoped to use litigation to transform state marriage laws, the opinions in *Baker* and *Jones* suggested that they would not achieve easy victories. The courts in Minnesota and Kentucky clearly did not take their claims very seriously. The opinions were short, and the outcomes were presented as though they were self-evident. Additional justifications were not required, the majority opinion writers seemed to suggest, because any reasonable person understood that marriage was the union of one man and one woman. All one had to do was look in a dictionary.

In retrospect, however, the legal arguments in these cases might have been poorly conceived, no doubt reflecting the lack of a coordinated litigation strategy at that time. The litigants in *Baker* and *Jones* cited a long list of grievances under the federal Constitution, but they did not argue that their state constitutional rights had been violated. Because the couples were filing the litigation in state courts, it would have made more sense for them to have grounded their arguments in state law. State

---

[27] *Id.* at 187.

[28] Jones v. Hallahan, 501 S.W.2d 588 (Ky. Ct. App. 1973).

[29] *Id.* at 590.

[30] The opinion quoted from BLACK'S LAW DICTIONARY (4th ed. 1968); CENTURY DICTIONARY AND ENCYCLOPEDIA; and WEBSTER'S NEW AMERICAN DICTIONARY (2d ed. 1934).

[31] *Jones*, 501 S.W.2d at 589.

courts were unlikely to have interpreted federal law more generously than the U.S. Supreme Court, given that state courts are not the final interpreters of federal law.

On the other hand, it is hard to think of any argument that would have been persuasive to the judges in *Baker* and *Jones*. Courts at the time seemed unwilling to give same-sex couples a sympathetic audience. In *Singer v. Hara*, which was the third case involving same-sex marriage that was decided by a state appellate court in this period, the litigants presented arguments under both the state and federal constitutions.[32] When John F. Singer and Paul Barwick were denied a marriage license in their home state of Washington, they argued as the litigants had done in *Baker* and *Jones* that their state marriage statutes did not specifically preclude same-sex couples from marrying and that a denial of their marriage licenses violated the Eighth, Ninth, and Fourteenth Amendments to the federal Constitution. However, they also maintained that the state's actions violated the equal rights amendment of the Washington constitution.[33]

Singer and Barwick maintained that the refusal of the state to permit them to marry constituted sex discrimination under the ERA, as they were prohibited from marrying because of the sex of their partners. In defense of this interpretation, Singer and Barwick cited a pamphlet that had been circulated to voters by the state attorney general before the ratification of the amendment, which had offered reasons for and against its passage. Listed in the "Statement against" was this argument: "Homosexual and lesbian marriage would be legalized, with further complication regarding adopting children into such a 'family.' People will live as they choose, but the beauty and sanctity of marriage must be preserved from such needless desecration."[34] Singer and Barwick observed that voters had read this statement and approved the ERA anyway.

The Court of Appeals of Washington was not convinced. Surely, the majority opinion argued, no one voting in favor of the ERA seriously thought that they were voting in favor of same-sex marriage. The language in the pamphlet was sensational propaganda designed to discourage votes for the amendment. The majority opinion cited a newspaper article from the time that described the arguments in the pamphlet as "emotional, irresponsible fantasies, misleading, deceptive and incorrect."[35] The court believed that a fair interpretation of the amendment could not support the interpretation that Singer and Barwick wanted to give it. The court also rejected their remaining arguments, for reasons similar to those provided in *Baker* and *Jones*.

Although the litigants in *Singer v. Hara* were no more successful than the same-sex couples in the previous cases, the majority opinion was longer than the other two

---

[32] Singer v. Hara, 522 P.2d 1187 (Wash. App. 1974).

[33] WASH. CONST. art. XXXI, §1 (1972) ("Equality of rights and responsibility under the law shall not be denied or abridged on account of sex.").

[34] *Singer*, 522 P.2d at 1191.

[35] *Id.*

and somewhat more sympathetic. "We are not unmindful of the fact that public attitude toward homosexuals is undergoing substantial, albeit gradual, change," the majority observed. "[W]e express no opinion upon the desirability of…revising our marriage laws to accommodate homosexuals and include same-sex relationships within the definition of marriage."[36] However, the court did not believe that it was the place of the judiciary to legalize same-sex marriage absent clear constitutional or statutory authority to do so. "That is a question for the people to answer through the legislative process. We merely hold such a legislative change is not constitutionally required."[37]

By the middle of the 1970s, the strategy of using state courts to produce social change did not seem to be very promising. Not one of the state courts that had been asked to evaluate state policies prohibiting same-sex marriage had ruled in favor of same-sex couples. The strategy also threatened to be counterproductive. With judges so unwilling to take the arguments of same-sex couples seriously, supporters of same-sex marriage risked creating a series of unfavorable precedents, leaving them worse off than they were before. As it was, the litigants in *Baker v. Nelson* inadvertently created a setback for the same-sex marriage movement when they appealed the Minnesota Supreme Court's decision to the U.S. Supreme Court. The setback occurred because of a procedural technicality relating to the form of the appeal that the litigants had filed. Today, when litigants appeal cases to the justices, they ordinarily file writs of certiorari, which are discretionary writs asking the justices to review their cases. Because denials of certiorari are not decisions on the merits, they have no precedential authority. However, the appeal in *Baker v. Nelson* was not filed as a writ of certiorari because the Supreme Court at the time had mandatory jurisdiction over state court decisions that raised federal questions.[38] Unlike denials of certiorari petitions, which have no precedential authority, dismissals of mandatory appeals constitute precedents that lower courts must follow.[39]

In practice, the justices did not treat mandatory appeals much differently from petitions for certiorari. Appellants would file a jurisdictional statement, explaining the grounds for the appeal, and if the justices decided that they did not want to take the case, they would dismiss the appeal "for want of substantial federal question."

---

[36] *Id.* at 1196.

[37] *Id.*

[38] Congress would later revise this policy, substantially reducing the size of the Supreme Court's mandatory docket. Supreme Court Case Selections Act, 28 U.S.C. § 1257 (1988).

[39] *See* Hicks v. Miranda, 422 U.S. 332, 344–45 (1975) ("unless and until the Supreme Court should instruct otherwise…the lower courts are bound by summary decisions by this Court until such time as the Court informs them that they are not") (internal quotation marks removed); and Mandel v. Bradley, 432 U.S. 173, 176 (1977) ("Summary affirmances and dismissals for want of a substantial federal question without doubt reject the specific challenges presented in the statement of jurisdiction.… They do prevent lower courts from coming to opposite conclusions on the precise issues presented and necessarily decided by those actions.").

When the justices decided not to review the Minnesota Supreme Court's opinion in *Baker v. Nelson*, they did so without making any statement on the merits. They simply released a routine order stating that the case did not present a substantial federal question. If the petition had been filed as a certiorari petition, the denial would have had no precedential value. But because the appeal in *Baker* was mandatory, the one-line dismissal mattered, suggesting that no substantial federal questions were presented by the litigants' constitutional claims, including their arguments under the Fourteenth Amendment's Due Process and Equal Protection Clauses. In one line, the Supreme Court effectively declared that the constitutional arguments of same-sex couples had no merit.

The justices might not have intended for their summary dismissal in *Baker v. Nelson* to be given this interpretation, but later federal and state courts treated the decision as authoritative. For example, in *McConnell v. Nooner*, the U.S. Court of Appeals for the Eighth Circuit cited *Baker* as authority for refusing to recognize a right under federal law for same-sex couples to marry.[40] "[T]he Supreme Court's dismissal of the appeal for want of a substantial federal question constitutes an adjudication of the merits which is binding on the lower federal courts," the majority wrote in *McConnell*. "The appellants have had their day in court on the issue of their right to marry under Minnesota law and under the United States Constitution."[41]

For litigants wishing to use the courts to bring an end to state bans on same-sex marriage, the prospects in the 1970s looked bleak. Aside from the losses that same-sex couples had suffered in state courts, an unfavorable Supreme Court precedent was now on the books. The few state appellate courts to have reviewed the claims of same-sex couples had been abruptly dismissive, and the U.S. Supreme Court itself had issued a judgment on the merits without providing same-sex couples with an opportunity to make their case in person. It would have been understandable if supporters of same-sex marriage thought that a litigation strategy looked hopeless. It would take another twenty years before the legal climate against same-sex marriage began to thaw.

Turning the Tide: Hawaii and Alaska

When same-sex couples renewed their challenges to state prohibitions of same-sex marriage in the 1990s, their legal strategy was different.[42] Litigants were less likely

---

[40] McConnell v. Nooner, 547 F.2d 54 (8th Cir. 1976).

[41] *Id.* at 56.

[42] In the intervening years a few state court decisions addressed the marriage question indirectly. *See In re* Succession of Bacot, 502 So.2d 1118 (La. App. 1987); Gajovski v. Gajovski, 610 N.E.2d 431 (Ohio App. 1991). For a more direct treatment of the marriage question, see De Santo v. Barnsley, 476 A.2d 952 (Pa. Super. 1984) (in which the Superior Court of Pennsylvania ruled that same-sex couples could not contract a common law marriage).

to base their arguments on the federal Constitution, as the litigants in the 1970s had done. Instead same-sex couples sought independent state constitutional grounds for invalidating same-sex marriage bans. If state supreme court justices were reluctant to interpret the U.S. Constitution more expansively than the U.S. Supreme Court, perhaps they would be willing to interpret their own constitutions broadly. After all, state supreme courts had the final word on what their state constitutions meant, and the U.S. Supreme Court had no power to overturn state court decisions unless they interfered with federal law.

Because same-sex marriage supporters had suffered decisive losses in the 1970s, there was some risk involved with pressing a litigation strategy further. Victories in court had the potential to grant same-sex couples the relief they sought, but losses could leave same-sex couples worse off than they were before. Once a state supreme court ruled that its constitution did not protect the right of same-sex couples to marry, that ruling would become a precedent that would guide future legal proceedings. Subsequent litigants seeking to use the courts to overturn state bans on same-sex marriage would have to argue not only that their rights were protected by the state constitution, but that previous rulings that had reached different conclusions were incorrect or obsolete.

There was also the possibility that state supreme court decisions in favor of same-sex marriage would not be accepted by the citizens in these states. If a court required the state to authorize same-sex marriage before the citizens were ready for it, there could be a backlash against the decision. Opponents of same-sex marriage might win enough support for a state constitutional amendment, which would bind the hands of the judges and make it even harder for same-sex marriage proponents to achieve their goals. Indeed, the legal climate was so discouraging that LGBT public interest groups such as Lambda Legal were not pressing the issue of marriage equality at the time and declined to become involved in the initial stages of *Baehr v. Lewin*, which challenged marriage laws in Hawaii.[43] The litigants in *Baehr* proceeded independently with their attorney, Dan Foley.

---

[43] Philosophical differences among LGBT advocates also explain the reluctance of groups such as Lambda Legal to pursue marriage equality. Paula Ettelbrick, the legal director at Lambda Legal at the time, doubted the wisdom of having same-sex couples assimilate into a patriarchal, heteronormative institution such as marriage. *See* Paula Ettelbrick, *Since When Is Marriage a Path to Liberation?* 6 OUT/LOOK: NAT'L GAY & LESB. Q. 8 (1989); *see also* Andersen, *supra* Chapter 1, note 57, at 177 ("The practical upshot of this intracommunity fissure was that, until 1993, none of the major gay legal groups treated same-sex marriage as an immediate priority."); Wolfson, *supra* Chapter 1, note 57, at 30 ("[T]he Hawaii couples first approached me to ask if I would be their lawyer, given my longstanding advocacy for the freedom to marry.... Lambda and other movement organizations... were divided internally over whether to challenge marriage discrimination. Because of these divisions, I was not allowed to take the case.").

The facts of *Baehr v. Lewin* were similar to those of previous same-sex marriage cases from the 1970s.[44] Nina Baehr and her partner Genora Dancel had sought to marry in the state of Hawaii, but were refused a license by the Department of Public Health and its director, John C. Lewin. Baehr and Dancel challenged the actions as an infringement on their constitutional rights, but unlike the litigants in the 1970s, Baehr and Dancel did not make any claims under the U.S. Constitution. They argued that the state's limitation of marriage to the union of one man and one woman violated the equal protection clause of Hawaii's constitution.[45] They also maintained that the same-sex marriage ban deprived them of the due process of law,[46] and the right to privacy.[47]

At first, it seemed as though Baehr and Dancel would be no more successful in court than the litigants in the 1970s had been. The trial court was unwilling to grant Baehr and Dancel a full hearing, dismissing the case for failure to state a claim, which meant that the trial judge believed that there was no set of facts upon which Hawaii laws could grant Baehr and Dancel relief. Hawaii's due process clause did not protect gay marriage, and sexual orientation was not a suspect class under the state's equal protection clause. The trial judge concluded that under a rational basis test, the state of Hawaii's interest in promoting the welfare of the community would be sufficient to survive any constitutional challenge, so it was unnecessary to conduct a full hearing.

The dismissal by the trial judge in Hawaii was not surprising when one considers the legal and social context of the time. Since the 1970s, supporters of same-sex marriage had met with little success in state courts. In states such as Minnesota, Kentucky, and Washington, judges had dispensed with the legal claims of same-sex couples using reasoning that was just as cursory as the trial judge's, and the federal legal context was not any better. A few years before *Lewin*, in *Bowers v. Hardwick*, the U.S. Supreme Court had ruled that the Due Process Clause of the Fourteenth Amendment did not protect consensual sodomy.[48] "Proscriptions against that conduct have ancient roots," Justice Byron White had written for the majority. "Against this background, to claim that a right to engage in such conduct is 'deeply rooted in this Nation's history and tradition' or 'implicit in the concept of ordered liberty'

---

[44] Baehr v. Lewin, 852 P.2d 44 (Haw. 1993).

[45] Haw. Const. art. I, § 5. At the time of the Hawaii Supreme Court's decision, the statute did not explicitly state that marriage must be limited to the union of one man and one woman, but in describing the institution the statute references only heterosexual partners. *See, e.g.*, Hawaii Revised Statutes (HRS) § 572-1, cl. 7 (1985) ("The marriage ceremony [is to] be performed in the State by a person or society with a valid license to solemnize marriages and the man and woman to be married and the person performing the marriage ceremony [are to] be all physically present at the same place and time for the marriage ceremony.").

[46] Haw. Const. art. I, § 5.

[47] Haw. Const. art. I, § 6.

[48] Bowers v. Hardwick, 478 U.S. 186 (1986).

is, at best, facetious."[49] As states could prohibit consensual gay sex, it was a small step for the trial court in Hawaii to rule summarily that same-sex couples were not entitled to marry.

The surprise came when the Hawaii Supreme Court ruled in favor of Baehr and Dancel on appeal. The justices ruled that the trial court had improperly dismissed the case because it had mischaracterized the nature of Baehr and Dancel's constitutional claims. The issue was not whether sexual orientation was a suspect classification under the state equal protection clause, but whether Baehr and Dancel could be denied marriage licenses solely because of their sex. "[B]y its plain language," Justice Steven H. Levinson wrote for the majority, the state's marriage law "restricts the marital relation to a male and a female.... It is the state's regulation of access to the status of married persons, on the basis of the applicants' sex, that gives rise to the question whether the applicant couples have been denied the equal protection of the laws."[50] Justice Levinson noted that classifications based on sex were entitled to higher scrutiny under the state's equal protection clause. As Levinson observed, "The equal protection clauses of the United States and Hawaii Constitutions are not mirror images of one another."[51] Whereas the U.S. Constitution guarantees "any person within its jurisdiction the equal protection of the laws,"[52] the Hawaii Constitution is more explicit, stating that "no person shall...be denied the enjoyment of... civil rights or be discriminated against in the exercise thereof because of race, religion, *sex*, or ancestry."[53] Because the Hawaii Constitution specifically mentions sex discrimination, sex-based classifications in Hawaii were accorded greater protections than they received under the federal Constitution.

The Hawaii Supreme Court remanded the case to the trial court with instructions to compile an evidentiary record and to evaluate the state's same-sex marriage ban using the standard of strict scrutiny. The burden would be on Lewin, as director of the Department of Public Health, to show that the exclusion of same-sex couples from marriage furthered "compelling interests" and was "narrowly tailored" to achieve these interests. The standard would be difficult for the state to meet because, as Justice Levinson instructed, the state's same-sex marriage ban would be "presumed to be unconstitutional."[54] Even though the Hawaii Supreme Court did not award a final victory to same-sex couples, the tone of the opinion seemed to indicate that a declaration was forthcoming.

The Hawaii Supreme Court's decision in *Baehr v. Lewin* was a landmark achievement for the same-sex marriage movement, even though in certain respects it was a

---

[49] *Id.* at 192–94 (quoting from Palko v. Connecticut, 302 U.S. 319, 326 (1937)).
[50] Baehr v. Lewin, 852 P.2d 44, 60 (Haw. 1993).
[51] *Id.* at 59.
[52] U.S. CONST. amend. XIV, § 1.
[53] HAW. CONST. art. I, § 5 (emphasis added).
[54] Baehr v. Lewin, 852 P.2d at 64.

conservative decision. For one thing, the Court did not rule that same-sex couples had under the state's due process clause a fundamental right to marry. Judge Levinson observed that federal courts had not interpreted the Fourteenth Amendment's Due Process Clause to protect same-sex marriage, and the Hawaii court was not prepared to interpret its own due process clause more expansively. "[W]e do not believe that a right to same-sex marriage is so rooted in the traditions and collective conscience of our people that failure to recognize it would violate the fundamental principles of liberty and justice that lie at the base of all our civil and political institutions," Judge Levinson wrote. "Neither do we believe that a right to same-sex marriage is implicit in the concept of ordered liberty, such that neither liberty nor justice would exist if it were sacrificed."[55] The justices also refused to identify sexual orientation as a suspect classification under the state's equal protection clause, instead framing the central issue as sex discrimination. Levinson observed that "it is irrelevant, for purposes of the constitutional analysis germane to this case, whether homosexuals constitute a 'suspect class' because it is immaterial whether the plaintiffs, or any of them, are homosexuals."[56] No one in the state, regardless of sexual orientation, could marry someone of the same sex.

Still, the Hawaii Supreme Court demonstrated much more sympathy for the legal claims of same-sex couples than any state supreme court had exhibited in the past, and on remand, the trial court realized the full promise of the *Lewin* decision. By the time the case got to trial, the title of the case had been changed to reflect the name of the new director of the Department of Public Health, Lawrence H. Miike. Lambda Legal also became involved, with Evan Wolfson joining Dan Foley as cocounsel. Applying strict scrutiny, Judge Kevin S.C. Chang in *Baehr v. Miike* found that Miike had not identified a compelling interest for maintaining the ban on same-sex marriage.[57] Among the potential interests rejected by Chang were the state's concerns that permitting same-sex marriage would impose hardships on couples who traveled to other states that did not recognize same-sex marriage, that there was inherent value to preserving the traditional definition of marriage, and that same-sex marriages had an adverse impact on the development of children. According to Judge Chang, "Defendant presented meager evidence with regard to the importance of the institution of traditional marriage, the benefits which that relationship provides to the community and, most importantly, the adverse effects, if any, which same-sex marriage would have on the institution of traditional marriage and how those effects would impact on the community and society."[58] Judge Chang ruled that the state's marriage statute was unconstitutional and that Miike could not deny marriage licenses to applicants solely on the basis of their sex. If the

[55] *Id.* at 57.
[56] *Id.* at 54, n.14.
[57] Baehr v. Miike, No. 91-1394 (Haw. Cir. Ct. 1996).
[58] *Id.*

decision stood up on appeal, same-sex couples in the state of Hawaii would finally have the opportunity to marry.

The victory for same-sex couples was short-lived. In November 1998 voters in Hawaii approved a constitutional amendment superseding the justices' interpretation of the state equal protection clause and empowering the state legislature to prohibit same-sex marriages.[59] On December 9, 1999, the Hawaii Supreme Court issued a brief order declaring the litigation moot.[60] In a concurrence, Justice Mario R. Ramil stated that the decision in *Baehr v. Lewin* had been unwise to begin with. "In my view," he wrote, "the debate over whether marriage should include unions between persons of the same sex involves a question of pure public policy that should have been left to the people of the state or their elected representatives."[61] Apparently the voters in Hawaii agreed.

Even though the Hawaii Supreme Court's decision in *Baehr v. Lewin* was ultimately overturned by a state constitutional amendment, it provided the blueprint for a litigation strategy that supporters of same-sex marriage could follow in other states. If state court judges were cautious about using the federal Constitution to provide rights and benefits to same-sex couples, judges might be willing to acknowledge the rights of same-sex couples under their own constitutions, as the justices in Hawaii had done. Under principles of judicial federalism, state supreme courts would not risk reversal by the U.S. Supreme Court as long as they did not impose on federal constitutional rights.

It turned out that Hawaii was not the only state in the 1990s in which the courts gave supporters of same-sex marriage a favorable reception. On August 4, 1994, shortly after the Hawaii Supreme Court's decision in *Baehr v. Lewin*, Jay Brause and Gene Dugan filed applications for marriage licenses in the state of Alaska, but were denied by the state's Office of Vital Statistics. Brause and Dugan filed suit in the Alaska Superior Court, arguing that the state's unwillingness to grant them a marriage license violated their right to privacy in the Alaska Constitution.[62] Brause and Dugan also maintained that the state had violated the equal protection clause of the state constitution.[63]

In the interim, the Alaska legislature revised the state's marriage law to define marriage as the union of one man and one woman and to deny same-sex relationships

---

[59] Specifically, the amendment revised Article I of the state Constitution to read, "The legislature shall have the power to reserve marriage to opposite-sex couples." HAW. CONST. art. I, § 23 (1998).

[60] Baehr v. Miike, No. 20371, 1999 Haw. LEXIS 391 (1999).

[61] *Id.* at 9 (Ramil, J., concurring).

[62] Unlike the federal Constitution, Alaska's constitution specifically mentions privacy. ALASKA CONST. art. I, §22 ("The right of the people to privacy is recognized and shall not be infringed.").

[63] ALASKA CONST. art. I, § 1 ("The constitution is dedicated to the principles that all persons have a natural right to life, liberty, the pursuit of happiness, and the enjoyment of the rewards of their own industry; that all persons are equal and entitled to equal rights, opportunities, and protections under the law; and that all persons have corresponding obligations to the people and to the State.").

the benefits of marriage.[64] The legislature's actions were in response to a decision by the Superior Court in Fairbanks, *Tumeo v. University of Alaska*.[65] In *Tumeo*, Judge Mary E. Green ruled that the University of Alaska could not deny health insurance benefits to same-sex partners. She also noted that the state's marriage laws were unclear about the status of same-sex unions, commenting that, "The Alaska Supreme Court has not been asked to decide whether Alaska's marriage statute allows for same-sex marriages."[66] After the Alaska legislature moved to clarify its intent, Brause and Dugan asked Judge Peter A. Michalski of the Superior Court in Anchorage to consider whether the new laws prohibiting same-sex marriage violated Alaska's constitution.

When Judge Michalski issued his decision in *Brause v. Bureau of Vital Statistics*, he accepted Brause and Dugan's state constitutional challenges.[67] Michalski observed that Alaska's constitution explicitly guaranteed a right to privacy, and that this right included the right of individuals to choose their life partners. It did not matter that the state had a long tradition of proscribing certain sexual practices. "The relevant question is not whether same-sex marriage is so rooted in our traditions that it is a fundamental right, but whether the freedom to choose one's own life partner is so rooted in our traditions," Judge Michalski wrote. "Government intrusion into the choice of a life partner encroaches on the intimate personal decisions of the individual."[68] If, in a hearing, the state did not present a compelling reason for denying same-sex couples the right to marry, the ban on same-sex marriage would not survive judicial review.

Judge Michalski also agreed with Brause and Dugan that Alaska's equal protection clause was implicated by the state's refusal to permit same-sex couples to marry, but he determined that the equal protection analysis was mooted by his conclusions about the due process clause. Michalski explained that Alaska's Constitution provided heightened protections to all individuals, regardless of sexual orientation, when the state infringed on their fundamental rights. The state's marriage statute would have to survive strict scrutiny, which required the state to have a compelling interest and for the legislation to be narrowly tailored to advancing that interest. It was unnecessary to inquire further into whether the equal protection clause was violated because the court was already applying its most exacting standard of review.

Judge Michalski's decision in *Brause* was not a final judgment on the merits, but it did provide the potential foundation for a subsequent decision striking down the

---

[64] ALASKA STAT. § 25.05.011(a) (May 7, 1996) ("Marriage is a civil contract entered into by one man and one woman"); ALASKA STAT. § 25.05.013(b) (May 7, 1996) ("A same-sex relationship may not be recognized by the state as being entitled to the benefits of marriage.").

[65] Tumeo v. Univ. of Alaska, No. 4FA-94–43 Civil (Alaska Super. Ct., Jan. 11, 1995).

[66] *Id.*

[67] Brause v. Bureau of Vital Statistics, No. 3 AN-95-6562 CI (Alaska Super. Ct. Feb. 27, 1998).

[68] *Id.*

state's same-sex marriage ban. Unfortunately for same-sex couples, the litigation never reached that point. The following fall, on November 3, 1998, voters in Alaska approved a ballot measure amending the state constitution to limit marriage to the union of one man and one woman.[69] On the same day that voters in Hawaii repudiated *Baehr v. Lewin*, Alaska voters amended their state constitution to overturn *Brause*.

The approval of state constitutional amendments in Hawaii and Alaska suggested that there were limits to what a litigation strategy could accomplish. Supporters of same-sex marriage might have been able to persuade judges in these states to strike down same-sex marriage bans, but the victories were not enough to produce the desired reform. If state courts interpreted their constitutions in ways that the public was unprepared to accept, then same-sex marriage opponents could muster the votes necessary to enact state constitutional amendments overturning the decisions. Future litigants would need to find ways of obtaining favorable rulings without creating such a public backlash.

Cautious Steps Forward: Vermont

The next major state court ruling on same-sex marriage was marked by greater caution from both the presiding judges and the litigants. *Baker v. Vermont* was also the first same-sex marriage decision in which LGBT public interest groups played a major organizational role from the outset.[70] Although many members of these groups continued to have misgivings about the wisdom of pressing the marriage question in court, they acknowledged the need to coordinate what had previously been an ad hoc series of lawsuits.[71] Part of this effort involved preparing elected officials in the state for a pro-marriage ruling. Beth Robinson and Susan Murray, who were cocounsel in *Baker*, spent two years lobbying Vermont legislators before they were prepared to move forward.[72] Their goal was to discourage the sort of backlash that had occurred in Hawaii and Alaska, where similar groundwork had not been laid. Evan Wolfson, the Lambda Legal attorney who participated in *Baehr*, first as an amicus and then as a cocounsel in later stages of the litigation, observed

[69] Ballot Measure 2 added ALASKA CONST. art. I, § 25 ("To be valid or recognized in this State, a marriage may exist only between one man and one woman.").

[70] Baker v. Vermont, 744 A.2d 864 (Vt. 1999).

[71] *See* Keck, *supra* Chapter 1, note 31, at 176 ("The actual choice faced by movement leaders was whether to join and help shape these efforts or to watch them continue as uncoordinated actions of individual plaintiffs and their private counsel. Since the latter choice would have left the advocacy organizations with no influence over important tactical decisions regarding when and where to file, what to argue, and whether to appeal—and since it might also appear as a significant rebuke of their own members and supporters—all the national LGBT rights organizations eventually signed on.").

[72] ANDERSEN, *supra* Chapter 1, note 57, at 197.

that LGBT interests in Hawaii "were completely unprepared to meet" the backlash that occurred in the state.[73] If LGBT interest groups were going to press forward with a litigation strategy, then they had to learn from their experiences in Hawaii and do what they could to facilitate implementation in subsequent venues.

The case facts in *Baker v. Vermont* were similar to earlier challenges to state marriage laws. Stan Baker and Peter Harrigan were among three couples to challenge Vermont's ban on same-sex marriage after the couples were denied marriage licenses by their town clerks. Baker and Harrigan argued that the state had interpreted its marriage statutes too narrowly because the statutes did not specifically limit marriage to opposite-sex couples. The plaintiffs also maintained that the state's construction of the statutes violated the Common Benefits Clause of Vermont's constitution.[74]

The state maintained that its primary reasons for denying same-sex couples the legal benefits of marriage were to protect children and to preserve "the link between procreation and child rearing."[75] Permitting same-sex couples to unite in legally sanctioned relationships "would diminish society's perception of the link between procreation and child rearing... [and] advance the notion that fathers or mothers...are mere surplusage to the functions of procreation and child rearing."[76] The trial court agreed and dismissed the case, arguing that the state's interests were reasonable enough to survive constitutional review. The trial court also ruled that there was no justification for reading the marriage statutes broadly to include same-sex couples.

On appeal, the Supreme Court of Vermont reversed the trial court's decision and sided with the same-sex couples, although not on every count. Writing for the majority in *Baker v. Vermont*, Chief Justice Jeffrey L. Amestoy agreed with the state that its marriage statutes, as currently written, limited marriage to the union of one man and one woman. Although the statutes did not explicitly define marriage so narrowly, Amestoy believed that the court's reading was consistent with the plain meaning of the term *marriage*, as found in most dictionaries.[77] He rejected the arguments by plaintiffs that the term *marriage* should be interpreted more broadly to include all committed couples because that definition would be contrary to legislative intent. According to Amestoy, "the evidence demonstrates a clear legislative assumption that marriage under our statutory scheme consists of a union between a man and a woman."[78]

[73] PINELLO, AMERICA'S STRUGGLE FOR SAME-SEX MARRIAGE, *supra* Chapter 1, note 57, at 27.

[74] VT. CONST. ch. I, art. 7 ("That government is, or ought to be, instituted for the common benefit, protection, and security of the people, nation, or community, and not for the particular emolument or advantage of any single person, family, or set of persons, who are a part only of that community.").

[75] *Baker*, 744 A.2d at 881.

[76] *Id.*

[77] Amestoy cited WEBSTER'S NEW INTERNATIONAL DICTIONARY (2d ed. 1955); and BLACK'S LAW DICTIONARY (7th ed. 1999).

[78] *Baker*, 744 A.2d at 869.

However, the Vermont Supreme Court did accept the plaintiffs' argument that the state's marriage statutes, so construed, violated Vermont's constitution. In reaching this judgment, Chief Justice Amestoy went out of his way to emphasize that it was the Common Benefits Clause of the state constitution—not the federal Constitution's Equal Protection Clause—that was the basis of the court's analysis. Amestoy observed that the Common Benefits Clause predated the Fourteenth Amendment "by nearly a century" and "differs markedly from the federal Equal Protection Clause in its language, historical origins, purpose, and development."[79] Amestoy noted that Vermont courts did not use suspect classifications or different tiers of review when interpreting the Common Benefits Clause. Instead there was a single common standard that was more rigorous than the rational basis review used in federal equal protection analysis. According to Amestoy, "Vermont courts ... engage in a meaningful, case-specific analysis to ensure that any exclusion from the general benefit and protection of the law would bear a just and reasonable relation to the legislative goals."[80]

Applying this standard, Chief Justice Amestoy ruled that the state's interests in protecting children and preserving the link between procreation and child rearing were neither reasonable nor just foundations for denying same-sex couples the common legal benefits of marriage. Amestoy observed that the state's position denied the reality that many same-sex couples were already raising children, and that the state of Vermont had encouraged the practice by making it easier for same-sex couples to adopt. It would provide no benefit to the children of same-sex couples for the state to deny their parents the benefits of marriage. "If anything," Amestoy wrote, "the exclusion of same-sex couples from the legal protections incident to marriage exposes their children to the precise risks that the State argues the marriage laws are designed to secure against."[81] The Court also considered and rejected other potential justifications that were provided by the state, including the interest in providing children with "both male and female role models" and "maintaining uniformity with other jurisdictions."[82]

The Court in *Baker* concluded that the interest that same-sex couples had in receiving the common benefits of marriage outweighed the competing state interests. "The legal benefits and protections flowing from a marriage license are of such significance that any statutory exclusion must necessarily be grounded on public concerns of sufficient weight, cogency, and authority that the justice of the deprivation cannot seriously be questioned," Chief Justice Amestoy wrote. "Considered in light of the extreme logical disjunction between the classification and the stated purposes of the law...the exclusion falls substantially short of this standard."[83]

[79] *Id.* at 870.
[80] *Id.* at 871.
[81] *Id.* at 882.
[82] *Id.* at 884–85.
[83] *Id.* at 884.

The state would have to provide same-sex couples the same rights and benefits that married couples received.

For the third time in a decade, a state court ruled that its legislature could not discriminate between same-sex couples and opposite-sex couples. However, unlike the courts in Hawaii and Alaska, Chief Justice Amestoy left open the possibility that the legislature could create an alternative institution for same-sex couples, such as domestic partnerships or civil unions, so long as they were equivalent to marriage. Recognizing the "deeply-felt religious, moral, and political beliefs" that the issue of same-sex marriage arouses, the justices believed that the name that was given to same-sex unions should be left to the political process. "Whatever system is chosen, however," Amestoy emphasized, "must conform with the constitutional imperative to afford all Vermonters the common benefit, protection, and security of the law."[84]

Considering the fact that voters the previous year had overturned same-sex marriage rulings in Alaska and Hawaii, the Vermont Supreme Court's decision to permit domestic partnerships was probably wise. *Baker v. Vermont* did not create the sort of backlash that the other two cases generated. A proposed constitutional amendment limiting same-sex marriage to the union of one man and one woman died in the state senate, and in 2000 the full legislature established the institution of civil unions for same-sex couples. It is uncertain whether legislators would have been so compliant had the Vermont Supreme Court required marriage, but it is not unreasonable to suppose that the court's caution mediated their response. Judges in the 1990s had discovered that on the issue of same-sex marriage there were limits to what voters and lawmakers would accept.

A few years later, in remarks delivered at Rutgers Law School, Chief Justice Amestoy basically admitted that strategy had guided his decision in *Baker*. "Considerations of strategy have long been held suspect by constitutional scholars," he said. "But I cannot agree that the same skepticism ought to attach to the examination of strategic considerations in state constitutionalism."[85] The chief justice observed that because state constitutional systems tended to be more participatory and responsive than the federal system, it was good strategy for judges to write opinions that reflected this reality, particularly on issues as explosive as marriage equality. "When confronted with such deeply divisive issues," Amestoy continued, "a state constitutional opinion may not be persuasive with the extra judicial actors who can alter it if it does not acknowledge their legitimate constitutional role and engage them in finding a solution."[86] The chief justice had learned that by attending to the political context and approaching decisions pragmatically, he could write a decision that would endure.

---

[84] *Id.* at 867.

[85] Jeffrey L. Amestoy, *Pragmatic Constitutionalism: Reflections on State Constitutional Theory and Same-Sex Marriage Claims*, 35 RUTGERS L.J. 1249, 1259 (2004).

[86] *Id.* at 1265.

CHAPTER 4

Massachusetts and Beyond

By the time litigation commenced in Massachusetts, the same-sex marriage movement had achieved only limited victories in state courts. Supporters of same-sex marriage had managed to persuade judges in a handful of states to rule in their favor, but two of these decisions, from Hawaii and Alaska, were soon overturned by state constitutional amendments. A third decision, from Vermont, was not overturned, but the justices in Vermont had not actually required the state to let same-sex couples marry, instead permitting the legislature to establish civil unions as alternative institutions.[1]

These limited victories were offset by more disappointing developments for supporters of same-sex marriage in other states. By 2002, voters in Nebraska and Nevada had approved state constitutional amendments limiting marriage to the union of one man and one woman, making it more difficult for same-sex couples in these states to use courts to achieve social reform. The federal Defense of Marriage Act, enacted in 1996, asserted that states did not have to recognize same-sex marriages from other states, and that the federal government would not recognize such marriages for purposes of federal law.[2] In light of these developments, it was uncertain whether litigation would provide meaningful or lasting relief for same-sex couples in Massachusetts or anywhere else. Nonetheless, LGBT public interest groups were determined to expand upon the victory in *Baker*, this time pressing the courts to accept full marriage equality.

[1] Andersen, *supra* Chapter 1, note 57, describes how reactions among LGBT advocates to *Baker v. Vermont* were mixed. On the one hand, Lambda Legal promoted the decision as a "thrilling victory" because it secured domestic partnership arrangements for same-sex couples. *Id.* at 187. On the other hand, "Beth Robinson, one of the three co-counsel in *Baker*, referred to the day she received news of the Vermont high court's decision as one of the worst days of her life. The decision, as she saw it, recognized the legal impermissibility of discrimination against same-sex couples but facilitated the continued imposition of social divisions between same-sex and opposite sex couples" *Id.* at 227–28.

[2] Defense of Marriage Act, 1 U.S.C. § 7 and 28 U.S.C. § 1738C (1996).

The litigation in Massachusetts began much like the same-sex marriage litigation in other states. Lead plaintiffs Hillary and Julie Goodridge had been together for thirteen years and were raising a five-year-old daughter when they decided that they wanted to get married. When the Goodridges were refused a license by their county clerk, they filed suit in a state trial court, citing a long list of constitutional violations under the state equal rights amendment and the state due process and free speech clauses.[3] However, the trial judge accepted the state's argument that the ban on same-sex marriage was rationally related to the state's interest in preserving the connection between procreation and marriage. The Goodridges appealed the case to the Supreme Judicial Court.

It was not apparent during oral arguments on March 4, 2003, that *Goodridge v. Department of Public Health* would become a landmark victory for same-sex couples, although there were signals.[4] Justice John Greaney announced to the plaintiffs' attorney, Mary Bonauto of GLAD, that he was "certain" her clients would win before he had even heard arguments from opposing counsel.[5] Chief Justice Margaret Marshall, who later wrote the majority opinion, also asked questions that seemed to be sympathetic to the same-sex couples. Yet, it was not obvious how several of the other justices would vote, including two justices who would become members of the majority coalition, Justices Judith Cowin and Roderick Ireland. The Goodridges would have to wait until November to learn whether the court would rule in their favor.

In the interim, the U.S. Supreme Court handed down its decision in *Lawrence v. Texas*, which profoundly shifted the status of gay people under federal law.[6] The timing was fortunate for same-sex couples, because it gave the justices in Massachusetts time to consider what, if any, legal implications *Lawrence* would have for their decision in *Goodridge*. Potentially more important were the political implications of *Lawrence*. If the U.S. Supreme Court was willing to give a sympathetic reception to gay couples, then perhaps the Massachusetts justices would be at greater liberty to produce an opinion in *Goodridge* that came out strongly in favor of same-sex marriage.

---

[3] MASS. CONST. part 1, art. 1 (1976) ("Equality under the law shall not be denied or abridged because of sex, race, color, creed or national origin."); MASS. CONST. part 1, art. 10 ("Each individual of the society has a right to be protected by it in the enjoyment of his life, liberty and property, according to standing laws"); MASS. CONST. part 1, art. 12 ("no subject shall be...deprived of his property, immunities, or privileges, put out of the protection of the law, exiled, or deprived of his life, liberty, or estate, but by the judgment of his peers, on the law of the land"); MASS CONST. part 1, art. 16: "The right of free speech shall not be abridged.").

[4] Goodridge v. Dep't of Public Health, 798 N.E.2d 941 (Mass. 2003).

[5] *Transcript of Oral Argument*, MASSNEWS.COM, http://www.massnews.com/2003_Editions/5_May/051203_mn_transcript_of_oral_argument_may_9.shtml. *See also* Kathleen Burge, *SJC Peppers Lawyers on Same-Sex Marriage*, BOS. GLOBE, Mar. 5, 2003, at A1.

[6] Lawrence v. Texas, 539 U.S. 558 (2003).

On the surface, *Lawrence v. Texas* had nothing to do with same-sex marriage. The question before the justices in *Lawrence* was whether a Texas law banning consensual gay sex violated the Due Process Clause of the Fourteenth Amendment.[7] Almost two decades earlier, in *Bowers v. Hardwick*, the justices considered a challenge to a similar law and concluded that same-sex couples were not protected.[8] The justices in *Lawrence v. Texas* reached a different conclusion, striking down Texas's antisodomy law, and explicitly overturning *Bowers*. Writing for the majority, Justice Anthony Kennedy explained that overruling *Bowers* was necessary because the justices in that case had conducted a flawed substantive due process analysis. In their attempt to give substantive content to the rights protected by the Due Process Clause, the justices in *Bowers* had assumed that the right in question was for gay persons to engage in sodomy, but in reality the case was about the liberty of individuals and "their dignity as free persons," which was surely within the scope of the Due Process Clause.[9]

Justice Kennedy also maintained that the justices in *Bowers* had misrepresented history when they had described the tradition of laws prohibiting sodomy. Kennedy acknowledged that gay people had long been the targets of discrimination, but he explained that laws actually criminalizing gay sex had been in place in the United States only since the 1970s. Previous laws had also banned heterosexual sodomy. By the time of *Bowers*, the majority of states did not ban any form of sodomy, and since then state laws had become even more permissive.[10] It would seem, then, that society was becoming more tolerant of gay rights. Justice Kennedy also observed that bans on consensual sodomy were inconsistent with the practices of other nations.[11]

Although *Lawrence v. Texas* did not directly concern same-sex marriage, at least two features of the decision were relevant to the same-sex marriage controversy.

---

[7] The Texas sodomy law in *Lawrence* was also challenged under the federal Equal Protection Clause, but the majority opinion focused on the due process argument. In a concurrence, Justice Sandra Day O'Connor believed that the Court in *Lawrence* should have based the decision on equal protection grounds, because the state irrationally discriminated against homosexuals in establishing its sodomy ban. *Id.* at 579 (O'Connor, J., concurring).

[8] Bowers v. Hardwick, 478 U.S. 186, 191 (1986) ("respondents would have us announce...a fundamental right to engage in homosexual sodomy. This we are quite unwilling to do."). The liberty protections of the Due Process Clause did not include a fundamental right to homosexual sodomy, according to Justice Byron White's majority opinion, because the right—so specified—was not among the rights that society has traditionally protected. With no specific constitutional language safeguarding gay rights, the Supreme Court in Bowers was not prepared to establish such a right by its own initiative.

[9] *Lawrence*, 539 U.S. at 567.

[10] *Id.* at 572–73. Kennedy explained that at the time of *Bowers*, sodomy bans were in place in twenty-four states and the District of Columbia, but by 2003 only thirteen states had retained their laws, and they were enforced in just four states.

[11] *Id.* at 573. Kennedy put particular emphasis on a decision from the European Court of Human Rights, Dudgeon v. United Kingdom, 45 Eur. Ct. H.R. 52 (1981), which five years before *Bowers* had outlawed sodomy bans under the European Convention of Human Rights.

First was the expansive language that Justice Kennedy used in the majority opinion to describe gay rights. From the outset, Kennedy made clear that the subject of *Lawrence* was not homosexual sodomy, as White had framed the issue, but the "liberty of the person both in its spatial and more transcendent dimensions."[12] Kennedy went on to write that "The petitioners are entitled to respect for their private lives," and that "The state cannot demean their existence or control their destiny by making their private sexual conduct a crime."[13] With the due process right defined so broadly, same-sex couples could reasonably argue that their right to control their destiny was burdened at least as much by a same-sex marriage prohibition as with a ban on consensual sodomy.

The other important signal came from one of the dissents, in which Justice Antonin Scalia predicted that *Lawrence* would make it easier for judges in the future to rule in favor of same-sex marriage. "Today's opinion dismantles the structure of constitutional law that has permitted a distinction to be made between heterosexual and homosexual unions, insofar as formal recognition in marriage is concerned," Justice Scalia wrote. "This case 'does not involve' the issue of homosexual marriage only if one entertains the belief that principle and logic have nothing to do with the decisions of this Court."[14] Justice Scalia could not see how, consistent with *Lawrence*, judges would be able to sustain prohibitions of same-sex marriage if moral disapproval of gay relationships was no longer a legitimate basis for legislation.

Five months later, on November 18, 2003, the Massachusetts Supreme Judicial Court issued its decision in *Goodridge*. It was good news for the same-sex couples. "We declare that barring an individual from the protections, benefits, and obligations of civil marriage solely because that person would marry a person of the same sex violates the Massachusetts Constitution," Chief Justice Margaret Marshall wrote for the majority.[15] The Commonwealth of Massachusetts "has failed to identify any constitutionally adequate reason for denying civil marriage to same-sex couples."[16] It is unclear whether *Lawrence* had an impact on the result in *Goodridge*. Chief Justice Marshall stated that the basis of *Goodridge* was the Massachusetts constitution, not *Lawrence* or the federal Constitution.[17] However, Marshall did cite *Lawrence* in the opening paragraphs of her majority opinion and made repeated references to the dignity and personal autonomy of gay people, as Justice Kennedy had

---

[12] *Lawrence*, 539 U.S. at 562.

[13] *Id.* at 578.

[14] *Id.* at 605 (Scalia, J., dissenting).

[15] Goodridge v. Dep't of Public Health, 798 N.E.2d 941, 948 (Mass. 2003).

[16] *Id.*

[17] *Id.* at 948–49 ("The Massachusetts Constitution is, if anything, more protective of individual liberty and equality than the Federal Constitution; it may demand broader protections for fundamental rights; and it is less tolerant of government intrusion into the protected spheres of private life.").

done in *Lawrence*.[18] Even if Marshall ultimately rested her decision in Massachusetts law, surely *Lawrence* gave her some cover to reach this result. Prior to *Lawrence*, the Massachusetts justices would have succeeded in expanding the federal floor of rights simply by permitting gay people to engage in consensual sex. A decision in favor of same-sex marriage would have seemed more radical in this context. By elevating the federal floor of protected rights for gay people, *Lawrence* helped to make the judgment in *Goodridge* come across as a more incremental expansion of rights than it would have seemed before *Lawrence*.

Like the Vermont Supreme Court, the justices in Massachusetts emphasized the many tangible and intangible benefits of marriage that the state was denying to same-sex couples.[19] Among the benefits described by the court were the joint filing of tax returns, the right to inherit property from spouses and to make medical decisions on their behalf, and the entitlement to the wages and benefits of deceased spouses. Also significant to the court were the benefits of marriage to children.[20] To evaluate the state's interest in denying these benefits to gay families, the court did not apply a heightened level of review under the state's equal protection or due process clauses. Strict scrutiny was unnecessary, the justices ruled, because the state's policy did not meet the minimum requirements of a rational basis test. The justices were not satisfied that gay people had to be barred from marriage to provide a "favorable setting for procreation" or to ensure "the optimal setting for child rearing."[21] These justifications were not rational because heterosexual marriages were not defined exclusively with reference to either procreation or child rearing.[22] The Supreme Judicial Court also did not accept the state's interests in conserving state resources or in preserving the traditional definition of marriage.

In the Court's view, the state's justifications smacked of prejudice, which could never be a rational basis for legislative classifications. "The marriage ban works a deep and scarring hardship on a very real segment of the community for no rational reason," Chief Justice Marshall wrote. "The absence of any reasonable relationship between, on the one hand, an absolute disqualification of same-sex couples who wish to enter into civil marriage and, on the other, protection of public health,

---

[18] *Id.* at 948 ("The Massachusetts Constitution affirms the dignity and equality of all individuals. It forbids the creation of second-class citizens.").

[19] *Id.* at 955 ("The benefits accessible only by way of a marriage license are enormous, touching nearly every aspect of life and death.").

[20] *Id.* at 957 ("Some of these benefits are social, such as the enhanced approval that still attends the status of being a marital child. Others are material, such as the greater ease of access to family-based State and Federal benefits that attend the presumptions of one's parentage.").

[21] *Id.* at 961.

[22] *Id.* at 962 ("Moreover, the Commonwealth affirmatively facilitates bringing children into a family regardless of whether the intended parent is married or unmarried, whether the child is adopted or born into a family, whether assistive technology was used to conceive the child, and whether the parent or her partner is heterosexual, homosexual, or bisexual.").

safety, or general welfare, suggests that the marriage restriction is rooted in persistent prejudices against persons who are (or who are believed to be) homosexual."[23]

The *Goodridge* decision was unquestionably a victory for same-sex couples, but its full implications would not be recognized until later, when the Massachusetts legislature was considering how to implement *Goodridge*. A month after the Supreme Judicial Court's ruling, on December 12, 2003, the Massachusetts Senate asked the justices for an advisory opinion clarifying whether civil unions were acceptable alternatives to same-sex marriage. The Senate proposed legislation that would provide same-sex couples with all of the rights and benefits of marriage, but would reserve the name *marriage* for heterosexual couples only. The Senate believed that the legislation would satisfy the requirements of *Goodridge* because there would be no tangible differences between marriages and civil unions under state law. The legislation also promoted what the Senate believed was the legitimate state interest in preserving "the traditional, historic nature and meaning of the institution of civil marriage."[24]

On February 3, 2004, the Supreme Judicial Court released the *Opinion of the Justices to the Senate*, ruling that civil unions were not valid substitutes for marriage.[25] The state's asserted interest in preserving the traditional definition of marriage was not a rational basis for treating same-sex couples differently, the justices ruled, because it served only to perpetuate discrimination against gay people. The state's denial of the title of marriage to same-sex couples was not trivial, but "a considered choice of language that reflects a demonstrable assigning of same-sex, largely homosexual, couples to second-class status."[26] The only appropriate remedy was to permit gay couples to marry.

The first marriages between same-sex couples in Massachusetts took place on May 17, 2004. Supporters of same-sex marriage had finally achieved the victory that had eluded them in other states, and they had used state courts to do it. However, it was unclear at the time how enduring this victory would be. In March 2004, the Massachusetts Senate and Assembly convened a special constitutional convention to consider overturning *Goodridge*. The General Court, as the assembled legislators were called, approved an amendment that would limit marriage to the union of one man and one woman but allow the legislature to create civil unions as alternative institutions. Before the amendment could be put to Massachusetts citizens for a vote, however, it had to be approved by a second convention in the next legislative session, and in September 2005, the General Court failed to produce the necessary votes.[27]

---

[23] *Id.* at 968.

[24] An Act Relative to Civil Unions, Senate No. 2175 (Mass. 2003).

[25] Opinion of the Justices to the Senate, 802 N.E.2d 565 (Mass. 2004).

[26] *Id.* at 570.

[27] *See* Lewis, *After Vote, Both Sides in Debate Energized, supra* Chapter 1, note 28; and Rutherford, *supra* Chapter 1, note 28.

In July 2006, following a citizen initiative, the Massachusetts General Court again convened to consider overturning *Goodridge*, but the vote on a proposed amendment was delayed until after the fall election. That November, after intense debate, lawmakers decided to recess the convention without voting on the amendment;[28] but in January 2007, legislators convened again after the Supreme Judicial Court ordered them to vote on the initiative.[29] Because the amendment was proposed by a citizen initiative, it required the support of only 25 percent of the legislature, or fifty votes, before it could be put on the ballot, and it received the required number of votes in the January session. However, just like amendments proposed by the legislature, the initiative amendment had to be approved in two successive legislative sessions before it could be put on the ballot, and in the next session the amendment did not receive the required fifty votes. Opponents of same-sex marriage would have to begin the initiative process again if they wanted to overturn *Goodridge*, winning the support of the state legislature in two successive sessions. In the meantime, same-sex marriages in Massachusetts would continue.

A Movement Stalled: New York and New Jersey

Supporters of same-sex marriage achieved a major victory in the Massachusetts courts, but subsequent developments would make it difficult for gay couples to extend this victory to other states. In November 2004, voters in eleven states amended their constitutions to limit marriage to the union of one man and one woman, joining two other states, Missouri and Louisiana, which had already approved constitutional amendments earlier in the year.[30] By November 2006, the total number of state constitutional amendments prohibiting same-sex marriage increased even further, to twenty-seven.[31]

The crush of amendments reduced the number of forums in which supporters of same-sex marriage could pursue litigation strategies. State supreme court justices would have a difficult time ruling in favor of same-sex couples when the

[28] *See* Pam Belluck, *Massachusetts Effort to End Same-Sex Marriage Is Dead for Now*, N.Y. Times, Nov. 10, 2006, at A16.

[29] *See* Belluck, *Same-Sex Marriage Vote Advances in Massachusetts*, *supra* Chapter 1, note 28; Phillips & Wangsness, *supra* Chapter 1, note 28.

[30] The states approving defense of marriage amendments in November 2004 were Arkansas, Georgia, Kentucky, Michigan, Mississippi, Montana, North Dakota, Ohio, Oklahoma, Oregon, and Utah. *See* Michael Kranish, *Gay Marriage Bans Passed. Measures OK'D in All 11 States Where Eyed*, Bos. Globe, Nov. 3, 2004, at A22; and Sarah Kershaw, *Constitutional Bans on Same-Sex Marriage Gain Widespread Support in 10 States*, N.Y. Times, Nov. 3, 2004, at P9.

[31] Additional marriage amendments were enacted in Kansas, Texas, Alabama, Idaho, South Carolina, South Dakota, Tennessee, Colorado, Virginia, and Wisconsin.

constitutions in their states were clear that same-sex marriages were prohibited.[32] In a number of these states, the amendments went even further, prohibiting state institutions from establishing civil unions or domestic partnerships as alternatives to marriage.[33] Supporters of same-sex marriage had little reason to expect the judges in these states to rule that the legislatures must treat same-sex couples equivalently to married couples.

Even in states that did not amend their constitutions, most judges who considered challenges to same-sex marriage bans in this period declined to interpret their constitutions as expansively as the justices in Massachusetts had done. Most judges flat-out rejected the possibility that their constitutions protected same-sex marriage. In Arizona, the Court of Appeals ruled in *Standhardt v. Superior Court* that "the fundamental right to marry protected by our federal and state constitutions does not encompass the right to marry a same-sex partner."[34] Similarly, a three-judge panel in Indiana refused to require the state to issue marriage licenses in *Morrison v. Sadler*.[35] "The differentiation between opposite-sex and same-sex couples in Indiana marriage law is based on inherent differences reasonably and rationally distinguishing the two classes: the ability to procreate 'naturally,'" wrote Judge Michael P. Barnes.[36]

The legal climate was not much better for same-sex couples back east. The Supreme Court of Rhode Island dealt the same-sex marriage movement a blow in *Chambers v. Ormiston*, ruling that same-sex couples who married in other states could not get divorced in Rhode Island.[37] The case did not directly challenge the constitutionality of Rhode Island's prohibition of same-sex marriage, but in refusing same-sex couples a divorce, the court made clear that only heterosexual marriages were recognized under state law. "In our judgment," the court wrote, "when the General Assembly accorded the Family Court the power to grant divorces from 'the bond of marriage,' it had in mind only marriages between people of different

---

[32] A potential approach would be for state supreme court justices to rule that the constitutional amendments were themselves unconstitutional because they violated the spirit of the original document. *See* R. George Wright, *Could a Constitutional Amendment Be Unconstitutional?*, 22 LOY. U. CHI. L.J. 741 (1991). The idea of imposing constitutional limits on the amending power is not well established in the United States but has gained traction in other countries, such as India, Germany, and Nepal. *See* Richard Stith, *Unconstitutional Constitutional Amendments: The Extraordinary Power of Nepal's Supreme Court*, 11 AM. U. J. INT'L L & POL'Y 47 (1996).

[33] *See, e.g.,* MICH CONST. art. I, § 25 (2004) ("To secure and preserve the benefits of marriage for our society and for future generations of children, the union of one man and one woman in marriage shall be the only agreement recognized as a marriage or similar union for any purpose."); and VA. CONST. art. I, § 15-A (2006) ("Nor shall this Commonwealth or its political subdivisions create or recognize another union, partnership, or other legal status to which is assigned the rights, benefits, obligations, qualities, or effects of marriage.").

[34] Standhardt v. Superior Court, 77 P. 3d 451, 465 (Ariz. App. 2003).

[35] Morrison v. Sadler, 821 N.E.2d 15 (Ind. Ct. App. 2005).

[36] *Id.* at 31.

[37] Chambers v. Ormiston, 935 A.2d 956 (R.I. 2007).

sexes."[38] A more direct challenge to a state marriage law came in Maryland, where the justices were asked to strike down a 1973 statute defining marriage as the union between one man and one woman. Maryland's highest court, the Court of Appeals, ruled in *Conaway v. Deane* that the exclusion of same-sex couples from marriage was not sex discrimination, and that the state had a legitimate interest in "safeguarding an environment most conducive to the stable propagation and continuance of the human race."[39]

Perhaps the most disappointing loss for same-sex couples in this period came from the state of New York. In 2006, the Court of Appeals of New York, which is the name given to New York State's highest court, considered a constitutional challenge to the state's prohibition of same-sex marriage. The plaintiffs in *Hernandez v. Robles*[40] made arguments that were similar to the constitutional challenges brought by plaintiffs in Massachusetts, claiming that New York's policy violated the due process and equal protection clauses of the state constitution.[41] A Manhattan trial judge, Doris Ling-Cohan, initially ruled in favor of the same-sex couples, using language echoing the *Goodridge* opinion.[42] "Similar to opposite-sex couples," Ling-Cohan wrote, "same-sex couples are entitled to the same fundamental right to follow their hearts and publicly commit to a lifetime partnership with the person of their choosing."[43] However, the trial judge's decision was overturned by an intermediate appellate court.

When the case reached New York's highest court, the judges ruled against the same-sex couples, although they could not agree on a majority rationale. The lead opinion by Judge Robert S. Smith garnered just two other votes, with a fourth judge, Victoria A. Graffeo, concurring separately. In a brief, eight-page opinion, with very little constitutional analysis, Judge Smith validated the state's interest in limiting marriage to opposite-sex couples, which he evaluated using a rational basis test. "The critical question," he wrote, "is whether a rational legislature could decide that these benefits should be given to members of opposite-sex couples, but not same-sex couples."[44] Judge Smith believed that a rational legislature could legitimately determine that heterosexual unions were the most optimal environments for raising children. "Intuition and experience suggest that a child benefits from having before his or her eyes, every day, living models of what both a man and a woman are like," Judge Smith wrote.[45]

---

[38] *Id.* at 964.

[39] Conaway v. Deane, 932 A.2d 571, 630 (MD 2007).

[40] Hernandez v. Robles, 855 N.E.2d 1 (N.Y. 2006).

[41] N.Y. CONST. art. I, § 6 ("No person shall be deprived of life, liberty or property without due process of law."); N.Y. CONST. art. I, § 11 ("No person shall be denied the equal protection of the laws of this state or any subdivision.").

[42] *See* Sabrina Tavernise, *Judge's Ruling Opens Window for Gay Marriage in New York City*, N.Y. TIMES, Feb. 5, 2005, at A1.

[43] *Id.*

[44] *Hernandez*, 855 N.E.2d at 7.

[45] *Id.*

Judge Graffeo elaborated on the constitutional arguments in her separate opinion concurring in the judgment. Judge Graffeo conceded that the rights protected by the New York constitution were more expansive than those protected by federal law, but she was not persuaded that sexual orientation was a basis for special protection. The right to marry, which was guaranteed by the federal and state due process clauses, had always been limited to couples of the opposite sex. New York's right to privacy, established in its precedents and traditions, was no more expansive than the federal right. "New York's Due Process Clause," she concluded, "simply does not encompass a fundamental right to marry the spouse of one's choice outside the one woman/one man construct."[46] Judge Graffeo was also unsatisfied that the state's equal protection clause provided relief for same-sex couples. She refused even to acknowledge that the state's marriage laws discriminated on the basis of sexual orientation, observing that gay people were free to marry partners of the opposite sex, just as heterosexual people were.[47] Consequently, there was no reason to consider whether sexual orientation was a suspect classification entitled to heightened protections under the state equal protection clause.

Both Judge Smith and Judge Graffeo believed it was appropriate for the court to exercise restraint. Judge Smith stated that without a clear constitutional foundation for ruling in favor of same-sex couples, the Court of Appeals should not substitute its own judgment for that of the legislature. "It is not for us to say whether same-sex marriage is right or wrong," he wrote.[48] Judge Graffeo likewise thought that the court should not intervene, even if the legislature was making bad policy. "It may well be that the time has come for the Legislature to address the needs of same-sex couples and their families, and to consider granting these individuals additional benefits through marriage or whatever status the Legislature deems appropriate," she wrote. "Because the New York Constitution does not compel such a revision of the Domestic Relations Law, the decision whether or not to do so rests with our elected representatives."[49]

Fortunately for gay couples, other officials in the state were prepared to secure their rights. In May 2008, Governor David Paterson ordered state agencies to recognize same-sex marriages that were performed in other states.[50] Then, in 2011, at the

---

[46] *Id.* at 18 (Graffeo, J., concurring).

[47] *Id.* at 20 ("In this respect, the Domestic Relations Law is facially neutral: Individuals who seek marriage licenses are not queried concerning their sexual orientation and are not precluded from marrying if they are not heterosexual.").

[48] *Id.* at 12 (majority opinion).

[49] *Id.* at 22 (Graffeo, J., concurring).

[50] In a memo to state agencies, Paterson wrote, "it is now timely to conduct a review of your agency's policy statements and regulations, and those statutes whose construction is vested in your agency, to ensure that terms such as 'spouse,' 'husband,' and 'wife' are construed in a manner that encompasses legal same-sex marriages, unless some other provision of law would bar your ability to do so."

urging of Governor Andrew Cuomo, the New York State Legislature voted to legalize same-sex marriage. The victory was an important one for the LGBT movement, but it occurred only in spite of the actions of the state high court. Indeed, the *Robles* decision showed that state supreme courts were not necessarily willing to interpret their constitutions expansively in the aftermath of *Goodridge*. If judges from a liberal state in the Northeast were unwilling to follow the lead of the Massachusetts Supreme Judicial Court, then what were the chances that judges in other states would be more receptive to same-sex marriage? Perhaps the favorable ruling in Massachusetts had been a fluke.

In October 2006, the Supreme Court of New Jersey weighed in on the same-sex marriage issue. The outcome of *Lewis v. Harris* was more favorable to same-sex couples than the decision in New York, but it was a less comprehensive victory than the decision in Massachusetts had been.[51] The Supreme Court of New Jersey ruled that the state only had to provide same-sex couples with the same legal benefits as opposite-sex couples; the legislature did not have to legalize same-sex marriage.[52] Writing for the majority, Justice Barry T. Albin explained that the state had traditionally recognized marriage as the union of one man and one woman, so there was no foundation for declaring same-sex marriage a fundamental right.[53] The justices were, however, more sympathetic to the claims of gay couples under the state constitution's equal protection guarantee. Applying a rational basis test, the justices could identify no legitimate basis for denying gay couples the same benefits as heterosexual couples, especially as the state already afforded them so many protections already. The legislature had enacted comprehensive civil rights legislation on behalf of same-sex couples in the 1991 Law Against Discrimination and had provided gay couples a partial list of rights and benefits under the 2004 Domestic Partnership Act. "There is no rational basis," Justice Albin wrote, "for, on the one hand, giving gays and lesbians full civil rights in their status as individuals, and, on the other, giving them an incomplete set of rights when they follow the inclination of their sexual orientation and enter into committed same-sex relationships."[54]

---

[51] Lewis v. Harris, 908 A.2d 196 (2006).

[52] The same-sex couples in New Jersey argued that the state's prohibition of same-sex marriage violated the state constitution's guarantees of equal protection and due process. *See* N.J. CONST. art. I, para. 1 "(All persons are by nature free and independent, and have certain natural and unalienable rights, among which are those of enjoying and defending life and liberty, of acquiring, possessing, and protecting property, and of pursuing and obtaining safety and happiness.") Although this provision does not specifically mention equal protection, the New Jersey Supreme Court has ruled that among the "unalienable rights" protected is the equal protection of the laws. *See* Sojourner v. New Jersey Dep't of Human Servs., 828 A.2d 306 (N.J. 2003).

[53] *Lewis*, 908 A.2d at 211 ("Despite the rich diversity of this State, the tolerance and goodness of its people, and the many recent advances made by gays and lesbians toward achieving social acceptance and equality under the law, we cannot find that a right to same-sex marriage is so deeply rooted in the traditions, history, and conscience of the people of this State that it ranks as a fundamental right.").

[54] *Id.* at 218.

However, the New Jersey Supreme Court stopped short of requiring the legislature to permit same-sex couples to marry. Like the judges in New York, the New Jersey justices believed it was appropriate to exercise restraint. Justice Albin observed that "a court must discern not only the limits of its own authority, but also when to exercise forbearance, recognizing that the legitimacy of its decisions rests on reason, not power."[55] It would be up to the state legislature to determine whether to permit same-sex couples to marry or to provide the same benefits in a separate institution. "We will not short-circuit the democratic process from running its course."[56]

At least the justices were unanimous in their determination that same-sex couples were entitled to the same benefits that opposite-sex couples received. Chief Justice Deborah T. Poritz would have gone further than the majority, explaining in her partial dissent that she would have extended the title of marriage to same-sex couples as well. According to Poritz, the right to marry includes more than just the tangible benefits of marriage; the intangible benefits also matter and are protected by the clause. "We must not underestimate the power of language," she wrote. "Labels set people apart as surely as physical separation on a bus or in school facilities. Labels are used to perpetuate prejudice about differences that, in this case, are embedded in the law."[57]

A majority of the justices refused to interpret the state constitution this expansively, however, and in this respect *Lewis v. Harris* was a disappointment for same-sex couples. Even though the New Jersey Supreme Court was much more favorable to same-sex couples than the judges in New York had been, the justices still did not go as far as Massachusetts in vindicating the couples' civil rights. In fact, no state supreme court had required full marriage equality for same-sex couples since *Goodridge*, and the number of forums for pursuing a litigation strategy was dwindling. The next few years would reveal whether continuing a litigation strategy made sense. Perhaps once the initial reaction to *Goodridge* subsided, and Americans saw same-sex marriages in practice, judges in other states would be emboldened to strike down same-sex marriage bans. Or perhaps *Goodridge* was just an isolated case, and the same-sex marriage movement would stall.

Later Developments: California and Connecticut

If same-sex marriage advocates encountered setbacks in New Jersey and New York, the decisions in 2008 from the state supreme courts in California and Connecticut were much more encouraging. They were also symbolic victories. At stake was not simply whether gay couples were entitled to receive the same legal rights and

---

[55] *Id.* at 223.

[56] *Id.*

[57] *Id.* at 226 (Poritz, J., dissenting in part).

benefits as heterosexual couples, but whether the term *marriage* must be used to describe same-sex unions.

Both California and Connecticut already treated committed same-sex partnerships almost identically to their gay counterparts. Same-sex couples in California were entitled to register as domestic partners,[58] whereas couples in Connecticut could join in civil unions, with the same rights and benefits as married partners.[59] The only real difference between these arrangements and marriages in the eyes of the law was the name. The title of marriage mattered, according to same-sex couples, because it would invest same-sex unions with a degree of legitimacy that they would not possess under a different label.[60] No matter how generous some state legislatures might be to gay couples, same-sex unions would not achieve true equality with heterosexual relationships as long as society continued to define them as something other than marriages.

A potential complication in the litigation in California and Connecticut was the issue of standing. Because the legislatures in both states had already provided committed same-sex couples with the same rights and privileges as married partners, the litigants were required to establish that they had suffered an actual harm that it was appropriate for the courts to redress. In federal constitutional law, the U.S. Supreme Court has established that for citizen suits to meet standing requirements, litigants must suffer an "injury in fact" that is "actual or imminent" and not "conjectural or hypothetical."[61] Some states have established similar requirements for standing to prevent citizens from using the courts to overturn policies they dislike.[62] Absent

---

[58] California Domestic Partner Rights and Responsibilities Act, AB 205 (Cal. 2003).

[59] An Act Concerning Civil Unions, Public Act No. 05-10 (Conn. 2005).

[60] Research indicates that many of those who oppose same-sex marriage also recognize that marriage will grant legitimacy to gay unions, and they oppose it for this reason. *See* KATHLEEN HULL, SAME-SEX MARRIAGE: THE CULTURAL POLITICS OF LOVE AND LAW 6 (2006) ("Many opponents of same-sex marriage … ground their objections to same-sex marriage in the broader cultural messages that legal recognition might send, that is, that homosexuality is normal or at least acceptable, and that committed same-sex relationships deserve the same treatment as heterosexual marriages.").

[61] Lujan v. Defenders of Wildlife, 504 U.S. 555 (1992).

[62] States vary considerably in their willingness to permit citizen suits. *Compare, e.g.,* Florida Wildlife Federation v. State Dep't of Envtl. Regulation, 390 So. 2d 64, 67 (Fla. 1980) (holding that "private citizens of Florida may institute suit under that statute without a showing of special injury"), *with* Gerst v. Marshall, 549 N.W.2d 810, 814 (Iowa 1996) (denying standing without "a causal relationship between a plaintiff's interests and the challenged conduct"). In Connecticut, the state supreme court prior to *Kerrigan* had ruled that "no one has standing to attack the constitutionality of a statute unless he alleges facts which, if proven, would establish that, in its impact upon him, the legislation attacked adversely affects his constitutionally protected rights." Hardware Mut. Cas. Co., v. Premo, 153 Conn. 465, 470–71 (1966). Furthermore, according to the court, the injury had to be concrete, and not premised on "some possible or hypothetical set of facts not proven to exist." *Id.* at 471. *See also* Susan George, William J. Snape III & Rina Rodriguez, *The Public in Action: Using State Citizen Suit Statutes to Protect Biodiversity,* 6 U. BALT. J. ENVTL. L. 1 (1997); and Thomas R. Phillips, *Speech: The Constitutional Right to a Remedy,* 78 N.Y.U. L. REV. 1309 (2003).

a concrete, identifiable harm, citizens must use the ballot box to express their disapproval of legislative policies.

The trial court in Connecticut was not satisfied that Elizabeth Kerrigan and the other litigants met the requirements for standing.[63] In July 2006, Superior Court Judge Patty Jenkins Pittman issued a summary judgment in favor of the Department of Public Health, ruling that "the plaintiffs have failed to prove that they have suffered any legal harm that rises to constitutional magnitude."[64] Judge Pittman observed that there were no legal distinctions between marriages and civil unions, and that any differences between the institutions were "nominal" and "inconsequential from a legal perspective."[65] The court could identify no harm that demanded judicial intervention.

On appeal, the Connecticut Supreme Court rejected the argument that same-sex couples had suffered no injury.[66] It was reasonable, the justices ruled, for same-sex couples to interpret their exclusion from marriage as a form of discrimination, and to demand redress. "Especially in light of the long and undisputed history of invidious discrimination that gay persons have suffered," Justice Palmer continued, "we cannot discount the plaintiffs' assertion that the legislature, in establishing a statutory scheme consigning same sex couples to civil unions, has relegated them to an inferior status, in essence, declaring them to be unworthy of the institution of marriage."[67] The Connecticut Supreme Court was satisfied the plaintiffs met the requirements for standing.

The plaintiffs in Connecticut presented the justices with a number of different constitutional challenges under the due process[68] and equal protection clauses[69] of the Connecticut constitution. The majority opinion in *Kerrigan* focused primarily on equal protection, ruling that sexual orientation was a quasi-suspect class entitled to a heightened level of review under the state constitution. Lacking its own precedents outlining the criteria for identifying suspect classes, the justices turned to the standards developed by the U.S. Supreme Court in its own equal protection cases.[70] The Connecticut Supreme Court believed that same-sex couples met all of

---

[63] Kerrigan v. Comm'r of Pub. Health, 49 Conn. Sup. 644 (Conn. Super. Ct. 2006).

[64] *Id.* at 646.

[65] *Id.* at 654.

[66] Kerrigan v. Comm'r of Pub. Health, 289 Conn. 135 (2008).

[67] *Id.* at 150.

[68] CONN. CONST. art. I, § 8 ("No person shall…be deprived of life, liberty or property without due process of law.").

[69] CONN. CONST. art. I, § 20 ("No person shall be denied the equal protection of the law nor be subjected to segregation or discrimination in the exercise or enjoyment of his civil or political rights because of religion, race, color, ancestry or national origin.").

[70] *Kerrigan*, 289 Conn. at 165–66. These standards included whether "the group has suffered a history of invidious discrimination" (United States v. Virginia, 518 U.S. 515 (1996), Massachusetts Bd. of Retirement v. Murgia, 427 U.S. 307 (1976)); "the characteristics that distinguish the group's members bear 'no relation to [their] ability to perform or contribute to society'" (Frontiero v. Richardson, 411

the criteria for quasi-suspect classes. The court described the long history of discriminatory treatment suffered by gay people inside and outside the state.[71] This discrimination had never fully subsided: the court cited statistics indicating that the number of hate crimes against gay persons had doubled between 2000 and 2004, and that Connecticut ranked thirteenth among states in the number of hate crimes targeted against sexual orientation.[72] The *Kerrigan* majority also believed that same-sex couples lacked political power. Although the justices acknowledged that gay rights advocates had managed to persuade the state legislature to enact legislation establishing civil unions in 2005, the legislation included a number of remarks that could be construed as antigay.[73] The Court also noted that an openly gay individual had never been elected to statewide office, and that gay people composed only a tiny fraction of the state legislature.

Having established sexual orientation as a quasi-suspect classification, the justices next considered whether the reasons offered by the state for denying same-sex couples the right to marry could be justified under heightened scrutiny, which requires the legislature to have an "exceedingly persuasive justification" and for legislation to be "substantially related to important and legitimate objectives."[74] Applying this test, the justices accepted neither of the justifications offered by the state: to promote consistency with the laws of other jurisdictions and to preserve the traditional definition of marriage. On the latter point, the Court observed that the legislature had already abandoned the traditional definition of marriage by

U.S. 677 (1973), City of Cleburne v. Cleburne Living Center, 473 U.S. 432 (1985)); "the characteristic that defines the members of the class as a discrete group is immutable or otherwise not within their control" (Lyng v. Castillo, 477 U.S. 635 (1986)); and "the group is a minority or politically powerless" (Bowen v. Gilliard, 483 U.S. 587 (1987), San Antonio Indep. Sch. Dist. v. Rodriguez, 411 U.S. 1 (1973)).

[71] *Kerrigan*, 289 Conn. at 176 ("For centuries, the prevailing attitude toward gay persons has been one of strong disapproval, frequent ostracism, social and legal discrimination, and at times ferocious punishment.").

[72] *Id.* at 199–201. Many of these data came from the Web site PARTNERSAGAINSTHATE.ORG (e.g., *2004 Federal Bureau of Investigation Hate Crime Statistics*, PARTNERSAGAINSTHATE.ORG, http://www. partnersagainsthate.org/statistics/connecticut-2004.html).

[73] *See* Conn. Gen. Stat. § 46a-81r (2007) (making clear that nothing in its gay-rights legislation should be "deemed or construed (1) to mean the state of Connecticut condones homosexuality or bisexuality or any equivalent lifestyle, (2) to authorize the promotion of homosexuality or bisexuality in educational institutions or require the teaching in educational institutions of homosexuality or bisexuality as an acceptable lifestyle, (3) to authorize or permit the use of numerical goals or quotas, or other types of affirmative action programs, with respect to homosexuality or bisexuality in the administration or enforcement of the [state's antidiscrimination laws], (4) to authorize the recognition of or the right of marriage between persons of the same sex, or (5) to establish sexual orientation as a specific and separate cultural classification in society."). These provisions suggested to the Court that gay people were not politically powerful, despite the legislative victories they had achieved. *Kerrigan*, 289 Conn. at 204–05.

[74] *Kerrigan*, 289 Conn. at 212–13.

creating the institution of civil unions for same-sex couples. The state was not arguing that children were better off raised by heterosexual partners or that prohibiting same-sex marriage would improve the quality of heterosexual unions, and tradition alone was not a persuasive justification. "[W]hen tradition is offered to justify preserving a statutory scheme that has been challenged on equal protection grounds," Justice Palmer wrote, "we must determine whether the *reasons* underlying that tradition are sufficient to satisfy constitutional requirements. Tradition alone never can provide sufficient cause to discriminate against a protected class."[75]

The Connecticut Supreme Court's decision in *Kerigan v. Commissioner of Public Health* was a decisive victory for supporters of same-sex marriage. The state legislature could not deny same-sex couples the right to marry, even if alternative institutions created by the state had equivalent benefits. *Kerrigan* also established that sexual orientation was a quasi-suspect classification under the state equal protection clause, a decision that had implications not only for same-sex marriage, but for any other classification based on sexual orientation that the legislature might try to make. From then on, such legislation would be subject to heightened judicial review.

The California Supreme Court, like the Connecticut Supreme Court in *Kerrigan*, based its decision on the state equal protection clause, but most of the first half of the opinion focused on why same-sex couples were also protected by the right to marry under the state's due process and privacy clauses.[76] The justices agreed with plaintiffs that the right to marry was expansive enough to include same-sex unions, based on California precedent, the text of the state constitution, and recent practices. The Court noted that California precedent had long defined marriage inclusively, as not simply the union of one man and one woman but as "the right of an individual to establish a legally recognized family with the person of one's choice."[77] This understanding of the marriage right dated back at least to *Perez v. Sharp*, in which the California Supreme Court struck down the state's ban on interracial marriage.[78] Although *Perez* did not specifically consider the status of same-sex unions, the *Perez* majority described the marriage right in broad terms that could apply to gay couples. The right to marry, Judge Roger J. Traynor wrote in *Perez*, was "the right to join in marriage with the person of one's choice."[79] The text of the California Constitution also, in the majority's view, supported an expansive interpretation of the right to marry. Unlike the federal constitution, the text of California's constitution specifically mentions the word "privacy" because of a state constitutional amendment in

---

[75] *Id.* at 221–22.
[76] *In re* Marriage Cases, 43 Cal. 4th 757 (2008).
[77] *Id.* at 814–15.
[78] Perez v. Sharp, 32 Cal.2d 711 (1948).
[79] *Id.* at 715.

1972.[80] The addition of this language had led the California Supreme Court in the past to recognize a special right of "autonomy privacy."[81] Finally, the Court defended its expansive interpretation of the right to marry by referencing the growing pattern of tolerance toward same-sex couples in the state. The majority opinion noted that in 1999 California established domestic partnerships for same-sex couples, and in the Domestic Partner Rights and Responsibilities Act of 2003 invested these relationships with virtually all of the benefits of marriage. Other legislation prevented discrimination against gay people in private businesses, on the job, in housing, and with state grants and other financial assistance. This recent history suggested to the justices that the state was becoming increasingly tolerant of gay rights.

Having defined the right to marry broadly to include same-sex partnerships, the California Supreme Court next considered whether the legislature's refusal to permit gay people to marry violated the state's equal protection clause. The majority opinion determined that sexual orientation was a suspect classification, for many of the same reasons that the Connecticut Supreme Court in *Kerrigan* determined that it was a quasi-suspect classification: sexual orientation was an immutable trait, it bore no relation to a person's ability to contribute to society, and gay people had suffered a history of discrimination.[82] Unlike the Connecticut Supreme Court, however, the majority in California did not think that a group's level of political power was a relevant criterion for identifying suspect classes.[83] The California court also identified sexual orientation as a suspect class rather than a quasi-suspect class because California law did not have an intermediate standard of equal protection review.[84]

Applying the standard of strict scrutiny, the majority ruled that tradition was not, by itself, a compelling justification for refusing same-sex unions the title of marriage.[85] There was simply too much at stake for same-sex partners. Providing

---

[80] CAL. CONST., art. I, § 1 ("All people are by nature free and independent and have inalienable rights. Among these are enjoying and defending life and liberty, acquiring, possessing, and protecting property, and pursuing and obtaining safety, happiness, and privacy.").

[81] *See* Hill v. Nat'l Collegiate Athletic Ass'n, 7 Cal.4th 1, 35 (1994) (defining autonomy privacy as an individual's interest "in making intimate personal decisions or conducting personal activities without observation, intrusion, or interference.").

[82] *Marriage Cases*, 43 Cal. 4th at 841–42.

[83] *Id.* at 843.

[84] *Id.* at 843–44.

[85] As in Connecticut, the state's principal justification for treating same-sex couples differently from opposite-sex couples was "retaining the traditional and well-established definition of marriage." *Id.* at 784. However, like the Connecticut Supreme Court, the majority in *In re Marriage Cases* concluded that tradition alone was not a sufficient justification for denying same-sex couples the right to marry. "[I]f we have learned anything from the significant evolution in the prevailing societal views and official policies toward members of minority races and toward women over the past half-century," Chief Justice George wrote, "it is that even the most familiar and generally accepted of social practices and traditions often mask an unfairness and inequality that frequently is not recognized or appreciated by those not directly harmed by those practices or traditions." *Id.* at 853–54.

only domestic partnerships sent the message that gay relationships were "to be viewed as of a lesser stature than marriage and, in effect, as a mark of second-class citizenship."[86] No matter how much the state legislature tried to equalize domestic partnerships and civil unions, the establishment of separate institutions was constitutionally suspect. "Even when the state affords substantive legal rights and benefits to a couple's family relationship that are comparable to the rights and benefits afforded to other couples," Chief Justice George wrote, "the state's assignment of a different name to the couple's relationship poses a risk that the different name itself will have the effect of denying such couple's relationship the equal respect and dignity to which the couple is constitutionally entitled."[87]

The victories for same-sex couples in Connecticut and California were important because they reinforced the decision of the Massachusetts Supreme Judicial Court in the *Opinion of the Justices*.[88] Now Massachusetts was no longer alone in its commitment to same-sex marriage. Four years after the *Opinion of the Justices*, two more state supreme courts had agreed that their constitutions prohibited legislatures from creating alternative institutions for same-sex couples, even when they received the same benefits as marriage. Symbolically, the decisions were also important because they suggested that gay relationships had the same worth as heterosexual unions, a move that supporters of marriage equality hoped would encourage broader social acceptance of gay rights and perhaps lead judges in other states to issue similar rulings.

Conclusion

After receiving important victories in California and Connecticut, the legal climate for same-sex couples seemed more promising than before, even if it was still not exactly favorable to the same-sex marriage movement. At the end of 2008, after voters in California overturned the state supreme court's decision in *In re Marriage Cases*, only two states provided full marriage equality for same-sex couples. In much of the country, amendments were in place that effectively blocked efforts by supporters of same-sex marriage to win favorable judgments in these states. It was not clear at the time whether the federal courts would step in to overturn these amendments.

Still, for supporters of same-sex marriage, there was reason for optimism. On April 3, 2009, the Iowa Supreme Court became the next state supreme court to rule in favor of same-sex marriage. Writing for a unanimous court in *Varnum v. Brien*,[89]

---

[86] *Id.* at 846.

[87] *Id.* at 844.

[88] Opinion of the Justices to the Senate, 802 N.E.2d 565 (Mass. 2004).

[89] Varnum v. Brien, 763 N.W.2d 862 (2009).

Justice Mark S. Cady ruled that a 1998 statute limiting marriage to the union of one man and one woman violated the equal protection clause of the state constitution.[90] The justices believed that, like gender, sexual orientation was a suspect classification entitled to heightened scrutiny under the state equal protection clause. Applying the standard of heightened scrutiny, the court was not satisfied that the exclusion of same-sex couples from civil marriage was substantially related to an important government objective. "We are firmly convinced the exclusion of gay and lesbian people from the institution of civil marriage does not substantially further any important governmental objective," Justice Cady wrote. "The legislature has excluded a historically disfavored class of persons from a supremely important civil institution without a constitutionally sufficient justification. There is no material fact, genuinely in dispute, that can affect this determination."[91] The justices maintained that the only suitable remedy to the constitutional infirmity was to provide same-sex couples access to civil marriage.

Four days after the Iowa Supreme Court's decision, lightning struck twice, when Vermont became the first state to legalize same-sex marriage through legislation. The move was a surprise at the time because Governor Jim Douglas vetoed the bill, and there did not appear to be enough votes in the state House of Representatives to override the veto. But in a sudden turnaround on April 7, 2009, supporters of same-sex marriage mustered the necessary two-thirds majority by a single vote.[92] In less than a week, the number of states permitting same-sex marriage had doubled, from two states to four.

The actions in Vermont marked a period of transition, in which progress on the issue of same-sex marriage shifted from state courts to state legislatures. On May 6, 2009, a month after Vermont acted on the issue, Maine became the fifth state to legalize same-sex marriage, with the unexpected support of Governor John Baldacci, who had previously opposed the bill.[93] New Hampshire then passed a same-sex marriage law in June. In the next few years, other state legislatures followed, and by the end of 2012 same-sex marriage had been approved in New York, Maryland, and Washington state.[94] Momentum seemed to be growing in favor of

---

[90] Iowa Const. art. I, § 6 ("All laws of a general nature shall have a uniform operation; the general assembly shall not grant to any citizen or class of citizens, privileges or immunities, which, upon the same terms shall not equally belong to all citizens.").

[91] Varnum, 763 N.W.2d at 906.

[92] See Jessica Garrison, Lawmakers Override the Governor's Veto of Their Legislation. Foes Plan to Respond with a TV Ad Campaign, L.A. Times, Apr. 8, 2009, at A14; and Abby Goodnough, Rejecting Veto, Vermont Backs Gay Marriage, N.Y. Times, Apr. 8, 2009, at A1.

[93] The actions of the Maine legislature were subsequently overturned by a referendum on November 3, 2009, but voters considered the issue once again and restored same-sex marriage in November 2012.

[94] The pro–same-sex marriage laws in Maryland and Washington both survived referenda in November 2012.

same-sex marriage, although it was uncertain how many other states would join the movement.

Concurrent with this activity, David Boies and Ted Olson filed suit in federal court challenging the constitutionality of Proposition 8 in California. Although many supporters of same-sex marriage questioned the wisdom of pursuing a federal litigation strategy at the time—especially given the conservative complexion of the U.S. Supreme Court—Boies and Olson secured favorable judicial outcomes, first at the district court level and then in the U.S. Court of Appeals for the Ninth Circuit.[95] With these victories in hand, and with appropriate venues for state court litigation dwindling, state supreme courts played a less prominent role than before in advancing marriage equality.

---

[95] *See* Perry v. Schwarzenegger, 704 F. Supp. 2d 921 (N.D. Cal. 2010); Perry v. Brown, Nos. 10-16696, 11-16577, 2012 WL 372713 (9th Cir. Feb. 7, 2012).

AN ANALYSIS OF STATE
JUDICIAL IMPACT

CHAPTER 5

Policy Initiation: The Diffusion of Same-Sex Marriage Cases across the States

After the victory in Iowa, the focus of same-sex marriage reform efforts shifted from the state courts to federal courts and to legislation in states such as Vermont and New York. It is appropriate, then, to reflect on what the legacy of the litigation in the states has been. The recent history raises a number of important questions about the capacity of state courts to influence policy. Why, for example, did only some judges rule in favor of same-sex marriage? Why was the public more accepting of same-sex marriage decisions in certain states? Why were only some decisions overturned by constitutional amendments? I consider these questions in the remainder of the book.

The subject of this chapter is *policy initiation*, by which I mean the willingness of judges to adopt new legal doctrines, or "innovations," such as the legalization of same-sex marriage. Following Canon and Baum, I define an innovation as "a program or policy which is new to the adopting unit, regardless of how old the idea may be or where it originates."[1] Policy initiation is, of course, required for judges to have any sort of impact on public policy development, but initiating policy is not necessarily as straightforward as finding judges who are personally supportive of policy change. Institutional and environmental conditions might impose constraints on judges, reducing their capacity to become policy innovators. If judges lack textual support for their decisions, if they can be voted out of office for unpopular rulings, or if the public objects strongly to their holdings, judges might be less willing to innovate.

Understanding judicial policy initiation is complicated by the fact that judges cannot initiate policy unless litigants give them the opportunity to do so. State supreme courts are, like other courts, reactive institutions. Unlike other policy

[1] Bradley C. Canon & Lawrence Baum, *Patterns of Adoption of Tort Law Innovations: An Application of Diffusion Theory to Judicial Doctrines*, 75 Am. Pol. Sci. Rev. 975, 976 (1981); *see also* Jack Walker, *The Diffusion of Innovations among the American States*, 63 Am. Pol. Sci. Rev. 1186 (1973).

makers, such as legislators or governors, judges are not at liberty to initiate policy on whatever issues they choose. Instead, judges must work within the parameters of the cases that come before them. Until supporters of same-sex marriage choose to litigate in particular states, judges must wait for the question to be presented to them. To some extent, then, variations in judicial policy initiation will reflect the behavior of the litigants who are challenging state marriage laws. If litigants—or the LGBT public interest groups that represent them—anticipate a greater likelihood of success in states in which the judges are liberal or retained for life, then judges will have a greater opportunity to innovate because appropriate cases will be available that will permit them to do so.

The behavior of litigants is not sufficient, however, to explain when policy initiation is likely to occur, as many judges have refused to legalize same-sex marriage even when asked. As the previous two chapters demonstrated, there has been considerable variation in how judges have approached the marriage question. Table 5.1 lists chronologically the twelve state high courts that, since the 1970s, have made substantive determinations about the legalization of same-sex marriage. The decisions of these courts have been evenly split. In five states (MN, NY, WA, MD, RI), judges did not recognize any form of marriage equality; in another five states (HI, MA, CA, CT, IA), high court judges mandated full marriage equality for same-sex couples; and in two states (VT, NJ), judges permitted a compromise, ruling that the state legislatures could create civil unions or domestic partnerships as alternative arrangements to marriage.

Of these decisions, perhaps the biggest surprise came from the Iowa Supreme Court. If previous decisions favoring same-sex marriage came from more traditionally liberal regions of the country, such as New England and the West Coast, *Varnum v. Brien* came down in the nation's heartland.[2] Iowa is somewhat more liberal than its neighbors in the West North Central division,[3] and before *Varnum* efforts to amend the state constitution to prohibit same-sex marriages had failed, unlike five of the other six states in the region.[4] But the *Varnum* decision was neither expected nor especially welcomed by the majority of citizens. A poll released by the University

---

[2] Varnum v. Brien, 763 N.W.2d 862 (Iowa 2009).

[3] My assessment of Iowa's liberalness is based on measures of citizen and government ideology developed by Berry et al., *supra* Chapter 2, note 76. The measures are scored on a 100-point scale, with higher values associated with more liberal ideologies. The citizen ideology score for Iowa in 2006 was 51.8, and the institutional ideology score was 69.9, which means that Iowa had the most liberal government that year of the seven states in its census division and the third most liberal citizenry.

[4] Constitutional amendments prohibiting same-sex marriages were enacted in Missouri (2004), Nebraska (2000), North Dakota (2004), Kansas (2005), and South Dakota (2006), but not Minnesota. On November 6, 2012, Minnesota voters narrowly rejected such an amendment, making Minnesota the first state in the nation in which an amendment prohibiting same-sex marriage failed a public vote.

Table 5.1 **State Supreme Court Decisions Concerning Same-Sex Marriage, 1971–2009**

Name	State	Year	Anti–Same-Sex Marriage	Civil Unions Only	Pro–Same-Sex Marriage
Baker v. Nelson	Minnesota	1971	X		
Baehr v. Lewin	Hawaii	1993			X
Baker v. Vermont	Vermont	1999		X	
Goodridge v. Department of Public Health	Massachusetts	2003			X
Hernandez v. Robles	New York	2006	X		
Anderson v. King County	Washington	2006	X		
Lewis v. Harris	New Jersey	2006		X	
Conaway v. Deane	Maryland	2007	X		
Chambers v. Ormiston	Rhode Island	2007	X		
In re Marriage Cases	California	2008			X
Kerrigan v. Commissioner of Public Health	Connecticut	2008			X
Varnum v. Brien	Iowa	2009			X
TOTAL			5	2	5

Note: The table includes only state supreme court decisions representing substantive determinations on the merits. Not included are decisions that dismissed litigation in light of the passage of a constitutional amendment or procedural challenges to state ballot initiatives. Rhode Island is included even though the case deals indirectly with same-sex marriage because the state supreme court made a substantive determination that same-sex couples may not wed under state law.

of Iowa just a day before *Varnum* was handed down found that only 26.2 percent of citizens in the state favored same-sex marriage, although more than half of its citizens would have supported civil unions for same-sex couples.[5] If *Varnum* was not dramatically out of step with public opinion, it went against the grain enough to constitute a real surprise.

The decision also posed something of a risk to the justices. With public opinion against the justices, the risk was real that the state would approve a constitutional amendment overturning *Varnum*, joining the thirty other states that had already

[5] See *University of Iowa Hawkeye Poll: Iowans' Views on Gay Marriage and Civil Unions* (Apr. 2, 2009), available at http://www.uiowa.edu/~c030111/HawkeyePoll-gaymarriageTopline.pdf.

enacted anti-marriage amendments by that time. "This is an unconstitutional ruling and another example of activist judging molding the Constitution to achieve their personal and political ends," Congressman Steve King (R—IA) announced in a statement released the same day as *Varnum*. "Now it is the Iowa legislature's responsibility to pass the Marriage Amendment to the Iowa Constitution, clarifying that marriage is between one man and one woman, to give the power that the Supreme Court has arrogated to itself back to the people of Iowa."[6] Assuming that the outcome in *Varnum* reflected their sincere policy preferences, the justices risked putting these policy goals in jeopardy by issuing a decision that the public would overturn with a constitutional amendment.[7]

The other risk of *Varnum* was that it would cost the justices their jobs. State supreme court justices in Iowa are appointed by the governor from a short list of candidates chosen by a nominating committee, but to keep their jobs the justices must stand for reelection in uncontested retention elections every eight years. There was a real possibility, then, that the justices would be held accountable for an unpopular decision in the next election, a possibility that was not lost on the justices at the time. "I can assure you that the members of our court were very much aware when we issued our decision in *Varnum* that we could lose our jobs because of our vote on that case," Chief Justice Marsha K. Ternus later commented in remarks delivered at Albany Law School.[8] As it turned out, all three of the justices up for reelection in 2010 lost their jobs, including Chief Justice Ternus and Justices Michael J. Streit and David L. Baker. Justice David Wiggins narrowly won reelection in 2012, following a strong campaign by same-sex marriage opponents to remove him from the bench. Three other judges face retention elections in 2016.

Although merit systems are supposed to emphasize the qualifications of judges, in fact they are not insulated from partisan politics.[9] Chief Justice Ternus observed that, following *Varnum*, "Iowa's retention election was hijacked by special interest groups intent on advancing their own agenda. In fact, the avowed purpose of ousting the three justices was to send a message across Iowa and the country that judges

---

[6] Steve King, *King Statement on Iowa Supreme Court Decision*, CONGRESSMAN STEVE KING: REPRESENTING THE 5TH DISTRICT OF IOWA (Apr. 3, 2009), http://steveking.house.gov/index.php?option=com_content&task=view&id=3905&Itemid=300099.

[7] There are no initiative amendments procedures in place in Iowa, so it would have taken at least two years for a constitutional amendment to appear on the ballot. IOWA CONST. art. X, § 1 provides that a proposed amendment to the state constitution must be approved by a majority of legislators in both houses convening in two separate legislative sessions, with the requirement that there be a general election before the second vote. The proposed amendment is then put before the citizens for a vote.

[8] Marsha Ternus, *Remarks*, 74 ALB. L. REV. 1569, 1576 (2011).

[9] See Hall, *State Supreme Courts in American Democracy*, *supra* Chapter 2, note 47, at 324. ("[R]etention elections are not impervious to partisan pressures, contrary to the claims of reformers. Supreme court justices who stand for retention in states characterized by competitive party politics or in elections with partisan cross-pressures... receive a significantly lower proportion of positive votes.").

ignore the wishes of the people at their peril."[10] With their jobs on the line, and the chance of a constitutional amendment overturning *Varnum* a real one, it is not immediately clear what would have encouraged the justices to act against public opinion as they did.

It is possible, of course, that the justices thought that the law compelled them to rule in favor of same-sex marriage. Writing for a unanimous court, Justice Mark S. Cady certainly presented the decision as though constitutional principles compelled the result. "We have a constitutional duty to ensure equal protection of the law," he wrote. "If gay and lesbian people must submit to different treatment without an exceedingly persuasive justification, they are deprived of the benefits of the principle of equal protection upon which the rule of law is founded."[11] No doubt the justices thought they were offering a defensible interpretation of Iowa law, but it is hard to imagine that they felt constrained to rule as they did. Because the relevant provisions of the Iowa Constitution are open-textured and the question was one of first impression, neither text nor precedent necessarily required marriage equality, had the justices wished to rule differently.

Why, then, did the Iowa Supreme Court come out with a decision that was so strongly supportive of same-sex marriage? More generally, the case of Iowa raises questions about when judges are more likely to adopt policy innovations such as the legalization of same-sex marriage. Why did the judges in Iowa vote to legalize same-sex marriage when judges in more liberal states, such as New York, Washington, and Rhode Island, declined to do so? Could there be systematic explanations that account for when judges are willing to adopt these types of innovations? Iowa is particularly interesting because its citizens and institutions are more conservative than other states in which supreme court justices have ruled in favor of same-sex marriage.[12]

On the other hand, Iowa has a relatively old, relatively well-established constitution, and the state has a long constitutional tradition of progressivism on equality issues. In fact, Iowa in 1998 became one of just twenty states to adopt an equal rights amendment, specifically prohibiting discrimination on the basis of sex.[13] As I discuss below, the justices were able to draw upon these progressive traditions to justify the decision in *Varnum*, and the justices might have thought that referencing these traditions would enhance the legitimacy of a pro-marriage outcome.

Indeed, it is possible that, as a general matter, judges are more willing to innovate in areas of policy such as same-sex marriage when their institutions are permissive

---

[10] Ternus, *supra* note 8, at 1574.

[11] Varnum v. Brien, 763 N.W.2d 862, 906 (Iowa 2009).

[12] For ideology data, see Berry et al., *supra* Chapter 2, note 76.

[13] Iowa Const. art. I, § 1 (1998) ("All men and women are, by nature, free and equal and have certain inalienable rights—among which are those of enjoying and defending life and liberty, acquiring, possessing and protecting property, and pursuing and obtaining safety and happiness.").

of such change. Liberal constitutional texts and traditions give flexibility to judges, as do judicial independence and professionalized institutions, which provide judges with the resources they need to give full attention to constitutional claims. It is probably no accident that most of the state supreme court justices who voted in favor of marriage equality were retained for life or by reappointment, making them relatively free of political pressures and electoral incentives. The California Supreme Court, which has less independence, ranks first in the country in its level of professionalism. These types of institutional variations might systematically influence whether courts are willing to adopt morality policy innovations.

In the rest of the chapter, I describe general characteristics of the state supreme courts that voted yes on the marriage question and develop a descriptive typology of these tribunals. I also use event history analysis to model the timing and sequence of state supreme court decisions favoring marriage equality. As the data will show, the decisions for the most part have been good reflections of their environments. Pro–same-sex marriage decisions have tended to come from states with liberal citizens and elected officials; low concentrations of evangelicals; and larger, more visible gay populations. However, the permissiveness of state institutions has also had an important explanatory role. Judges who have voted in favor of marriage equality have tended to sit on independent, professionalized courts, in states with constitutions that include broader equal rights protections than are found in the federal constitution.

Judicial Ideology

When trying to understand judicial policy initiation, the most reasonable place to start is by looking at the ideological preferences of the judges. It is well established that judges vote consistently with their policy preferences at most levels of the federal and state judiciaries.[14] Not surprisingly, this research has found that judges who are liberal tend to favor liberal policy outcomes, and conservative judges tend to prefer conservative outcomes. Looking specifically at gay rights controversies, Pinello affirmed that attitudes drive judicial behavior in this area, including on courts of

---

[14] See Jeffrey A. Segal & Harold J. Spaeth, The Supreme Court and the Attitudinal Model Revisited (2002) (concerning the influence of sincere judicial policy preferences on the U.S. Supreme Court); Michael W. Giles, Virginia A. Hettinger & Todd Peppers, Picking Federal Judges: A Note on Policy and Partisan Selection Agendas, 54 Pol. Res. Q. 623 (2001) (showing that there is a link between the behavior of judges on the U.S. Courts of Appeals and the preferences of the political actors who were responsible for their appointment); and Paul Brace, Laura Langer & Melinda Gann Hall, Measuring the Preferences of State Supreme Court Judges, 62 J. Pol. 387 (2000) (showing that party-adjusted surrogate judge ideology scores provide "a valid, stable measure of judge preferences in state supreme courts").

last resort.[15] The ability of judges to vote sincerely, however, is not absolute. Judges might be constrained depending on their places in the judicial hierarchy and the holdings of earlier decisions. Judges on lower state and federal courts are expected to adhere to policies set by their judicial superiors,[16] but even judges on courts of last resort must work within frameworks established by their own precedents.[17] Judges who decline to adhere to these legal norms might find that their decisions have less legitimacy.

In the area of same-sex marriage policy, these traditional constraints on judicial behavior have had much less force because the cases have been primarily matters of first impression. State judges who have ruled on the issue of marriage equality have had no direct state court precedents to guide their decisions or competing federal precedents to take into account. At least in theory, then, the judges have had more flexibility to vote consistently with their sincere policy preferences. It is little surprise, then, that there is a correlation between the ideology of state judges and policy initiation in the area of same-sex marriage policy. Table 5.2 ranks states by their median high court ideologies, based on aggregate data from 1993 to 2006.[18] The data show that states that have more liberal judges have been more likely to rule in favor of the legalization of same-sex marriage. In fact, the most liberal court, Hawaii (91.0), was the first court to rule in favor of marriage equality, followed by Vermont (84.5) and Massachusetts (70.9). On the other hand, none of the states with the ten most conservative supreme courts have had decisions legalizing same-sex marriage, nor have high courts even considered the issue.

Complicating the analysis is the fact that supporters of same-sex marriage have been more likely to file litigation in states with liberal high courts. Litigation was filed in seven of the states with the ten most liberal courts and none of the states with the ten most conservative courts. We therefore cannot know with certainty

[15] *See* Pinello, Gay Rights and American Law, *supra* Chapter 2, note 2 at 84 ("judges' attitudes, as measured by their age, gender, political party affiliation, prior career experience, race, and religion, were vitally important in fashioning appellate court response to the issues most intimate to lesbians and gay men").

[16] *See* Charles M. Cameron, Jeffrey A. Segal & Donald Songer, *Strategic Auditing in a Political Hierarchy: An Informational Model of the Supreme Court's Certiorari Decisions*, 94 Am. Pol. Sci. Rev. 101 (2000).

[17] *See* Jack Knight & Lee Epstein, *The Norm of Stare Decisis*, 40 Am. J. Pol. Sci. 1018 (1996); Herbert H. Kritzer & Mark J. Richards, *Jurisprudential Regimes and Supreme Court Decisionmaking: The* Lemon *Regime and Establishment Clause Cases*, 37 Law & Soc'y Rev. 827 (2003); Herbert H. Kritzer & Mark J. Richards, *Jurisprudential Regimes in Supreme Court Decision Making*, 96 Am. Pol. Sci. Rev. 305 (2002). *But see* Jeffrey R. Lax & Kelly T. Rader, *Legal Constraints on Supreme Court Decision Making: Do Jurisprudential Regimes Exist?*, 72 J. Pol. 273 (2010).

[18] Data are from Stephanie A. Lindquist, State Politics and the Judiciary Database (2007) (constructed pursuant to National Science Foundation Grant SES #0550618, *Predictability and the Rule of Law: Overruling Decisions in State Supreme Courts*). Ideology scores are based on the median party-adjusted judge ideology (PAJID) scores. *See* Brace et al., *supra* note 13.

Table 5.2 **Median High Court Ideology**

State	Median High Court Ideology	Any Same-Sex Marriage Decision	Pro–Same-Sex Marriage Decision
Hawaii	91.0	X	X
Vermont	84.5	X	X*
Massachusetts	70.9	X	X
New York	66.6	X	
Maryland	63.8	X	
Connecticut	60.8	X	X
Rhode Island	60.3	X	
Illinois	57.5		
Michigan	52.6		
Pennsylvania	51.5		
Washington	50.4	X	
Oregon	50.2		
Tennessee	49.6		
Maine	48.4		
North Carolina	46.2		
Wisconsin	44.2		
Georgia	43.9		
South Carolina	42.9		
Minnesota	39.5	X	
New Mexico	39.1		
Oklahoma	39.0		
Alabama	38.9		
Arkansas	38.4		
Mississippi	37.0		
Colorado	36.9		
West Virginia	36.4		
Louisiana	35.9		
Florida	35.7		
Kentucky	35.5		

State	Median High Court Ideology	Any Same-Sex Marriage Decision	Pro–Same-Sex Marriage Decision
North Dakota	34.0		
New Jersey	32.8	X	X*
Montana	31.0		
Nebraska	30.7		
Idaho	28.9		
Ohio	28.5		
Wyoming	28.3		
Texas	27.6		
Iowa	24.8	X	X
Missouri	24.7		
California	23.8	X	X
Nevada	23.5		
Virginia	23.4		
South Dakota	23.4		
Indiana	23.3		
Alaska	22.9		
Delaware	22.6		
Arizona	22.1		
Utah	20.1		
New Hampshire	11.1		
Kansas	9.4		
AVERAGE	**39.3**		

*Note: These state courts required civil unions only.

Source: LINDQUIST, STATE POLITICS AND THE JUDICIARY DATABASE (2007).

how these conservative courts would have ruled on the marriage question had they been asked. That said, it is possible to make some inferences by focusing just on the behavior of the judges in the states in which litigation was filed. Among the top twenty-five most liberal courts, the three most liberal who were asked to legalize same-sex marriage (HI, VT, MA) did so, whereas the three most conservative

(RI, WA, MN) did not. It would appear, then, that more liberal courts have tended to rule in favor of marriage equality.

To be sure, Table 5.2 does not take into account other potentially confounding alternative explanations, nor is the correlation between state judge ideology and policy initiation as close as it could be. Although the three most liberal courts ruled in favor of marriage equality, the next two, New York (66.6) and Maryland (63.8), refused to legalize same-sex marriage when given the opportunity.[19] Judges in Rhode Island (60.3), who also rank high in liberalism, also ruled against marriage equality when presented with the question. Moreover, judges in Iowa (24.8) and California (23.8) voted for marriage equality despite serving on more conservative tribunals.[20] It is possible, then, that some other quality of these tribunals, apart from ideology, encouraged supporters of same-sex marriage to litigate and the judges to support legalization.[21]

Institutional Differences

Another set of explanations that might help to account for variations in judicial policy initiation relates to the institutional design of state courts. As I discussed in the second chapter, judicial institutions differ from one another in a number of respects. State courts of last resort vary in their levels of professionalism, as reflected in the salaries of the justices, the sizes of their staffs, and control over their dockets.[22] State courts also differ in terms of the reputations of their members, with judges in some states more widely cited, and thus more prestigious, than others.[23]

---

[19] In the case of Maryland, there is evidence to suggest that the median ideology of the court had become more conservative by the time of the *Conaway* decision. Between 2000 and 2001, the median ideology of the Maryland Supreme Court dropped from 70.9 to 35.7. No comparable decline occurred in New York.

[20] The behavior of the judges in these states is not attributable to an increase in the liberalism of the courts over time. The ideology of the membership in Iowa and California has been relatively stable over time.

[21] It is also possible that a general ideology score does not do a good job of capturing the particular attitudes of judges on the same-sex marriage issue. Courts that rank as conservative generally might nonetheless have members who support same-sex marriage. Unfortunately, we do not have data measuring the policy preferences of state court judges on this issue, so we are left to make inferences from general measures.

[22] See Squire, *Measuring the Professionalization of State Courts of Last Resort, supra* Chapter 1, note 59; *see also* GLICK & VINES, *supra* Chapter 1, note 59; and Brace & Hall, *"Haves" versus "Have Nots" in State Supreme Courts, supra* Chapter 1, note 59.

[23] For more on the link between citations and judicial prestige, see Gregory A. Caldeira, *On the Reputation of State Supreme Courts,* 5 POL. BEHAV. 83 (1983); Stepher J. Choi, Mitu Gulati & Eric A. Posner, *Judicial Evaluations and Information Forcing: Ranking State High Courts and Their Judges,* 58 DUKE L. J. 1313 (2009); and David Klein & Darby Morrisroe, *The Prestige and Influence of Individual Judges on the U.S. Courts of Appeals,* 28 J. LEGAL STUD. 371 (1999).

It is possible that these types of variations influence the willingness of judges to adopt policy innovations.

When it comes to policy initiation in the area of same-sex marriage, perhaps the most important types of institutional variations are the methods of judicial selection and retention. There are several reasons for expecting elected judges to be less likely to initiate policy in this area. First, elected judges are more likely to share the values of their communities than judges who are less directly accountable. Elections give the public an opportunity to change the composition of the judiciary and to select judges who reflect their values. Because same-sex marriage lacked popular support in much of the country during the years I examined, I would expect states with elected supreme courts to be more likely to have been staffed with justices who opposed same-sex marriage.

Second, even when elected judges personally favor same-sex marriage, they might fear being voted out of office for acting on these beliefs. We know from research on state supreme courts that justices have these types of concerns. In one of her earliest articles on the subject, Hall described an interview that she conducted with one of the members of the Louisiana Supreme Court, Justice "A," who was personally opposed to the death penalty but was reluctant to dissent in cases in which a majority of the court upheld a death sentence.[24] Justice "A" expressed concerns about reelection and believed that it would be politically unwise to vote against constituent preferences on the issue, especially as death penalty cases tended to be high profile. "Since a liberal voting pattern in this highly visible and emotional set of decisions would place the justice at odds with his more conservatively oriented constituency," Hall reported, "Justice 'A' stated that he does not dissent in death penalty cases against an opinion of the court to affirm a defendant's conviction and sentence, expressly because of a perceived voter sanction, in spite of his deeply felt personal preferences to the contrary."[25]

In subsequent work, Hall and Brace affirmed that this tendency was not unique to Justice "A," but was in fact a common dimension of the behavior of elected state supreme court justices.[26] In controversial public policy areas, such as death penalty cases, electoral incentives encourage state supreme court justices to vote cautiously. Cann and Wilhelm reinforced these findings, observing that state supreme court justices are more responsive to constituent preferences in highly visible cases.[27]

---

[24] Hall, *Constituent Influence in State Supreme Courts*, *supra* Chapter 1, note 7.

[25] *Id.* at 1120.

[26] *See* Brace & Hall, *Integrated Models of Judicial Dissent*, *supra* Chapter 1, note 7; Brace & Hall, *The Interplay of Preferences, Case Facts, Context, and Rules in the Politics of Judicial Choice*, *supra* Chapter 1, note 7; Brace & Hall, *Neo-Institutionalism and Dissent in State Supreme Courts*, *supra* Chapter 1, note 7; Brace & Hall, *Studying Courts Comparatively*, *supra* Chapter 1, note 7; Hall, *Electoral Politics and Strategic Voting in State Supreme Courts*, *supra* Chapter 1, note 7; Hall & Brace, *supra* Chapter 1, note 7.

[27] *See* Damon M. Cann & Teena Wilhelm, *Case Visibility and the Electoral Connection in State Supreme Courts*, 39 AM. POL. RES. 557 (2011).

One might therefore expect that judges who are retained in partisan or nonpartisan elections will be more resistant to issuing a decision in favor of same-sex marriage. Same-sex marriage cases are surely even more salient than the death penalty cases that Brace and Hall studied,[28] and public attitudes about the issue tend to be strong. A decision in favor of same-sex marriage would most certainly be the focus of a state supreme court justice's next bid for reelection, and an unpopular vote might lose the justice the seat.

Table 5.3 ranks states by the method of retention used for associate supreme court justices.[29] Listed first are states in which judges are appointed for life and are therefore the most independent.[30] Next are states in which high court judges are reappointed after a fixed term of service by the governor, the legislature, or a nominating commission. Then come states that use retention elections, in which the public votes for candidates who run unopposed, followed by states that use competitive nonpartisan and partisan elections. These latter states contain the most democratically accountable selection systems. I expect that as retention systems become more accountable, judges will be less likely to vote in favor of the legalization of same-sex marriage.

After ranking states by the method of retention used for high court judges, Table 5.3 next orders states by their level of high court professionalization, as reflected by the size of judicial staffs and salaries and the amount of control that judges have over their dockets. Following Squire, I define high court professionalization as "a court's ability to generate and evaluate information."[31] Some of the earliest research on the adoption of judicial policy innovations by state high courts hypothesized that professionalized courts would be more likely to innovate because of their improved institutional capacity.[32] For example, Canon and Baum suggested that states with

---

[28] Indeed, Vining and Wilhelm provide evidence that death penalty appeals are not necessarily salient, at least as measured by front-page newspaper coverage and amicus participation. *See* Richard L. Vining, Jr. & Teena Wilhelm, *Measuring Case Salience in State Courts of Last Resort*, 64 POL. RES. Q. 559, 564 (2011) ("Interestingly, we find that popular notions about the salience of death penalty appeals may be mistaken. While 25.62 percent (31 of 121) of criminal appeals cases on the front page involved capital punishment, only 2.31 percent of death penalty appeals received front-page coverage and 2.54 percent attracted amici. . . . Given the relative infrequency of coverage of death penalty rulings by state high courts, scholars should reconsider the notion that capital punishment appeals are necessarily salient.").

[29] Data are from *Judicial Selection in the States: Initial Selection, Retention, and Term Length*, AMERICAN JUDICATURE SOCIETY, *available at* http://www.judicialselection.us.

[30] Only in Rhode Island do high court judges actually have life tenure. In both Massachusetts and New Hampshire, judges retain their offices to age seventy.

[31] Squire, *Measuring the Professionalization of State Courts of Last Resort*, *supra* Chapter 1, note 59, at 223.

[32] *See* Canon & Baum, *supra* note 1; and Gregory A. Caldeira, *The Transmission of Legal Precedents: A Study of State Supreme Courts*, 79 AM. POL. SCI. REV. 178 (1985) [hereinafter Caldeira, *The Transmission of Legal Precedents*].

Table 5.3 **Method of Retention and Professionalism of State High Courts**

State	Method of Retention	Professionalism	Any Same-Sex Marriage Decision	Pro– Same-Sex Marriage Decision
New Hampshire	Life Tenure	0.69		
Massachusetts	Life Tenure	0.58	X	X
Rhode Island	Life Tenure	0.53	X	
South Carolina	Reappointment	0.73		
New York	Reappointment	0.72	X	
New Jersey	Reappointment	0.71	X	X*
Virginia	Reappointment	0.66		
Delaware	Reappointment	0.62		
Connecticut	Reappointment	0.57	X	X
Hawaii	Reappointment	0.53	X	X
Maine	Reappointment	0.41		
Vermont	Reappointment	0.35	X	X*
California	Retention Election	1.00	X	X
Pennsylvania	Retention Election	0.88		
Tennessee	Retention Election	0.72		
Florida	Retention Election	0.71		
Alaska	Retention Election	0.69		
Illinois	Retention Election	0.69		
Missouri	Retention Election	0.64		
Arizona	Retention Election	0.60		
Indiana	Retention Election	0.58		
Nebraska	Retention Election	0.56		
Maryland	Retention Election	0.51	X	
Colorado	Retention Election	0.49		
Kansas	Retention Election	0.48		
New Mexico	Retention Election	0.47		
Iowa	Retention Election	0.46	X	X
Oklahoma	Retention Election	0.45		

(Continued)

Table 5.3 (Continued)

State	Method of Retention	Professionalism	Any Same-Sex Marriage Decision	Pro–Same-Sex Marriage Decision
Wyoming	Retention Election	0.39		
South Dakota	Retention Election	0.34		
Utah	Retention Election	0.33		
Michigan	Nonpartisan Election	0.88		
Georgia	Nonpartisan Election	0.64		
Washington	Nonpartisan Election	0.64	X	
Wisconsin	Nonpartisan Election	0.63		
Kentucky	Nonpartisan Election	0.62		
Ohio	Nonpartisan Election	0.60		
Minnesota	Nonpartisan Election	0.59	X	
North Carolina	Nonpartisan Election	0.55		
Oregon	Nonpartisan Election	0.53		
Arkansas	Nonpartisan Election	0.51		
Idaho	Nonpartisan Election	0.51		
Montana	Nonpartisan Election	0.47		
Nevada	Nonpartisan Election	0.41		
Mississippi	Nonpartisan Election	0.36		
North Dakota	Nonpartisan Election	0.25		
West Virginia	Partisan Election	0.81		
Louisiana	Partisan Election	0.67		
Texas	Partisan Election	0.67		
Alabama	Partisan Election	0.51		
AVERAGE		**0.58**		

*Note: These state courts required civil unions only.

Sources: (a) Retention Methods: American Judicature Society; (b) Professionalization: Squire, *Measuring the Professionalization of State Courts of Last Resort*, 8 St. Pol. & Pol'y Q. 223 (2008).

professional administrators and intermediate appellate courts might function more effectively and be more receptive to legal change. "Professional administrators and intermediate appellate courts may give supreme court justices more time to become aware of innovative doctrines and to consider their implications," they wrote.[33] Brace and Hall later affirmed that judges on professionalized courts are more likely to intervene in cases involving disadvantaged parties and to rule in favor of "underdog" parties on the merits.[34]

Altogether, then, I expect that the judges who are the most likely to become innovators in the area of same-sex marriage policy will be the ones who live in states with the most independent, professionalized courts. For the most part, the trends in Table 5.3 are consistent with these expectations. Notably, no court has ruled in favor of same-sex marriage in states with partisan or nonpartisan elections—the only states with contested judicial elections in which courts were even asked to address the issue were Washington and Minnesota. These states both use nonpartisan elections, and their courts rank higher in their professionalization than other courts in nonpartisan election states. However on neither court were judges willing to rule in favor of marriage equality.[35]

Courts have been more likely to rule in favor of the legalization of same-sex marriage when judges have life tenure or they are reappointed. Courts have ruled on the issue of same-sex marriage in seven of the twelve states that use these types of retention methods, and judges have sided with marriage equality in five of these states. Additionally, judges from two states that use retention elections have also voted in favor of marriage equality. One of these states, California, is ranked first in professionalism. Although the trends reported in Table 5.3 do not control for other factors that might influence policy initiation, they do suggest that there is a relationship between policy initiation and the institutional design of state courts.[36]

Of course, there are exceptions to the general trends reported in Table 5.3. Judges in New Hampshire, which has one of the most independent, professionalized courts, never took up the same-sex marriage issue. Nor did judges in South Carolina, which also ranks highly in both independence and professionalism. In contrast, judges in Iowa, which ranks relatively low in its level of professionalism, did issue a decision

---

[33] Canon & Baum, *supra* note 1, at 981.

[34] *See* Brace & Hall, *"Haves" versus "Have Nots" in State Supreme Courts*, *supra* Chapter 1, note 59.

[35] These findings are in slight tension with Pinello, Gay Rights and American Law, *supra* Chapter 2, note 2, at 91, who found that "appointed judges were not necessarily more liberal than elected jurists on lesbian and gay rights." However, Pinello did find that as the term of service of appointed judges increases, their likelihood of voting in favor of gay rights increases. A way of accounting for the discrepancies between Pinello's findings and my own might relate to issue salience. Haider-Markel & Meier, *supra* Chapter 1, note 63, report that most gay rights issues have low salience. Elected judges might have fewer concerns about a public backlash in routine gay rights controversies if they are not salient, as these issues are less likely to affect the judges' chances of reelection. Because Pinello was looking at a more comprehensive set of cases relating to gay rights than I am studying here, many of which were not salient, it makes sense to think that the effects of judicial selection would be different.

[36] Perhaps the most important control is citizen ideology. States that use appointment systems tend to have more liberal political cultures than other states, so it is possible that the method of retention is capturing a dimension of the state's political culture, not institutional effects. I control for the effects of citizen ideology in the event history analysis reported below.

favoring the legalization of same-sex marriage. On the whole, however, the trends in Table 5.3 suggest that institutional considerations influence state court behavior.

Constitutional Differences

A third explanation for the variation in policy initiation by state high courts in same-sex marriage policy relates to differences in the quality of the constitutional resources that judges have to work with. Perhaps judges are more likely to legalize same-sex marriage when litigants can muster persuasive justifications for doing so. Variations in state constitutions and state constitutional systems might make litigants unequally situated in their capacities to construct persuasive legal arguments. These variations might also affect the ability of justices to construct legal justifications for marriage equality that will be perceived as legitimate within their states.

State constitutions vary considerably in their substantive rights protections. For example, Table 5.4 reports whether a state's constitution includes an equal rights amendment specifically prohibiting discrimination on the basis of sex. As Table 5.4 shows, by 2008 twenty states had explicit constitutional prohibitions of sex discrimination in place.[37] I expect for at least two reasons the presence of ERAs to be associated with court decisions favoring the legalization of same-sex marriage. First, state ERAs provide a specific textual justification for a decision favoring marriage equality. Notably, the Hawaii Supreme Court in *Baehr v. Lewin* identified state prohibitions of same-sex marriage as a form of sex discrimination.[38] According to the supreme court justices in Hawaii, denying marriage licenses to couples based solely on the sexes of their partners qualified as sex discrimination.

No other state supreme court decision legalizing same-sex marriage explicitly relied upon their state's ERA, at least in the majority opinion, but there is good reason to suspect that the presence of an ERA in the Massachusetts constitution helped to forge the majority coalition in *Goodridge*. Justice John M. Greaney, who was a member of the narrow 4–3 majority coalition, stated in his concurrence that he thought the state's prohibition of same-sex marriage counted as sex discrimination. "That the classification is sex based is self-evident," he wrote. "As a factual matter, an individual's choice of marital partner is constrained because of his or her own sex. Stated in particular terms, Hillary Goodridge cannot marry Julie Goodridge because she (Hillary) is a woman."[39] Because classifications based on sex were analyzed using

---

[37] As mentioned above, New Jersey is sometimes counted as a twenty-first state because it amended its constitution in 1947 to make the language gender neutral. *See* Williams, *supra* Chapter 2, note 69. However, this amendment is not universally recognized as an ERA, and I do not treat it as one here.

[38] Baehr v. Lewin, 852 P.2d 44, 59 (Haw. 1993).

[39] Goodridge v. Dep't of Public Health, 798 N.E.2d 941, 971(Mass. 2003) (Greaney, J. concurring).

Table 5.4 **The Inclusion of an Equal Rights Amendment**

State	Equal Rights Amendment	Any Same-Sex Marriage Decision	Pro–Same-Sex Marriage Decision
Alaska	X		
California	X	X	X
Colorado	X		
Connecticut	X	X	X
Florida	X		
Hawaii	X	X	X
Illinois	X		
Iowa	X	X	X
Louisiana	X		
Maryland	X	X	
Massachusetts	X	X	X
Montana	X		
New Hampshire	X		
New Mexico	X		
Pennsylvania	X		
Texas	X		
Utah	X		
Virginia	X		
Washington	X	X	
Wyoming	X		
Alabama			
Arizona			
Arkansas			
Delaware			
Georgia			
Idaho			
Indiana			
Kansas			
Kentucky			

(Continued)

Table 5.4 (Continued)

State	Equal Rights Amendment	Any Same-Sex Marriage Decision	Pro–Same-Sex Marriage Decision
Maine			
Michigan			
Minnesota		X	
Mississippi			
Missouri			
Nebraska			
Nevada			
New Jersey**		X	X*
New York		X	
North Carolina			
North Dakota			
Ohio			
Oklahoma			
Oregon			
Rhode Island		X	
South Carolina			
South Dakota			
Tennessee			
Vermont		X	X*
West Virginia			
Wisconsin			

*Note: These state courts required civil unions only.

**Note: Although lacking an ERA, the New Jersey constitution was amended in 1947 to clarify that references to "persons" in the document referred to both men and women.

strict scrutiny under the Massachusetts constitution, Greaney believed the state had to have a compelling interest for denying marriage benefits based on sex.

The second reason that ERAs can be important is that they provide judges with a foundation for extending equal rights protections to other unprotected but analogous classifications, such as sexual orientation, which exhibit characteristics similar to gender. When supreme court justices in Connecticut, which has an ERA, were determining whether sexual orientation should be considered a quasi-suspect class, they observed that gay rights groups, like women's rights groups, lacked political power, even though, like women, LGBT groups had achieved some legislative victories. "Today, women, like African-Americans, continue to receive heightened protection under the equal protection clause even though they are a potent and growing political force," Justice Palmer wrote for the majority. "Consequently, a group satisfies the political powerlessness factor if it demonstrates that, because of the pervasive and sustained nature of the discrimination that its members have suffered, there is a risk that that discrimination will not be rectified, sooner rather than later, merely by resort to the democratic process."[40]

Because LGBT groups resembled women's rights groups in these respects, it made sense to treat them similarly. Justice Palmer explained that "gay persons are entitled to have their claim for heightened constitutional protection under the state constitution given the same, evenhanded consideration of the political powerlessness standard that other historically maligned groups, including women, have received."[41] These types of statements suggest that judges might be more likely to rule in favor of marriage equality when their state constitutions include equal rights amendments.

In fact, Table 5.4 suggests that the presence of an ERA is associated with state court decisions favoring marriage equality. In states with ERAs, five of the seven high courts that were asked to legalize same-sex marriage did so, compared to just two of the five courts asked to legalize same-sex marriage in non-ERA states. Notably, both California and Iowa, which ranked low in terms of high court ideology, have ERAs in their constitutions. It is possible, then, that the presence of permissive constitutional language induced the supreme court justices in these states to act.

Of course, the correlation between the presence of ERAs and rulings in favor of the legalization of same-sex marriage is not perfect. Judges in Washington and Maryland, which both have ERAs, voted against marriage equality when they were asked to consider the question. Vermont and New Jersey ruled in favor of marriage equality without ERAs—although in both of these states, judges required only that the legislature establish civil unions, not marriage. Perhaps with more permissive constitutional texts, the justices would have gone further.

Once again, the absence of controls is important here. It is possible that the same factors that contribute to the adoption of state ERAs also affect the activity of judges on the marriage question. One might expect, for example, that states with more liberal citizens and institutions are more likely to produce both ERAs and pro-marriage decisions. Yet, as I discuss below, four of the states that lack ERAs—New Jersey,

---

[40] Kerrigan v. Comm'r of Public Health, 289 Conn. 135, 196–97 (Conn. 2008).
[41] *Id.* at 216.

New York, Rhode Island, and Vermont—rank among the highest in their degree of liberalness, and in none of these states did judges require full marriage equality. It is defensible, then, to conclude that constitutional texts have a unique, independent effect.

Another attribute of state constitutions that might influence the tendency of judges to innovate is the age of a state constitution. Some states, such as Massachusetts, New Hampshire, and Vermont, have constitutions that date back to the eighteenth century. Other states such as Louisiana, Montana, and North Carolina have much more recent constitutions, dating from the 1970s. Georgia's constitution is the youngest, from 1983. It is possible that judges from states with older constitutions are more likely to innovate than judges with less well-established constitutions. By standing the test of time, older constitutions might gain legitimacy, and this legitimacy might transfer to decisions written under their authority. Lacking this sort of constitutional cover, judges in states with less-established constitutions might be more reluctant to act.

Judges in states with older constitutions might also find that they have a richer catalog of precedents interpreting the state constitution that they can use to support decisions favoring the legalization of same-sex marriage. For example, the California Supreme Court drew upon a variety of precedents from over 130 years of state constitutional law to establish that the state had long been progressive on matters of marriage equality. Perhaps most important was *Perez v. Sharp*,[42] in which the California Supreme Court struck down state prohibitions of interracial marriages, twenty years before the U.S. Supreme Court did so in *Loving v. Virginia*.[43] With the *Perez* precedent available to them, the California justices could more persuasively argue that their constitution required them to strike down state laws that limited access to marriage.

Table 5.5 ranks states by the ages of their state constitutions. Overall, the trends suggest that, contrary to expectations, the relationship between constitution age and the tendency of state courts to innovate is not close. Although Massachusetts, which has the oldest constitution, ruled in favor of same-sex marriage, so too did Hawaii and Connecticut, which have much more recent constitutions. Older constitutions also do not appear to be the special target of litigation strategies, with litigation just as likely to be filed in states with older and younger constitutions. This is not to say that the age of a state constitution might not be important in particular states. As I discussed above, there is reason to think that the age of the California constitution yielded a rich catalog of precedents to justify the outcome in *In re Marriage Cases* and that justices in Iowa drew upon their own state's rich history to justify the decision in *Varnum*.

It is possible that, in some circumstances, newer constitutions actually provide better opportunities for protecting minority rights. Miriam Smith found that the

[42] Perez v. Sharp, 32 Cal.2d 711 (1948).
[43] Loving v. Virginia, 388 U.S. 1 (1967).

Table 5.5 **Constitution Age**

State	Constitution Age (2009)	Any Same-Sex Marriage Decision	Pro–Same-Sex Marriage Decision
Massachusetts	229	X	X
New Hampshire	225		
Vermont	216	X	X*
Maine	189		
Rhode Island	166	X	
Wisconsin	161		
Indiana	158		
Ohio	158		
Iowa	152	X	X
Minnesota	151	X	
Oregon	150		
Kansas	148		
Nevada	145		
Maryland	142	X	
Tennessee	139		
West Virginia	137		
California	135	X	X
Nebraska	134		
Colorado	133		
Texas	133		
Delaware	122		
Washington	120	X	
North Dakota	120		
South Dakota	120		
Wyoming	119		
Idaho	119		
Mississippi	119		
Kentucky	118		
New York	114	X	

(Continued)

Table 5.5 (Continued)

State	Constitution Age (2009)	Any Same-Sex Marriage Decision	Pro–Same-Sex Marriage Decision
Utah	113		
South Carolina	113		
Alabama	108		
Oklahoma	102		
New Mexico	97		
Arizona	97		
Arkansas	97		
Missouri	64		
New Jersey	61	X	X*
Alaska	50		
Hawaii	50	X	X
Michigan	45		
Connecticut	44	X	X
Pennsylvania	41		
Florida	40		
Illinois	38		
Virginia	38		
North Carolina	38		
Montana	36		
Louisiana	34		
Georgia	26		
AVERAGE	**112**		

*Note: These state courts required civil unions only.

relatively recent adoption of the Canadian constitution facilitated the adoption of same-sex marriage in that country because the new text included language favorable to gay rights.[44] Perhaps, then, the effect of constitution age is variable. In some circumstances older constitutions work to the advantage of judges by providing them

[44] *See* Miriam Smith, Political Institutions and Lesbian and Gay Rights in the United States and Canada 21 (2008) ("The Canadian constitution provides openings for gay and lesbian litigants in part because it is a newer constitution and because the jurisprudential structure of rights in Canada does not create blockages as does American equal protection doctrine.").

with a greater catalog of precedents and by conferring legitimacy on judicial pronouncements, but in other circumstances older constitutions work against judges by providing them with outmoded language and fewer textual hooks for identifying new rights. The point is not that the age of a state constitution can never be important, but rather that Table 5.5 provides no evidence that the age of a state constitution has a systematic effect. The content of a constitution is more systematically important than its age.

Environmental Differences

My final expectation is that state judges are more likely to initiate policy when the environments in which they are located are sympathetic to policy change. The importance of environmental considerations on judicial policy innovation has been recognized by scholars at least since Canon and Baum studied the diffusion of tort law innovations across state supreme courts.[45] Canon and Baum observed that states are more likely to adopt tort law innovations when they have large populations or high levels of urbanization because these states are more likely to generate test cases than sparsely populated rural areas. The implication of Canon and Baum's research is that environmental conditions influence the diffusion of judicial policy innovations, providing justices with differing levels of opportunity to innovate.

Morality policy innovations, which are highly salient and technically simple, are likely to transmit differently from routine innovations such as the tort law innovations that Canon and Baum studied. We know from the literature on morality policies that, in general, the politics of morality policies is quite different from the politics of other types of policies because they are much more likely to engage the public.[46] Public attitudes are therefore likely to play a more critical role in defining the policy environment than they would if a less-salient issue area was involved. I suspect, then, that judges will be more likely to rule in favor of the legalization of same-sex marriage when their environments are liberal and secular, such as when citizens in the state are ideologically liberal, when state institutions are controlled by the Democratic Party, when states have fewer religious interest groups, and when their gay populations are politically active.

The willingness of state court judges to innovate in liberal, secular environments stems from at least three considerations. First, because judges come from the

[45] *See* Canon & Baum, *supra* note 1; and Caldeira, *The Transmission of Legal Precedents*, *supra* note 32.

[46] *See* Haider-Markel & Meier, *supra* Chapter 1, note 63; Lowi, *American Business, Public Policy, Case-Studies, and Political Theory*, *supra* Chapter 1, note 63; Lowi, *Four Systems of Policy, Politics, and Choice*, *supra* Chapter 1, note 63; Lowi, *Forward: New Dimensions in Policy and Politics*, *supra* Chapter 1, note 63; and Mooney & Lee, *supra* Chapter 1, note 63.

communities over which they preside, judges in states with liberal, secular communities are likely to be sympathetic to the values of these communities, making them more likely to favor the legalization of same-sex marriage. A second consideration is that judges might be less concerned about a backlash from citizens when the political culture is predominantly liberal. In more conservative states, judges might be concerned that their decisions will be overturned by constitutional amendments, or they might anticipate that they will not be reelected or reappointed at the expiration of their terms. Finally, when public support for same-sex marriage is relatively high, there is likely to be a greater number of litigants who are available to bring cases asking state supreme court justices to consider the marriage question. LGBT public interest groups might also be more willing to file suit because they anticipate that it will be easier to lay the groundwork for pro-marriage rulings in states that are already relatively progressive on rights issues.

The first environmental factor that has the potential to influence policy initiation on same-sex marriage policy is the ideology of a state's citizenry. Table 5.6 organizes states by their mean levels of citizen support for same-sex marriage, using scores developed by Lax and Philips.[47] Listed first are the more liberal states, which have higher levels of public support. My expectation is that same-sex marriage decisions will be more likely in liberal states, and in fact the data are mostly consistent with this expectation. In five of the ten most liberal states (MA, VT, CT, CA, HI), judges issued decisions favoring the legalization of same-sex marriages or civil unions. In three other states in the top ten (RI, NY, WA), judges had the opportunity to legalize same-sex marriage but declined to do so. In two other states (NH, ME), there was no litigation, but in 2009 the legislatures in both of these states voted in favor of legalization. Same-sex marriage policy initiation therefore does appear to be correlated with citizen attitudes about the issue.

A second, related environmental factor that has the potential to influence policy initiation is the ideology of state institutions. For the same reasons that one might expect judges to issue decisions that reflect the preferences of their citizens, policy initiation might also be more likely when the other institutions of state government are more supportive. Research suggests that judges are unlikely to have much of an impact on government policy when they stand alone, opposed by the rest of the government establishment.[48] Judges might anticipate that other state institutions will attempt to limit the effects of their decisions or to curb judicial power in other ways, making them more reluctant to issue decisions that will generate this sort of opposition.

Table 5.7 ranks states by the ideology of their government institutions, using data created with a procedure described by Berry et al.[49] The institutional ideology

---

[47] *See* Lax & Phillips, *supra* Chapter 2, note 77.

[48] *See* ROSENBERG, *supra* Chapter 1, note 3.

[49] *See* Berry et al., *supra* Chapter 2, note 76. At the time I conducted research, data were available through 2008 from Richard Fording's Web site (http://www.bama.ua.edu/~rcfording/stateideology.html).

Table 5.6 **Mean Citizen Support for Same-Sex Marriage**

State	Mean Citizen Support for Same-Sex Marriage	Any Same-Sex Marriage Decision	Pro–Same-Sex Marriage Decision
Massachusetts	56.0	X	X
Rhode Island	53.0	X	
Vermont	53.0	X	X*
Connecticut	52.0	X	X
New York	52.0	X	
New Hampshire	51.0		
California	50.0	X	X
Hawaii	49.0	X	X
Maine	49.0		
Washington	49.0	X	
New Jersey	48.0	X	X*
Colorado	47.0		
Nevada	46.0		
New Mexico	45.0		
Oregon	45.0		
Arizona	44.0		
Pennsylvania	43.0		
Alaska	42.0		
Illinois	42.0		
Minnesota	42.0	X	
Wisconsin	42.0		
Delaware	41.0		
Maryland	41.0	X	
Montana	41.0		
Florida	39.0		
Michigan	39.0		
Ohio	39.0		
Iowa	38.0	X	X
Virginia	37.0		

(Continued)

Table 5.6 (Continued)

State	Mean Citizen Support for Same-Sex Marriage	Any Same-Sex Marriage Decision	Pro–Same-Sex Marriage Decision
Kansas	36.0		
Wyoming	36.0		
Indiana	35.0		
South Dakota	35.0		
Idaho	34.0		
Missouri	34.0		
North Dakota	33.0		
West Virginia	33.0		
Nebraska	32.0		
Texas	32.0		
North Carolina	31.0		
Georgia	30.0		
Louisiana	30.0		
Kentucky	28.0		
South Carolina	28.0		
Tennessee	26.0		
Arkansas	25.0		
Oklahoma	25.0		
Utah	25.0		
Alabama	23.0		
Mississippi	23.0		
AVERAGE	**39.0**		

*These state courts required civil unions only.

Source: Lax & Phillips, *Gay Rights in the States: Public Opinion and Policy Responsiveness,* 103 Am. Pol. Sci. Rev. 367 (2009).

scores reflect the ideologies of the governor and the upper and lower houses of the state legislature and are reported on a 100-point scale, with higher values associated with higher amounts of institutional liberalism. The values reported in Table 5.7 are mean scores, which are based on the average institutional ideology scores for each state from 1993 to 2008. The table reports that the states with the most liberal political institutions were Vermont (69.6), followed by Hawaii (67.2), Maryland (65.5),

Table 5.7 **State Institutional Ideology**

State	Institutional Ideology	Any Same-Sex Marriage Decision	Pro–Same-Sex Marriage Decision
Vermont	69.6	X	X*
Hawaii	67.2	X	X
Maryland	65.5	X	
North Carolina	62.7		
Washington	62.4	X	
Rhode Island	62.3	X	
Maine	61.5		
West Virginia	61.0		
Massachusetts	60.8	X	X
Oregon	59.8		
Delaware	59.7		
New Mexico	59.7		
California	55.2	X	X
Connecticut	54.1	X	X
Louisiana	53.5		
Georgia	53.5		
Arkansas	53.2		
Alabama	53.2		
New Jersey	52.5	X	X*
Kentucky	52.2		
Iowa	51.3	X	X
New York	51.3	X	
Tennessee	51.1		
Missouri	51.0		
Mississippi	50.5		
Illinois	49.8		
Alaska	48.4		
Minnesota	47.1	X	
Oklahoma	47.0		

(Continued)

Table 5.7 (Continued)

State	Institutional Ideology	Any Same-Sex Marriage Decision	Pro–Same-Sex Marriage Decision
Virginia	46.8		
Pennsylvania	46.6		
Indiana	46.2		
Nevada	45.2		
North Dakota	44.6		
Michigan	44.3		
Wisconsin	42.7		
Nebraska	42.4		
New Hampshire	41.9		
Colorado	41.1		
Montana	40.5		
Florida	40.4		
Texas	38.8		
South Carolina	38.7		
Kansas	38.3		
Wyoming	37.9		
South Dakota	36.8		
Ohio	36.5		
Arizona	34.8		
Utah	30.1		
Idaho	29.3		
AVERAGE	**46.3**		

*These state courts required civil unions only.

Source: Berry et al., *Measuring Citizen and Government Ideology in the American States: A Re-Appraisal*, 10 Sᴛ. Pᴏʟ. & Pᴏʟ'ʏ Q. 117 (2010).

North Carolina (62.7), and Washington (62.4). The most conservative governments were in Idaho (29.3), followed by Utah (30.1), Arizona (34.8), Ohio (36.5), and South Dakota (36.8).

Based on the data from Table 5.7, there does appear to be a relationship between institutional ideology and the likelihood of a decision favoring marriage equality. However, the fit is not as strong as with citizen ideology. All of the pro–same-sex marriage decisions occurred in states with relatively liberal institutions, but among these states, there does not appear to be a close relationship between institutional ideology and innovation. Instead, there appears to be a tendency for supporters of same-sex marriage to file suit in states with liberal institutions. Excluding Minnesota, where the marriage question was litigated in the 1970s, all of the states in which litigation occurred were among the twenty-five with the most liberal institutions. It would appear, then, that institutional ideology has a stronger influence on litigation strategies than on the behavior of state judges. Supporters of same-sex marriage preferred to file suit in states with liberal institutions, but once the question was asked, the liberalism of a state's institutions did not determine which state supreme courts favored marriage equality.

A third environmental factor that has the potential to influence state supreme court activity is the religiosity of the citizenry. States with a high proportion of citizens who are members of religions that disapprove of same-sex marriage might be especially resistant to state supreme court decisions favoring it. For example, states with a large evangelical population might be more likely to take action against these decisions because of the conservatism and political activism of many evangelical denominations.[50] Moore reports that, although evangelical attitudes about gay people are more tolerant than before, disapproval among these groups remains high.[51]

Table 5.8 ranks states according to the evangelical population by state, based on data from 2000.[52] The data show that the states with the highest evangelical populations are primarily South Central states such as Arkansas (43.2 percent), Oklahoma (41.5 percent), Alabama (40.6 percent), Mississippi (39.7 percent), and Tennessee (37.0 percent), whereas the states with the smallest proportions of evangelicals are in the Northeast, including Rhode Island (1.6 percent), New Hampshire

---

[50] *See* MICHAEL LIENESCH, REDEEMING AMERICA: PIETY AND POLITICS IN THE NEW CHRISTIAN RIGHT (1993); Robert G. Moore, *Political Participation and Tolerance: American Evangelicals in Transition* (Paper Presented at the Annual Meeting of the Midwest Political Science Association, Chicago, IL, 2007); CHRISTIAN SMITH, AMERICAN EVANGELICALISM, EMBATTLED AND THRIVING (1998); and CAL THOMAS & ED DOBSON, BLINDED BY MIGHT: WHY THE RELIGIOUS RIGHT CAN'T SAVE AMERICA (1999).

[51] Moore, *supra* note 50; *see also* JAMES M. PENNING & CORWIN SMIDT, EVANGELICALISM: THE NEXT GENERATION (2002).

[52] Data are from the Association of Religion Data Archive (http://www.thearda.com), which has assembled the information from a series of studies published by the Glenmary Research Center. For 1980, see B. QUINN, HERMAN ANDERSON, MARTIN BRADLEY, PAUL GOETTING & PEGGY SHRIVER, CHURCHES AND CHURCH MEMBERSHIP IN THE UNITED STATES, 1980 (1982); for 1990, see M.B. BRADLEY, NORMAN M. GREEN, JR., DALE E. JONES, MAC LYNN & LOU McNEIL, CHURCHES AND CHURCH MEMBERSHIP IN THE UNITED STATES, 1990 (1992); for 2000, see DALE E. JONES, SHERRY DOTY, CLIFFORD GRAMMICH, JAMES E. HORSCH, RICHARD HOUSEAL, MAC LYNN, JOHN P. MARCUM, KENNETH M. SANCHAGRIN & RICHARD H. TAYLOR, RELIGIOUS CONGREGATIONS AND MEMBERSHIP IN THE UNITED STATES 2000: AN ENUMERATION BY REGION, STATE AND COUNTY BASED ON DATA REPORTED FOR 149 RELIGIOUS BODIES (2002).

Table 5.8 **Percentage of Citizens Who Are Evangelical**

State	% Evangelical	Any Same-Sex Marriage Decision	Pro–Same-Sex Marriage Decision
Arkansas	43.2		
Oklahoma	41.5		
Alabama	40.6		
Mississippi	39.7		
Tennessee	37.0		
Kentucky	33.7		
South Carolina	29.4		
Georgia	27.8		
North Carolina	25.6		
Missouri	24.8		
Texas	24.4		
Louisiana	21.5		
Virginia	17.1		
Indiana	16.0		
Kansas	15.7		
Nebraska	14.6		
South Dakota	14.4		
Florida	14.1		
New Mexico	13.1		
Wisconsin	12.7		
Arizona	12.5		
Iowa	11.8	X	X
Wyoming	11.4		
Oregon	11.4		
Minnesota	11.2	X	
Montana	11.2		
Michigan	10.9		
North Dakota	10.6		
Colorado	10.6		

State	% Evangelical	Any Same-Sex Marriage Decision	Pro–Same-Sex Marriage Decision
Illinois	10.3		
Ohio	10.0		
West Virginia	9.9		
Washington	9.9	X	
Idaho	9.0		
Maryland	7.7	X	
California	7.2	X	X
Pennsylvania	5.8		
Nevada	5.4		
Delaware	5.2		
Maine	3.3		
New York	3.0	X	
Connecticut	2.4	X	X
New Jersey	2.4	X	X*
Massachusetts	2.4	X	X
Vermont	2.4	X	X*
New Hampshire	2.4		
Utah	1.9		
Rhode Island	1.6	X	
AVERAGE	**14.8**		

*Note: These state courts required civil unions only.

Source: The Association of Religion Data Archive. Data were unavailable for Alaska and Hawaii.

(2.4 percent), Vermont (2.4 percent), Massachusetts (2.4 percent), New Jersey (2.4 percent), and Connecticut (2.4 percent). Utah (1.9 percent), which is not in the Northeast, also has only a very small evangelical population, but it has a large conservative Mormon population.

I expect that judicial policy initiation in the area of same-sex marriage policy will be less likely in religiously conservative states, both because judges might anticipate a backlash from evangelical groups and judges themselves might be sympathetic to religiously conservative values. The data in Table 5.8 are consistent with these expectations. In none of the states with a high population of evangelicals did judges rule in favor of marriage equality. However, for the most part, judges in these states were not even asked to legalize same-sex marriage. We therefore do not know how judges would have responded to the marriage question in religiously conservative states.

The final environmental condition that is likely to influence judicial policy innovation is the size of the state's gay population. A larger gay population encourages judicial policy initiation by providing a larger pool of potential test cases challenging state marriage laws. It also has the potential to transform public opinion in a state, making judges more willing to rule in favor of marriage equality. Research suggests that when people know gay people personally they are more likely to evaluate them positively,[53] although some research suggests that this "contact theory" only holds true outside of the South.[54] If public opinion is more tolerant toward gay rights in states with larger, more politically active gay populations, there might be less threat of a backlash against decisions favoring marriage equality, making judges more likely to act.

The size of a state's gay population of course varies with the size of the overall population. Table 5.9 lists the number of same-sex households per state, based on data obtained from the 2000 census, and finds not surprisingly that more-populous states tend to have a larger number of gay households than less-populous states. The most populous state, California, also has the largest number of same-sex households, at 92,138, followed by New York at 46,490 and Texas at 42,912. Wyoming, which was the state with the smallest number of coupled households in 2000, had the second smallest number of same-sex households, at 807. The state with the smallest number of same-sex households was North Dakota, at 703.

Because I am ultimately interested in the relative size, or visibility, of the state's gay population, I ranked states not by the number of same-sex households, but by the percentage of all coupled households in each state that identified as same-sex.[55] Table 5.9 reports that in 2000 the states with the most-visible populations of same-sex couples were California, at 1.4 percent of coupled households, and Vermont and Massachusetts, at 1.3 percent. States with similar levels of visibility were Florida (1.2 percent), Nevada (1.2 percent), and Washington (1.2 percent). The states with the least-visible populations of same-sex couples were Iowa (0.5 percent), New Jersey (0.5 percent), North Dakota (0.5 percent), and South Dakota (0.5 percent). Of

[53] See L. Marvin Overby & Jay Barth, *Contact, Community Context, and Public Attitudes toward Gay Men and Lesbians*, 34 POLITY 433 (2002).

[54] See Jay Barth & L. Marvin Overby, *Are Gay Men and Lesbians in the South the New "Threat"? Regional Comparisons of the Contact Theory*, 31 POL. & POL'Y 1 (2003).

[55] The measure surely underreports the actual number of gay households in the state, as many citizens may be unwilling to identify themselves as gay. I suspect, however, that these households are also likely to be less visible, so they are appropriately excluded from the visibility measure.

Table 5.9 **Percentage of Households That Are Same-Sex**

State	% Same-Sex	Same-Sex Households	All Coupled Households	Any Same-Sex Marriage Decision	Pro–Same-Sex Marriage Decision
California	1.4	92,138	6,560,600	X	X
Massachusetts	1.3	17,099	1,328,836	X	X
Vermont	1.3	1,933	144,492	X	X*
Florida	1.2	41,048	3,561,888		
Nevada	1.2	4,973	427,103		
Washington	1.2	15,900	1,321,464	X	
Arizona	1.1	12,332	1,104,499		
Colorado	1.1	10,045	949,895		
Delaware	1.1	1,868	171,434		
Georgia	1.1	19,288	1,694,543		
Maine	1.1	3,394	310,033		
Oregon	1.1	8,932	777,166		
Rhode Island	1.1	2,471	219,937	X	
Connecticut	1.0	7,386	745,340	X	X
Hawaii	1.0	2,389	239,593	X	X
Louisiana	1.0	8,808	893,061		
Maryland	1.0	11,243	1,104,884	X	
Texas	1.0	42,912	4,316,987		
Alaska	0.9	1,180	132,886		
Illinois	0.9	22,887	2,573,438		
New Hampshire	0.9	2,703	294,998		
North Carolina	0.9	16,198	1,789,026		
South Carolina	0.9	7,609	853,564		
Virginia	0.9	13,802	1,552,409		
Alabama	0.8	8,109	965,453		
Kentucky	0.8	7,114	929,210		
Minnesota	0.8	9,147	1,118,603	X	
Mississippi	0.8	4,774	567,582		

(Continued)

Table 5.9 (Continued)

State	% Same-Sex	Same-Sex Households	All Coupled Households	Any Same-Sex Marriage Decision	Pro–Same-Sex Marriage Decision
Missouri	0.8	9,428	1,251,876		
Ohio	0.8	18,937	2,514,887		
Pennsylvania	0.8	21,166	2,705,295		
Tennessee	0.8	10,189	1,267,908		
Arkansas	0.7	4,423	606,944		
Indiana	0.7	10,219	1,376,309		
Kansas	0.7	3,973	610,223		
Michigan	0.7	15,368	2,149,930		
New York	0.7	46,490	7,056,860	X	
Oklahoma	0.7	5,763	770,918		
Utah	0.7	3,370	467,035		
West Virginia	0.7	2,916	432,254		
Wisconsin	0.7	8,232	1,226,564		
Wyoming	0.7	807	116,560		
Idaho	0.6	1,873	299,075		
Montana	0.6	1,218	210,008		
Nebraska	0.6	2,332	390,533		
New Mexico	0.6	4,496	677,971		
Iowa	0.5	3,698	690,076	X	X
New Jersey	0.5	16,604	3,064,645	X	X*
North Dakota	0.5	703	148,812		
South Dakota	0.5	826	171,282		
Total	**1.0**	594,391	59,969,000		

*Note: These state courts required civil unions only.

Source: U.S. Census Bureau, *Married-Couple and Unmarried-Partner Households for the United States, Regions, States, and for Puerto Rico: 2000* (http://www.census.gov/prod/2003pubs/censr-5.pdf).

course, in no state is the gay population visible in an absolute sense, because the percentage of coupled households never exceeds about 1.4 percent. However, Table 5.9 establishes that there is variability in the level of visibility, and it is possible that this variability influences whether judges will innovate on same-sex marriage policy.

An examination of the trends, however, suggests that the relationship is not as strong as it could be. First, and perhaps most surprisingly, there does not appear to be a strong correlation between the visibility of the gay population and the initiation of same-sex marriage litigation. Litigation has been about as likely in low-visibility states as in high-visibility states. There is, however, a stronger relationship between the visibility of the gay population and the issuance of decisions favoring same-sex marriage. The three states with the most-visible gay populations (CA, MA, VT) all had courts that ruled in favor of marriage equality. Once again Iowa stands out. According to the data in Table 5.9, at the time of *Varnum*, Iowa had one of the smallest gay populations, relative to the overall population in the state, but the judges still ruled in favor of marriage equality.

A Descriptive Typology of Same-Sex Marriage Decisions

Table 5.10 summarizes the information from the previous tables, organizing states into a descriptive typology that presents characteristics of states in which high court judges ruled on the legalization of same-sex marriage. Because I am interested in judicial policy innovation, I have not included states in which judges did not consider the marriage question. Studying these other states might teach us about the conditions in which public interest groups are more likely to file lawsuits, but they teach us very little about judicial behavior. To understand judicial policy innovation, it is more useful to look at states in which judges had the opportunity to legalize same-sex marriage.

I organized states along two dimensions: the permissiveness of their institutions and the liberalism of their environments. These classifications are made based only on comparisons to other states in the typology, not to other states that are not included. Minnesota's placement in Table 5.10, for example, does not mean that Minnesota is the most conservative state in the country or that it has the most-restrictive institutions. Many other states rank lower than Minnesota on these dimensions. However, when Minnesota is compared to other states that have considered the legalization of same-sex marriage, it does rank as the most conservative and the least permissive. States that rank lower than Minnesota were not included in the typology because their high courts did not rule on the same-sex marriage issue. Most likely LGBT public interest lawyers anticipated that they would be unable to secure victories in these states.

I classified states as having permissive institutions when they had professionalized courts and their judges had life tenure or were retained through executive or legislative reappointment. I considered these institutional conditions to be the most permissive because judges were the least likely to face political reprisals for issuing unpopular decisions. I also classified states as permissive when their constitutions were older and included equal rights amendments, because these constitutions were the most likely to provide cover for judges choosing to legalize same-sex marriage.

Table 5.10 **A Descriptive Typology of Same-Sex Marriage Decisions**

| | | Institutions | | |
		Restrictive		*Permissive*
	Liberal	Washington	Vermont*	Hawaii*
			Rhode Island	Massachusetts*
			California*	Connecticut*
Environment			New York	
			New Jersey*	
			Maryland	
	Conservative	Minnesota	Iowa*	

*Note: Judges in these states voted in favor of same-sex marriage or civil unions.

Of the states in the typology, only Massachusetts meets all of these criteria, but Hawaii and Connecticut are close. The constitutions in Hawaii and Connecticut were drafted more recently than the one in Massachusetts, and the states reappoint judges after fixed terms instead of granting them life tenure. However, compared to other states, all three states present institutional conditions that are the most permissive of decisions favoring marriage equality. Less-permissive states are those that fall short on one or more of these indicators. For example, the least-permissive states, Washington and Minnesota, use nonpartisan elections to retain judges. States identified as having moderately permissive institutions tended to lack an equal rights amendment (VT, RI, NY, NJ) or use uncontested retention elections for the retention of judges (CA, MD, IA).

The liberalism of a state's political environment was also based on several measures, specifically the ideology of a state's citizens and institutions, Democratic control of state government, the religiosity of a state's citizenry, and the visibility of the state's gay population. Most states in the typology ranked highly on these indicators. In fact the most-conservative states in the typology, Minnesota and Iowa, would have been placed at the national median if all fifty states had been included. LGBT civil rights lawyers simply did not pursue litigation strategies in more-conservative states, so we do not know how judges would have behaved in these environments.

How, then, do states in which judges ruled in favor of the legalization of same-sex marriage compare to states in which judges ruled against it? Obviously, the number of states in the typology is very small, but a few interesting trends stand out. First, in all three states that were classified as having the most liberal, permissive environments, judges ruled in favor of the legalization of same-sex marriage. In fact, Massachusetts, which was the first state in which justices actually required marriage, ranks high on virtually all of the dimensions that I examined. Massachusetts has the oldest constitution, it includes an equal rights amendment, the justices have life tenure, and its Supreme Judicial Court ranks relatively highly among the states in its level of professionalism.

In contrast, judges in Washington and Minnesota, which both use nonpartisan elections for the retention of judges, ruled against marriage equality. Judges from states with moderate levels of permissiveness and liberalism have also been less likely to rule in favor of marriage equality, although their behavior has been less consistent. Judges in three states with moderately permissive institutions (RI, NY, MD) declined to rule in favor of same-sex marriage, but judges in two states (CA, IA) required full marriage equality, and judges in two other states (VT, NJ) required civil unions but not marriage.

Modeling the Timing of Same-Sex Marriage Decisions

Because so few states have voted in favor of the legalization of same-sex marriage, it is difficult to conduct rigorous hypothesis testing. However, it is possible to gain some insight into the factors that systematically influence policy initiation using event history analysis. Event history analysis focuses on the timing and sequence of events and has become the leading method of studying the diffusion of policy innovations across states.[56] With event history analysis, one can gain insight into which of the institutional and environmental conditions outlined above are the most strongly associated with state supreme court decisions favoring the legalization of same-sex marriage.

Results of the event history analysis are presented in Table 5.11. I used two dependent variables, one measuring the year in which a state court decided a case favoring the legalization of same-sex marriage, and one measuring the year in which a state court actually ruled in favor of legalization. The reason for including two dependent variables was to distinguish the activity of litigants from the behavior of judges. If certain variables influence the likelihood that a decision is handed down but not the likelihood of a pro-marriage ruling, then one might reasonably infer that these variables relate more to litigant activity than to the behavior of high court judges.

---

[56] *See* Frances Stokes Berry & William D. Berry, *State Lottery Adoptions as Policy Innovations: An Event History Analysis*, 84 AMER. POL. SCI. REV. 395 (1990); Frances Stokes Berry & William D. Berry, *Tax Innovation in the States: Capitalizing on Political Opportunity*, 36 AMER. J. POL. SCI. 715 (1992); Henry R. Glick & Scott P. Hays, *Innovation and Reinvention in State Policymaking: Theory and the Evolution of Living Will Laws*, 53 J. POL. 835 (1991); Michael J. Faber, *Defense of Marriage Acts: A Policy Diffusion Study* (Paper Presented at the Annual Meeting of the Western Political Science Association, Las Vegas, NV, March 2007); Haider-Markel, *supra* Chapter 2, note 79; Michael Mintrom, *Policy Entrepreneurs and the Diffusion of Innovation*, 41 AM. J. POL. SCI. 738 (1997); Christopher Z. Mooney, *Modeling Regional Effects on State Policy Diffusion*, 54 POL. RES. Q. 103 (2001).

Table 5.11 **Cloglog Model of Same-Sex Marriage Decisions, 1993–2009**

	Any Decision	*Pro-SSM Decision*
Reappointment/Life Tenure	—	2.429** (0.947)
High Court Reputation	0.123* (0.052)	0.237** (0.080)
High Court Ideology	0.041* (0.020)	0.049* (0.024)
Citizen Ideology	0.182* (0.078)	—
Institutional Ideology	0.098* (0.049)	—
Spline	1.562*** (0.441)	1.734** (0.574)
Constant	−15.428** (4.992)	−3.832 (2.671)
Wald Chi^2	19.350**	16.040**
N	737	763

*p < 0.05; ** p < 0.01; *** p < 0.001 (2-tailed)

Note: Table 5.11 reports only variables that attained statistical significance.

The data were organized in long form, with the first dependent variable (ANY DECISION) coded 0 for every state year in which a state supreme court did not issue a decision considering the marriage question, and 1 for the year that it did take up the question, with no further observations recorded for that state. The second dependent variable (PRO-SSM DECISION) was measured using a similar methodology, with 1 recording the year, if any, that a state supreme court issued a decision favoring the legalization of same-sex marriage. I set the date of entry into the risk set at 1994, the year after the Hawaii Supreme Court's decision in *Baehr v. Lewin*.[57] Even though the Minnesota Supreme Court issued a decision on the marriage question as early as 1971, it was the Hawaii Supreme Court that was the first to actually innovate in this area by ruling that the state constitution required marriage equality. Because the Minnesota decision predates the period, I excluded the state from the analysis.

As the number of state courts to legalize same-sex marriage is so small, the model would not converge with the addition of too many variables. It was therefore necessary to test small clusters of independent variables and construct the final models containing only those variables that remained consistently robust after controlling

[57] Baehr v. Lewin, 852 P.2d 44 (Haw. 1993).

for other variables. These variables are reported in Table 5.11. Before generating the final list, I tested all of the variables detailed in the preceding tables. I also tested measures of HIGH COURT REPUTATION and HIGH COURT INDEPENDENCE developed by Choi et. al.[58] The measure of HIGH COURT REPUTATION, based on data from 1998 through 2006, estimates high court prestige by looking at the number of citations to a state high court's opinions by out-of-state judges, including judges on other state courts, the U.S. Supreme Court, and other federal courts outside the home circuit. The HIGH COURT INDEPENDENCE measure records the percentage of the time that high court judges vote with judges from the opposite party. In addition to these variables, I also introduced variables controlling for the region of the country in which an opinion occurred as well as the number of state high courts in the same census division to have considered the marriage question. Finally, I controlled for whether the state had previously approved a constitutional amendment prohibiting same-sex marriage, which would have served to preempt state court activity.

The results reported in Table 5.11 show that, despite the small number of cases to consider the marriage question, several variables attain statistical significance.[59] Turning first to the factors that influence the likelihood of a state court issuing any decision concerning the legalization of same-sex marriage, Table 5.11 reports that litigation is more likely to be filed when courts have prestigious reputations (HIGH COURT REPUTATION) as well as ideologically liberal judges (HIGH COURT IDEOLOGY). Decisions are also more likely from judges in states where citizen support for same-sex marriage is high (CITIZEN IDEOLOGY) and in which government institutions are liberal (INSTITUTIONAL IDEOLOGY). Decisions actually favoring the legalization of same-sex marriage are more likely in states that retain justices for life or that use reappointment for the retention of judges (REAPPOINTMENT/ LIFE TENURE), in which high court judges have prestigious reputations (HIGH COURT REPUTATION), and in which high court judges are liberal (HIGH COURT IDEOLOGY).[60]

Overall, then, it would appear that a combination of institutional and environmental considerations influence when state judges have been more likely to take up the marriage question. Same-sex marriage supporters have tended to file suit in states where judges are ideologically liberal and have prestigious reputations. They

---

[58] Choi et al., *supra* note 22.

[59] I used a complementary log-log model ("cloglog"), which is appropriate for rare events. *See* Jack Buckley & Chad Westerland, *Duration Dependence, Functional Form, and Corrected Standard Errors: Improving EHA Models of State Policy Diffusion*, 4 ST. POL. & POL'Y Q. 94 (2004). I controlled for duration dependence by including cubic spline terms for each model using a "spline" macro for Stata. *See* Peter Sasieni, *Natural Cubic Splines*, STATA TECHN. BULL. 19, Nov. 1994.

[60] The fact that the remaining variables do not attain statistical significance does not mean that the conditions they measure have no effect on policy initiation. The relatively small number of state courts legalizing same-sex marriage makes it difficult for the effects of any of the variables to register significantly. Instead of discounting the possibility that other types of institutional and environmental considerations matter, it would be fairer to say that the variables reported in Table 5.11 are those that have been shown to systematically influence policy initiation.

have also tended to litigate in states with liberal institutions and high levels of public support for same-sex marriage. No doubt supporters of same-sex marriage anticipated that judges in these states would be more likely to rule in favor of the legalization of same-sex marriage and that the public would be more likely to support rulings favoring marriage equality.

Environmental considerations have been less influential, however, in determining which state supreme courts have been more likely to rule in favor of same-sex marriage. The relative liberalism of a state's citizens and institutions has been less important than characteristics of the state high courts. Policy initiation has been more likely to occur when state supreme court justices sit on liberal, prestigious courts. Policy initiation has also been more likely to come from independent tribunals, where the justices are retained for life or are reappointed by governors or state legislators. It should be noted once again, however, that since the Hawaii Supreme Court voted in favor of marriage equality in 1993, the number of elected judges to have been asked to rule on the marriage question is small, composed of judges from Washington state, which uses nonpartisan elections, and California, Maryland, and Iowa, which use uncontested retention elections.

Event history analysis does not simply measure whether courts have ruled in favor of same-sex marriage, but the timing and sequence of these decisions as well. The relative position of cases in the time line makes a difference, and in this respect there has been a fairly consistent trend, with elected judges acting on the marriage question only after more independent tribunals innovated first. Minnesota, Washington, and Maryland were the first elected courts to address the issue, and they all voted no. California and Iowa voted yes, but only at the end of the study period. These findings are important, suggesting that policy innovations originate in relatively independent tribunals and then spread to elected tribunals later, when the policies have become better established.

Conclusion

Overall, the portrait of morality policy diffusion that emerges is of a wave of innovation broken by a succession of environmental and institutional barriers. Morality policy innovation is frustrated first by the need for litigation, which requires environments that are capable of producing appropriate test cases. For morality policies such as the legalization of same-sex marriage, public attitudes may be central to determining how supportive particular environments are likely to be. Also relevant are the interests of certain key constituencies, such as evangelicals, and the ideological composition of state institutions.

The second barrier to policy innovation is the need for judges who are willing to innovate. Not only must judges sincerely support policy change; they must also sit on tribunals that are structured in ways that permit innovation to occur. The guarantee of independence is particularly important, but there is also evidence to suggest that professionalized courts, and courts with more prestigious reputations, have also had a greater tendency to innovate. Additionally, pro-marriage rulings have been more common in states with equal rights amendments. The implication of these findings is that when state institutions or constitutional texts do not provide adequate cover for state supreme court justices, policy innovation is less likely to occur.

Why, then, did the Iowa Supreme Court in 2009 take the risk of ruling in favor of same-sex marriage? Unfortunately, the data do not provide a clear answer. In many respects, the *Varnum* decision stands apart. The judges in Iowa were, for the most part, more conservative than their counterparts in other states. The judges were also in a conservative political environment in which the gay population had relatively low visibility. Based on the patterns observed in other states, one would not have expected the justices to have produced a decision favoring the legalization of same-sex marriage.

It is possible that *Varnum* was simply an anomaly. However, there are at least three potential explanations that might account for the justices' actions. The first possibility is that the justices thought that the political climate in Iowa was changing. Although majorities of citizens in Iowa did not favor same-sex marriage in 2009, a majority did support civil unions.[61] The state also supported Barack Obama over John McCain in the 2008 presidential election, by a vote of 53.9 percent to 44.4 percent.[62] A decision in favor of same-sex marriage might not have been an obvious fit for Iowa at that time, but it was not clearly a mismatch either. Perhaps the justices thought that their decision would be accepted because the political environment was becoming more moderate.

A second possibility is that the justices felt that the Iowa constitution provided adequate cover for their decision. Iowa's constitution ranks among the ten oldest in the country, and it has long been used to protect disadvantaged groups. Justice Cady emphasized this point in his majority opinion. He observed that the Iowa Supreme Court stood against slavery seventeen years before *Dred Scott v. Sandford*, the notorious U.S. Supreme Court decision that rejected the citizenship claims of African Americans.[63] Justice Cady described the case *In re Ralph*,[64] in which the justices "refused to treat a human being as property to enforce a contract for slavery and held our laws must extend equal protection to persons of all races and conditions."[65] Justice Cady went on to observe that the Iowa Supreme Court had "struck blows to the concept of segregation" nearly a century before *Brown v. Board of Education*

[61] *See University of Iowa Hawkeye Poll, supra* note 5.

[62] Federal Election Commission, Federal Elections 2008: Election Results for the U.S. President, the U.S. Senate and the U.S. House of Representatives 31 (July 2009), *available at* http://www.fec.gov/pubrec/fe2008/federalelections2008.pdf.

[63] Dred Scott v. Sandford, 60 U.S. 393 (1856).

[64] *In re* Ralph, 1 Morris 1 (Iowa 1839).

[65] Varnum v. Brien, 763 N.W.2d 862, 877 (Iowa 2009).

desegregated public education,[66] and that Iowa was the first state to admit women to the bar, three years before another infamous U.S. Supreme Court decision permitted states to exclude them.[67] The adoption by Iowa of an equal rights amendment in 1998 was also consistent with this trend. "In each of those instances," Justice Cady wrote, "our state approached a fork in the road toward fulfillment of our constitution's ideals and reaffirmed the absolute equality of all persons before the law as the very foundation principle of our government."[68]

Justice Cady then proceeded to the central question: "How can a state premised on the constitutional principle of equal protection justify exclusion of a class of Iowans from civil marriage?"[69] By this point, it was obvious how Justice Cady would answer this question. Justice Cady was able to take advantage of Iowa's rich constitutional history, and in particular his state's history of progressivism on equality issues, to justify an outcome in *Varnum* favoring marriage equality. Indeed, Justice Cady was quite explicit on this point. "The path we have taken as a state has not been by accident," he explained, "but has been navigated with the compass of equality firmly in hand, constructed with a point balanced carefully on the pivot of equal protection."[70]

It seems clear, then, that the state constitution provided some cover for the Iowa justices and perhaps made them more willing to reach a pro-marriage ruling. Although the text of Iowa's constitution does not clearly define equality, the state's precedents do permit the expansive interpretation the justices gave it. By relying on the state's permissive constitutional traditions, the justices might have thought— albeit incorrectly, given the political reprisals against the justices the next year— that they could avoid charges of judicial activism and produce a ruling that Iowans would accept.

A third possibility is that the judges in Iowa were willing to act because several other state supreme courts had already ruled in favor of marriage equality by that point. Each successive marriage decision has used as part of its justification the same-sex marriage decisions from other states that were decided previously. The Supreme Judicial Court of Massachusetts in *Goodridge v. Department of Public Health* cited Hawaii's decision in its own judgment in favor of marriage equality.[71] The California Supreme Court then cited Hawaii and Massachusetts in *In re Marriage Cases,*[72] and so forth. The Iowa Supreme Court cited all of these decisions. Each of the same-sex marriage decisions became a precedent that, while not binding in

---

[66] Brown v. Bd. of Educ., 347 U.S. 483 (1954). For the Iowa precedents, see Clark v. Bd. of Dirs., 24 Iowa 266 (1868); and Coger v. North West. Union Packet Co., 37 Iowa 145 (1873).

[67] Bradwell v. Illinois, 83 U.S. 130 (1873).

[68] *Varnum,* 763 N.W.2d at 877 (internal quotation marks removed).

[69] *Id.* at 878.

[70] *Id.*

[71] Goodridge v. Dep't of Public Health, 798 N.E.2d 941, 949, n.3 (Mass. 2003).

[72] *In re* Marriage Cases, 43 Cal. 4th 757, 778–79, 799, n.20, & 836, n.54 (2008).

other states, further established the plausibility of same-sex marriage on the national stage, making it easier for the judges in subsequent states to rule in favor of same-sex couples. What might have seemed radical in 1993 or even 2003 would have seemed less so in 2009, especially as two state high courts had just ruled in favor of same-sex marriage the year before.

Justice Cady relied heavily on the language of the other same-sex marriage rulings in his opinion. At one key point in his opinion, for example, when explaining why classifications based on sexual orientation require closer scrutiny, Justice Cady stated that "it would be difficult to improve upon the words of the Supreme Court of Connecticut."[73] He then quoted extensively from the Connecticut Supreme Court's decision in *Kerrigan* from the year before. The message Justice Cady was sending was clear: that the justices were not going out on a limb by ruling in favor of same-sex marriage. Other peer tribunals had reached the same results using similar reasoning.

Perhaps, then, an explanation for why the judges in Iowa were willing to act, despite the conservatism of their environment, was that the judges were not required to be policy innovators, but rather imitators of other judges who had come before them. The true innovators, in Hawaii and Massachusetts, acted only because their environments were the most permissive and supportive of decisions favoring marriage equality—and even in these states, the same-sex marriage decisions were challenged. Hawaii's decision was overturned by a state constitutional amendment, and the Massachusetts decision very nearly was. Once judges in these more permissive environments acted, however, and the issue of same-sex marriage became more familiar to a national audience, it was possible for judges in more-conservative, less-permissive environments to step in.

Even so, it was probably no accident that the decision in *Varnum* was unanimous. Too many other states in the region and across the country had enacted constitutional amendments prohibiting same-sex marriage, and there was the real possibility that Iowa would join them. A majority of the justices would also have to face retention elections within the next few years, and the justices understood that an unpopular same-sex marriage decision would put their jobs at risk. Morality policies such as same-sex marriage are so high profile and elicit such strong public attitudes that, without total insulation from the public, judges are unlikely to issue decisions on controversial public policies free of concern about the political consequences. This could be a reason the number of state supreme courts to have ruled in favor of same-sex marriage has been so small.

---

[73] *Varnum*, 763 N.W.2d at 895.

CHAPTER 6

Policy Legitimation: Evaluating the Capacity of State Courts to Change Public Opinion

Once a state court has decided to initiate policy by issuing a decision, the next step that is required for judges to have an impact on government policy is for the decision to be implemented by the individuals or groups who are responsible for putting the holding into effect. Depending on the issue, different government officials might be involved in policy implementation and the officials might have varying degrees of flexibility about how to respond. If a court's mandate is open-ended, or if government officials have discretion about how to proceed, judges might find that implementing groups are less willing to act consistently with the letter or spirit of the court's judgment.

To some extent, the implementation of state court decisions requiring marriage equality has been relatively straightforward because the holdings have left little room for government officials to defy or evade them. If a state court requires the legalization of same-sex marriage, there is nothing left to interpret: county clerks must issue marriage licenses.[1] However, implementation is complicated by the strong interest of the public. Unlike many of the cases that state courts decide, cases involving morality policies such as same-sex marriage are closely followed by the public.[2] If the public disapproves of a state court decision on such a highly salient issue, citizens might take action to limit the effects of the decision, or encourage government officials to do so. Citizens might, for example, push for a constitutional amendment or the removal of the judges from office.

Judges are more likely to influence morality policies if they can persuade the public to support their decisions, or at least to accept them—and in fact many courts are well equipped to do just that. What sets judging apart from the behavior of other government actors such as legislators is that, in the public's mind, judges are not

[1] *But see* Thomas Kaplan, *Rights Collide as Town Clerk Sidesteps Role in Gay Marriages*, N.Y. Times, Sept. 27, 2011, at A1 (describing the efforts of some town clerks to evade their obligation to administer marriage licenses to same-sex couples).

[2] *See* Haider-Markel & Meier, *supra* Chapter 1, note 63; and Mooney & Lee, *supra* Chapter 1, note 63.

guided by bare politics but legal principles.[3] Even though social science research suggests that ideology influences judicial behavior in gay rights cases[4] and other controversies,[5] these myths about judges persist.[6] The public's sense that judges are engaged in principled decision making gives judges a moral authority that enables them to confer legitimacy on the policy alternatives they endorse.

Or at least that is the conventional wisdom. The truth is that not all judges may possess this legitimacy-conferring capacity. When courts are structured in ways that undermine perceptions that the judges are engaged in principled decision making judges might find that they are less capable of building the public's support. Judicial elections might be particularly consequential in this respect. In this chapter, I examine the conditions under which state judges are more likely to build public support for government policies, a process that I refer to as *policy legitimation*. When discussing policy legitimation, I do not mean to suggest that state judges deliberately cultivate public opinion, although it is possible that some judges do think about the public's responses to their decisions. Instead, I suggest that there are particular characteristics of state courts and their environments that affect how the public receives their decisions.

A problem for any court intervening in same-sex marriage policy is that public opinion about the issue has tended to be strong and, for the most part, negative. Table 6.1 presents the results of a national survey of approximately one thousand adults that I conducted in October 2008, around the time that California and Connecticut both ruled in favor of marriage equality.[7] The survey asked respondents whether they favored the legalization of same-sex marriages in their own states and the recognition of same-sex marriages performed in other states.[8] The data show that in 2008, the majority of the American public still believed that the term *marriage* should be reserved for opposite-sex partnerships. Overall, 43.6 percent of respondents said they supported same-sex marriage, while 45.5 percent said they would recognize marriages from other states.

---

[3] *See* Casey, *supra* Chapter 2, note 37; and Michael J. Petrick, *The Supreme Court and Authority Acceptance*, 21 W. POL. Q. 5 (1968).

[4] *See* PINELLO, GAY RIGHTS AND AMERICAN LAW, *supra* Chapter 2, note 2.

[5] *See* Brace et al., *supra* Chapter 5, note 14.

[6] *See* John M. Scheb II & William Lyons, *Judicial Behavior and Public Opinion: Popular Expectations regarding the Factors That Influence Supreme Court Decisions*, 23 POL. BEHAV. 181 (2001); and John M. Scheb II & William Lyons, *The Myth of Legality and Public Evaluation of the Supreme Court*, 81 SOC. SCI. Q. 928 (2000).

[7] Data are from the 2008 Cooperative Congressional Election Study (CCES), an Internet survey that was administered in October 2008 by YouGov/Polimetrix of Palo Alto, CA.

[8] The precise question wording depended on the treatment condition to which survey respondents were assigned, consistent with procedures for the survey experiment that I describe below. For example, for the first question, I asked, "If the [governor/state legislature/judges in your state] legalized same-sex marriage, would you support the decision?" The 1000 respondents were randomly assigned to one of three treatment conditions, with one-third given questions that assigned the policy to the governor, one-third assigned to questions featuring the state legislature, and one-third assigned to questions featuring state judges.

Table 6.1 **Public Attitudes about Same-Sex Marriages and the Recognition of Same-Sex Marriages from Other States, October 2008**

	Legalization of Same-Sex Marriages in Home State		Recognition of Marriages from Other States	
	For	*Against*	*For*	*Against*
General	43.6%	56.4%	45.5%	54.5%
Sex				
Male	40.4%	59.6%	42.2%	57.8%
Female	46.9%	53.1%	49.0%	51.0%
Race				
White	42.3%	57.7%	44.3%	55.7%
Black	45.1%	54.9%	47.4%	52.6%
Hispanic	50.0%	50.0%	52.0%	48.0%
Other	48.0%	52.0%	49.0%	51.0%
Age				
18–34	61.9%	38.1%	63.0%	37.0%
35–54	45.2%	54.8%	47.3%	52.7%
55+	31.5%	68.5%	33.7%	66.3%
Education				
No High School	43.6%	56.4%	43.6%	56.4%
High School Graduate	34.8%	65.2%	35.9%	64.1%
Some College	37.5%	62.5%	40.3%	59.7%
2-Year	43.8%	56.2%	50.0%	50.0%
4-Year	58.3%	41.7%	59.7%	40.3%
Post-Grad	58.1%	41.9%	61.2%	38.8%
Household Income				
Under $29,999	39.8%	60.2%	42.1%	57.9%
$29,999–79,999	40.7%	59.3%	42.3%	57.7%
$80,000 or more	52.7%	47.3%	55.3%	44.7%
Party Identification				
Strong Democrat	70.9%	29.1%	72.9%	27.1%

	Legalization of Same-Sex Marriages in Home State		Recognition of Marriages from Other States	
	For	Against	For	Against
Not Very Strong Democrat	59.4%	40.6%	60.6%	39.4%
Lean Democrat	76.3%	23.7%	76.0%	24.0%
Independent	45.0%	55.0%	49.0%	51.0%
Lean Republican	19.5%	80.5%	24.7%	75.3%
Not Very Strong Republican	24.7%	75.3%	24.4%	75.6%
Strong Republican	6.9%	93.1%	8.6%	91.4%
Religion				
Very Important	23.1%	76.9%	24.0%	76.0%
Somewhat Important	45.9%	54.1%	49.4%	50.6%
Not Too Important	70.1%	29.9%	74.4%	25.6%
Not at All Important	81.5%	18.5%	81.7%	18.3%
Region				
Northeast	56.5%	43.5%	56.8%	43.2%
Midwest	38.5%	61.5%	39.9%	60.1%
South	38.7%	61.3%	41.0%	59.0%
West	45.4%	54.6%	48.9%	51.1%

Note: The margin of error is ± 3.2%.

Source: 2008 Cooperative Congressional Election Study   N = 920

To be sure, public attitudes have softened somewhat since the Hawaii Supreme Court first ruled in favor of marriage equality in 1993. Keck traced public opinion about same-sex marriage since *Baehr v. Lewin* and found a steady increase in public support in the years following the decision.[9] For example, Keck reports that before *Baehr*, a Gallup poll found public support for same-sex marriage to be at 23.0 percent, but by the time of California's decision in 2008, Gallup was reporting support

[9] See Keck, *supra* Chapter 1, note 31.

as high as 46.0 percent, consistent with the level of support in Table 6.1.[10] These figures rose above 50.0 percent in 2011.[11]

Of course, the public attitudes that matter the most to state court judges are the attitudes of citizens in their own states. After all, it is the state citizenry, not the national citizenry, which has the power to vote elected justices out of office for unpopular decisions or to press for state constitutional amendments. Table 6.1 does not break down support for same-sex marriage by state, but from other research we know that the public has tended to disapprove of decisions favoring same-sex marriage, even in liberal states that might be expected to sympathize with such a ruling. Pinello reports that in February 2004, around the time of the second *Goodridge* decision, 53.0 percent of Massachusetts residents opposed same-sex marriage, up from 44.0 percent of residents who said in a poll conducted seven months before *Goodridge* that they opposed it.[12] In both Hawaii and California, court decisions were overturned by popularly supported constitutional amendments. The only state in which a pro-marriage decision met an immediately positive public response was Connecticut, where 53.0 percent of residents expressed support for *Kerrigan*.[13] It would seem, then, that the national attitudes that are reported in Table 6.1 are mostly consistent with public attitudes in particular states.

What is less clear is whether these negative public attitudes can be mediated by institutional or environmental conditions. Perhaps certain institutional conditions encourage the public to trust judges with the marriage question and to support court decisions when judges do get involved. I investigate these possibilities using survey research that I conducted shortly before the 2008 presidential election as part of the Cooperative Congressional Election Study. I also analyze a 2005 *Washington Post/ABC News* poll that asked a substantially similar question to the one I employed in my own survey. These surveys were administered concurrently with the same-sex marriage decisions and are therefore reflective of public attitudes at the time of the marriage cases.

The data will show that, in general, state supreme courts are no more likely than other institutions to build public support for morality policies such as same-sex marriage. However, these aggregate trends mask important differences in how the

---

[10] *Id.* at 165.

[11] *See* Frank Newport, *For First Time, Majority of Americans Favor Legal Gay Marriage*, GALLOP. COM (May 20, 2011), http://www.gallup.com/poll/147662/first-time-majority-americans-favor-legal-gay-marriage.aspx; and Lydia Saad, *U.S. Acceptance of Gay/Lesbian Relations Is the New Normal*, GALLOP.COM (May 14, 2012), http://www.gallup.com/poll/154634/acceptance-gay-lesbian-relations-new-normal.aspx.

[12] *See* PINELLO, AMERICA'S STRUGGLE FOR SAME-SEX MARRIAGE, *supra* Chapter 1, note 57, at 183.

[13] *See* Christopher Keating, *A Majority Backs Gay Marriage Ruling; Overall, 53 Percent Endorse Decision, but Poll Finds Sharp Differences among Democrats, Republicans*, HARTFORD COURANT, Oct. 14, 2008, at A9.

decisions of different state courts are received. Specifically, I find that judges who are reappointed, retained for life, or retained with uncontested retention elections are more likely to win public support for the legalization of same-sex marriage than judges who are retained with contested elections. Levels of public trust in state courts to deal with the marriage question are also lower in contested election states.[14]

State Courts and Policy Legitimation

The conventional wisdom is that courts in general are better equipped than other institutions to build public support for government policies such as same-sex marriage. Legitimacy theory suggests that judges build support for public policy alternatives by persuading the public to trust in the integrity of their decision-making processes.[15] The use of reasoned decision making permits judges to influence public opinion in even the most controversial areas of policy. As Petrick wrote about the U.S. Supreme Court, "the Supreme Court, amidst a setting of dignity and somberness which other branches of American government so often seem to lack, can pursue activities and promote policies which other agencies practicably cannot, such as upholding the rights of Communists, outlawing school desegregation, forbidding recitation of nondenominational prayers in public schools, and requiring access to counsel during police interrogations."[16]

An implication of legitimacy theory is that, by maintaining a perception that they are principled decision makers who are above politics, judges can be more effective than other officials at increasing public support for government policies. A series of experiments affirmed that citizens are more likely to support policies attributed to the U.S. Supreme Court than to other institutions.[17] Hoekstra found that laboratory

---

[14] I focus primarily on the effects of judicial selection and retention methods because they are the institutional features that are the most likely to be familiar to the public, whose attitudes matter the most when it comes to understanding the politics of morality policies like same-sex marriage. I am less persuaded that public attitudes about state court decisions will be influenced by other institutional and constitutional differences, such as the presence of an equal rights amendment or a state constitution's age, although they might be important in other contexts.

[15] *See* Dahl, *supra* Chapter 2, note 6; Petrick, *supra* note 3; Murphy & Tanenhaus, *supra* Chapter 2, note 35; MURPHY ET AL., *supra* Chapter 2, note 37; Casey, *supra* Chapter 2, note 37; Caldeira & Gibson, *supra* Chapter 2, note 35; Gibson et al., *On the Legitimacy of National High Courts, supra* Chapter 2, note 37.

[16] Petrick, *supra* note 3, at 16.

[17] *See* Jeffery J. Mondak, *Institutional Legitimacy, Policy Legitimacy, and the Supreme Court,* 20 AM. POL. Q. 457 (1992); Jeffery J. Mondak, *Perceived Legitimacy of Supreme Court Decisions: Three Functions of Source Credibility,* 12 POL. BEHAV. 363 (1990); Valerie J. Hoekstra, *The Supreme Court and Opinion Change: An Experimental Study of the Court's Ability to Change Opinion,* 23 AM. POL. Q. 109 (1995); Rosalee A. Clawson, Elizabeth R. Kegler & Eric N. Waltenberg, *The Legitimacy-Conferring Authority of the U.S. Supreme Court: An Experimental Design,* 29 AM. POL. RES. 566 (2001); and James L. Gibson,

subjects were more likely to support policies when they were associated with the Supreme Court than with Congress or a nonpartisan think tank.[18] Clawson et al. corroborated these findings in another laboratory experiment, but found that the legitimacy-conferring capacity of courts was moderated by group-centric attitudes and citizen interest in politics.[19] Using a survey experiment, Gibson et al. found the Court to be only slightly ahead of Congress in its capacity to make the public willing to accept objectionable policy alternatives, but affirmed that the Court does enjoy some advantage.[20]

The problem is that there are good reasons for thinking that many state supreme courts do not possess this sort of legitimacy-conferring capacity. One of the limitations of legitimacy theory is that it has been developed primarily based on observations of the U.S. Supreme Court, so we know very little about whether judges in other institutional contexts have the same capacity to build support for government policies. It could be that when courts are structured differently, judges will fare no better than other government officials at building public support for policies such as same-sex marriage.

Specifically, one might expect that the independence of U.S. Supreme Court justices, guaranteed by life tenure, reinforces the public's perception that the justices are principled decision makers. Casey found that among the myths the public holds about the U.S. Supreme Court is that the justices "uphold the laws of the land" and that "their main job is to see that equal rights is performed."[21] It is possible that when courts are structured in ways that emphasize accountability over independence, these myths break down, and judges lose their special capacity to win support for government policies. As I discussed at length in Chapter 2, judges in many states are directly accountable to the voting public through a variety of electoral mechanisms. It is unclear what, if any, effect that these judicial elections have had on the legitimacy-conferring capacity of courts. On the one hand, elections ensure that courts reflect public values, which might improve public support for their decisions.[22] On the other hand, the lack of independence might make elected judges seem less principled, making it more difficult for judges to speak with special authority on issues such as same-sex marriage. Because legitimacy theory maintains that

Gregory A. Caldeira & Lester Kenyatta Spense, *Why Do People Accept Public Policies They Oppose? Testing Legitimacy Theory with a Survey-Based Experiment*, 58 POL. RES. Q. 187 (2005) [hereinafter Gibson et al., *Why Do People Accept Public Policies They Oppose?*].

[18] Hoekstra, *supra* note 17; *but see* Larry R. Baas & Dan Thomas, *The Supreme Court and Policy Legitimation: Experimental Tests*, 12 AM. POL. Q. 335 (1984) (finding no evidence that the U.S. Supreme Court possesses a legitimacy-conferring capacity).

[19] Clawson et al., *supra* note 17.

[20] Gibson et al., *Why Do People Accept Public Policies They Oppose?*, *supra* note 17.

[21] Casey, *supra* Chapter 2, note 37, at 393.

[22] *See* Wenzel et al., *supra* Chapter 1, note 8, at 196 ("we expect that more citizens are populists than elitists and that they prefer having an influence over political outcomes").

independence is the mechanism that permits judges to speak with special authority, it follows that when judges are retained through contested elections, they will be less capable of building public support for government policies.

Indeed, research by Gibson and Caldeira bolsters this theoretical expectation.[23] Gibson and Caldeira investigated whether public acceptance of the tenets of legal realism has undermined the institutional legitimacy of the U.S. Supreme Court. They found that, in general, support for the Court was not damaged when respondents accepted that political views are relevant to judicial decision making. However, they found that support declines when judges appear to resemble ordinary politicians.[24] "Support for the Court is not damaged by acceptance of the basic tenets of legal realism," they concluded, "but support depends upon seeing judges as different from ordinary politicians, in part because, unlike politicians, they are principled in their decisionmaking."[25] If judicial elections contribute to a perception that judges are simply "politicians in robes," not principled decision makers, then elections might reduce the capacity for judges to build support for government policies.

Notably, I do not predict that the capacity of judges to build support for government policies is diminished in states that use uncontested retention elections. I distinguish between contested and uncontested elections because of empirical research that has found that the electoral connection is weaker in merit selection states. Although it is true that Hall has found that judges in merit states "are not impervious to partisan pressures,"[26] Cann and Wilhelm found that high court judges are the most responsive to public opinion in states with contested elections.[27] They explained "that state supreme court justices in these electoral systems have an inherently engendered sense of political vulnerability, whether they are in a current reelection campaign or whether elections within their state tend to be 'noisy' and competitive."[28]

Cann and Wilhelm found that uncontested retention elections, in contrast, have low levels of turnout and rarely result in losses for incumbents, reducing the incumbents' feelings of vulnerability. Voters are also less informed about candidates when elections are uncontested because there are no rival candidates to challenge incumbents' voting records. Such considerations led Cann and Wilhelm to conclude that "due to the low

[23] James L. Gibson & Gregory A. Caldeira, *Has Legal Realism Damaged the Legitimacy of the U.S. Supreme Court?*, 45 Law & Soc'y Rev. 196 (2011).

[24] Specifically, Gibson and Caldeira found that the public was less supportive of the Supreme Court when the respondent agreed with the statement, "Supreme Court judges are little more than politicians in robes." *Id.* at 209.

[25] *Id.* at 209.

[26] Hall, *State Supreme Courts in American Democracy, supra* Chapter 2, note 47, at 324.

[27] Cann & Wilhelm, *supra* Chapter 5, note 27.

[28] *Id.* at 568.

levels of voter turnout, low levels of voter information, and low defeat rates in these elections...there will be little responsiveness to public opinion in these states."[29]

Because the strength of the electoral connection between state supreme court justices and their constituents is likely to be weaker in states with uncontested retention elections, it is reasonable to expect that judges in merit systems will more closely resemble appointed judges in their ability to build public support for government policies. Merit judges are more likely to appear "above" politics because they are less responsive to public opinion. The low levels of voter turnout and information in retention elections also help to maintain distance between judges and the public, reinforcing myths that they are principled decision makers who operate outside of ordinary politics.

Comparing Levels of Public Trust across State Institutions

One way of evaluating the potential for state courts to influence public opinion on issues such as same-sex marriage is to examine the extent to which the public trusts courts, compared to other state institutions, to decide morality policy issues. If my suspicions about legitimacy theory are correct, then levels of public trust in courts should vary depending on the methods of judicial retention used in respondents' home states. In June 2005, ABC News/Washington Post conducted a poll asking a national random sample of approximately one thousand adults who they trusted to set policy in three issue areas: same-sex marriage, the death penalty, and abortion.[30] The timing of the survey was ideal because it occurred after the Massachusetts supreme court had ruled in favor of same-sex marriage, but before judges had acted in California, Connecticut, and Iowa. State court activity on the issue was therefore active and still developing.

A breakdown of the responses is provided in Table 6.2. If we look generally across the issue areas, it appears that, at the time the survey was taken in 2005, the public was less willing to trust state courts with the issue of same-sex marriage than their state legislatures. Table 6.2 reports that 39.7 percent of respondents trusted their state courts to deal with the issue of gay marriage, compared to 44.4 percent who trusted their state legislatures. Public trust in courts was considerably stronger on the issue of the death penalty, with 53.3 percent trusting state courts to deal with the issue, compared to 39.8 percent of respondents trusting state legislatures. On abortion, the public was more evenly divided, with 43.9 percent supporting state courts and 43.0 percent supporting their legislatures to deal with the issue.

[29] Id.

[30] ABC/WASHINGTON POST POLL #2005–983: CONGRESS/SOCIAL SECURITY/WAR IN IRAQ/ STEM CELL RESEARCH (June 2–5, 2005), distributed by the Roper Center for Public Opinion Research. The survey asked, "Who do you trust more to deal with the issue of...[gay marriage/abortion/the death penalty], your state legislature, or your state court?"

Table 6.2 **"Who do you trust more to deal with the issue of . . . [gay marriage/ abortion/the death penalty], your state legislature, or your state court?" General Results**

	Gay Marriage	*Death Penalty*	*Abortion*
State Court	396 (39.7%)	531 (53.3%)	438 (43.9%)
State Legislature	443 (44.4%)	397 (39.8%)	429 (43.0%)
Both/neither/ don't know	159 (15.9%)	69 (6.9%)	130 (13.0%)
TOTAL	998 (100.0%)	997 (100.0%)	997 (100.0%)

Note: Data are from a 2005 *Washington Post*/ABC News poll (#2005–983: Congress/Social Security/War in Iraq/Stem Cell Research), based on a random national sample of 1000 respondents.

It is not immediately clear why the public would be less trusting of courts on the issue of same-sex marriage than on abortion and the death penalty. However, for present purposes the important point is that, contrary to the expectations of legitimacy theory, the public does not automatically think of state courts as being more trustworthy to deal with morality policies such as same-sex marriage. In fact, the results for same-sex marriage suggest that the opposite is true. Overall the public has a slight preference for state legislatures to deal with the issue of same-sex marriage, not state courts.

I suspect, however, that these aggregate numbers mask differences in public trust between elected and appointed courts. To explore this possibility, I obtained the original data used in the survey and organized responses based on the method of judicial retention used in the respondents' home states. These results are reported in Table 6.3, with separate categories for respondents from states that retain judges through reappointment/life tenure, retention elections, partisan elections, and nonpartisan elections.[31] If we look first at reappointment/life tenure states, Table 6.3 reports that the public trusts state courts (41.4 percent) about as much as state legislatures (42.1 percent) to deal with the marriage issue. Courts enjoy a marginal advantage (42.3 percent) over legislatures (40.3 percent) in retention election states. However, the differences become more pronounced, to the detriment of courts, in states that use contested elections to retain their judges. In states with nonpartisan elections, just 35.2 percent of respondents report trusting their state courts to deal

[31] The classification of retention methods for state supreme court justices is mostly consistent with Table 2.1 except that states that use partisan elections for the initial selection or nomination of state supreme court justices were classified as partisan election states.

Table 6.3 **"Who do you trust more to deal with the issue of . . . [gay marriage/ abortion/the death penalty], your state legislature, or your state court?" Breakdown by Judicial Retention Method**

A. Reappointment/Life Tenure States

	Gay Marriage	*Death Penalty*	*Abortion*
State Court	68 (41.4%)	95 (57.9%)	81 (49.1%)
State Legislature	69 (42.1%)	56 (34.2%)	61 (37.0%)
Both/neither/don't know	27 (16.5%)	13 (7.9%)	23 (13.9%)
TOTAL	164 (100.0%)	164 (100.0%)	165 (100.0%)

B. Retention Election States

	Gay Marriage	*Death Penalty*	*Abortion*
State Court	146 (42.3%)	188 (54.5%)	153 (44.6%)
State Legislature	139 (40.3%)	130 (37.7%)	144 (42.0%)
Both/neither/don't know	60 (17.4%)	27 (7.8%)	46 (13.4%)
TOTAL	345 (100.0%)	345 (100.0%)	343 (100.0%)

C. Nonpartisan Election States

	Gay Marriage	*Death Penalty*	*Abortion*
State Court	95 (35.2%)	134 (49.8%)	100 (37.0%)
State Legislature	130 (48.2%)	116 (43.1%)	128 (47.4%)
Both/neither/don't know	45 (16.7%)	19 (7.1%)	42 (15.6%)
TOTAL	270 (100.0%)	269 (100.0%)	270 (100.0%)

D. Partisan Election States

	Gay Marriage	*Death Penalty*	*Abortion*
State Court	59 (38.1%)	77 (49.7%)	68 (43.9%)
State Legislature	77 (49.7%)	70 (45.2%)	71 (45.8%)

	Gay Marriage	*Death Penalty*	*Abortion*
Both/neither/don't know	19 (12.3%)	8 (5.2%)	16 (10.3%)
TOTAL	155 (100.0%)	155 (100.0%)	155 (100.0%)

Note: Data are from a 2005 *Washington Post*/ABC News poll (#2005–983: Congress/Social Security/War in Iraq/Stem Cell Research), based on a random national sample of 1000 respondents.

with the marriage question, compared to 48.2 percent who trust legislatures, a difference of about thirteen percentage points. In partisan election states, 49.7 percent of respondents trust state legislatures compared to 38.1 percent who trust state courts.

These trends hold up across issue areas. When it comes to the death penalty, Table 6.3 reports that the public generally trusts state courts more than state legislatures to deal with the issue. However, the magnitude of the public's preference for state courts is less pronounced in contested election states. In states with nonpartisan elections the public prefers state courts (49.8 percent) to state legislatures (43.1 percent) by about six percentage points, while in partisan election states the difference between trust in courts (49.7 percent) and legislatures (45.2 percent) is about four percentage points. In contrast, there is a twenty-three point difference between courts (57.9 percent) and legislatures (34.2 percent) in reappointment/life tenure states. In states that use uncontested retention elections, the difference between courts (54.5 percent) and legislatures (37.7 percent) is comparable.

On the issue of abortion, the trends are once again similar. In judicial reappointment/life tenure states, 49.1 percent of respondents said that they trust their courts to deal with the abortion issue, compared to 37.0 percent who trust their legislatures, a difference of about twelve percentage points. In nonpartisan election states, the clear preference is for state legislatures (47.4 percent), with only 37.0 percent of respondents trusting state courts to deal with the abortion issue in these states. In partisan election states and merit systems, the differences are less pronounced, with a slight preference for state legislatures in partisan election states (45.8 percent to 43.9 percent) and a slight preference for state courts in states that use uncontested retention elections (44.6 percent to 42.0 percent).

Despite some differences across issue areas, the general trends reported in Table 6.3 are remarkably consistent. When respondents are asked whether they prefer to have their state legislatures or their state courts deal with salient morality policies, their responses vary depending on the method of judicial retention used in their home states. Respondents from states that use reappointment for the retention of high court judges, or that retain their high court judges for life, tend to trust state courts, whereas citizens in states with contested judicial elections tend to trust their legislatures.

To be sure, the trends in Table 6.3 do not take other potentially confounding influences on public opinion into account, so in Table 6.4 I report the results of

Table 6.4 **Probit Model of Public Trust in State Courts to Decide Morality Policy Issues**

	Gay Marriage	*Death Penalty*	*Abortion*
Key Variables			
Reappointment/Life Tenure	0.213* (0.105)	0.270** (0.096)	0.286** (0.105)
Policy Views			
Ideology	−0.127* (0.053)	−0.160* (0.076)	−0.142* (0.056)
Party ID	−0.133* (0.056)	−0.071 (0.054)	−0.109* (0.050)
Demographics			
Education Level	0.056* (0.028)	0.017 (0.028)	0.023 (0.033)
Age	−0.002 (0.002)	−0.001 (0.003)	0.002 (0.003)
Male	0.005 (0.076)	0.033 (0.065)	0.193* (0.086)
White	0.108 (0.187)	0.420* (0.174)	0.233 (0.160)
Black	0.071 (0.203)	0.282 (0.208)	0.287 (0.212)
Hispanic	0.457* (0.198)	0.249* (0.236)	0.222 (0.273)
Region			
New England	0.135 (0.335)	0.306 (0.246)	0.043 (0.258)
Middle Atlantic	0.204 (0.211)	0.275* (0.137)	0.113 (0.205)
East North Central	0.301 (0.231)	0.197 (0.180)	0.083 (0.211)
West North Central	−0.068 (0.201)	−0.049 (0.165)	−0.395* (0.202)
Southern Atlantic	0.123 (0.213)	0.046 (0.128)	−0.012 (0.203)
West South Central	0.089 (0.191)	0.273** (0.095)	−0.073 (0.188)

	Gay Marriage	Death Penalty	Abortion
Mountain	−0.202	0.099	−0.236
	(0.252)	(0.233)	(0.225)
Pacific	0.362[a]	0.362***	0.097[a]
	(0.211)	(0.104)	(0.217)
Constant	−0.439	−0.311	−0.428
	(0.313)	(0.279)	(0.412)
Chi^2	141.950***	69.880***	75.320***

*$p < 0.05$; **$p < 0.01$; ***$p < 0.001$; [a]$p < 0.10$ N = 953

a probit model of public trust in state courts. The dependent variable is a dichotomous variable coded 1 when respondents indicated that they trusted their state courts instead of their state legislatures to deal with a particular issue. The key independent variable (REAPPOINTMENT/LIFE TENURE) is a dummy variable coded 1 when respondents were located in states that either used reappointment for the retention of high court judges or retained their judges for life. The baseline category of 0 includes all other judicial selection types. I controlled for respondents' ideology using IDEOLOGY and PARTY ID variables from the Washington Post/ABC News poll. For both variables, higher values are associated with more conservative responses. I also controlled for the respondents' EDUCATION LEVEL, AGE, gender (MALE), race (WHITE, BLACK, HISPANIC, OTHER, with OTHER as the baseline), and census division (NEW ENGLAND, MIDDLE ATLANTIC, EAST NORTH CENTRAL, WEST NORTH CENTRAL, SOUTHERN ATLANTIC, EAST SOUTH CENTRAL, WEST SOUTH CENTRAL, MOUNTAIN, and PACIFIC, with EAST SOUTH CENTRAL as the baseline), and I controlled for within-state correlation.

The results in Table 6.4 indicate that, even after taking other potentially confounding factors into account, the public is more likely to prefer courts to deal with morality policy issues in states that reappoint their judges or grant them life tenure. The significance levels are higher for the death penalty and abortion, but otherwise the effects of REAPPOINTMENT/LIFE TENURE are comparable. These trends are consistent with my hypothesis that judges are more capable of building public support for morality policies when they are independent of electoral processes. Elected judges are less likely to appear "above" politics and to be basing their decisions on principled criteria.

Comparing Levels of Public Support across State Institutions

The preceding analysis provides initial support for my hypothesis that judicial selection methods influence the capacity of state courts to build public support for government policies. However, there are limits to the conclusions that one can make from the Washington Post/ABC News poll. Ultimately that poll only asked respondents to report who they trust to deal with the same-sex marriage issue, not to evaluate actual policy choices that have been made by, or have been attributed to, their state institutions.

To address this issue, and to corroborate the results of the first survey, I designed a survey experiment patterned after previous laboratory experiments comparing the legitimacy-conferring capacity of courts with that of other institutions. Respondents were randomly assigned to one of three conditions associating the legalization of same-sex marriage with a different state institution. In the first group, I asked respondents, "If the judges in your state legalized same-sex marriage, would you support the decision?" For the second group, I replaced the words "judges in your state" with "governor." In the third group, I associated same-sex marriage policy with a "state legislature." Questions were posed hypothetically because by 2008 only a handful of states had legalized same-sex marriage. To keep the effects of the treatment equivalent across respondents, I excluded respondents from states in which judges had already ruled in favor of same-sex marriage (HI, MA, CT, CA) or civil unions (VT, NJ). I did not want some respondents to be evaluating hypothetical court decisions and others to be evaluating actual same-sex marriage decisions. At the time data were collected, in October 2008, same-sex marriages had become legal only because of court orders, so in all cases the proposed legislative activity was hypothetical. In the end, each of the treatment conditions had a roughly equal number of respondents, approximately 250 to 265 respondents per group.

Data are from the 2008 Cooperative Congressional Election Study (CCES), a national internet survey of one thousand respondents.[32] CCES uses nonprobability sampling, so it is not appropriate for all types of survey research, but the data are suited to survey experiments randomly assigning subjects to different treatment conditions. A report by the American Association of Public Opinion Research (AAPOR) affirmed that nonprobability online surveys can be used in these types of experimental conditions.[33] As long as sampling bias is distributed randomly across the treatment conditions, one can be confident that observed differences among the groups are attributable to the treatments. It should also be noted that the results of this survey are corroborated by the Washington Post/ABC News poll, which does employ a probability sample.

If courts are more likely than other state institutions to increase public support for government policies, then one would expect respondents to be more likely to express support for same-sex marriage when the policy is attributed to a state court than when it is attributed to another state institution. These results would be consistent with research that has found that the U.S. Supreme Court has a greater capacity to legitimate public policies than other institutions. However, as I discovered in

[32] Further information is available at the CCES Web site (http://projects.iq.harvard.edu/cces/book/cces-2008).

[33] Reg Baker et al, *AAPOR Report on Online Panels*, AMERICAN ASSOCIATION FOR PUBLIC OPINION RESEARCH (Mar. 2010), *available at* http://www.aapor.org.

Table 6.5 **"If the [state legislature/governor/judges in your state] legalized same-sex marriage, would you support the decision?" General Results**

	State Legislature	*Governor*	*State Judges*	*TOTAL*
Anti-SSM	150 (58.4%)	152 (60.6%)	155 (58.5%)	457 (59.1%)
Pro-SSM	107 (41.6%)	99 (39.4%)	110 (41.5%)	316 (40.9%)
TOTAL	257 (100.0%)	251 (100.0%)	265 (100.0%)	773 (100.0%)

Note: Data are from the 2008 Cooperative Congressional Election Study, based on questions developed by the author. Responses were excluded when respondents were from states in which courts had already mandated same-sex marriage (HI, MA, CT, CA) or civil unions (VT, NJ).

the previous section, state courts enjoy no automatic advantage. In fact, Table 6.5 reports no meaningful differences between the three groups: 41.5 percent of respondents supported the legalization of same-sex marriage when it was attributed to "judges in your state," compared to 39.4 percent when the policy was associated with the "governor" and 41.6 percent when the policy was linked with the "state legislature." These differences are not statistically significant.[34] The public, *in general*, is no more likely to support the legalization of same-sex marriage when the policy comes from a court than from another institution.

However, just like before, it is still possible that the potential for courts to influence policy is heightened in certain conditions. Table 6.6 breaks down the raw data by the method of judicial retention used for judges in respondents' home states. I am interested, once again, in comparing differences in the response rate of the treatment subjects, who received prompts attributing the legalization of same-sex marriage to state judges, and control subjects, who received prompts attributing the policy to a governor or legislature. I expect the differences in support for the legalization of same-sex marriage between treatment and control subjects to be smaller in states that use contested elections. Because elected judges lack independence, their policies are likely to seem less distinct from those of other government officials, making the public less likely to defer to them.

Of course, this manipulation introduces a quasi-experimental component to the research design, which might raise concerns about the validity of the comparisons. Although I have randomly assigned individuals to receive a prompt associating the

---

[34] The statistical significance of the survey experiment was estimated using Green and Gerber's Web software. *See* Don Green & Alan Gerber, *Web Software for Analyzing Experimental Data*, YALE INSTITUTION FOR SOCIAL AND POLICY STUDIES, http://research.yale.edu/. The estimated treatment effect (i.e., the influence of associating the legalization of same-sex marriage with a state court) was +2.9 percent, with a standard error of 3.5 percent. A one-tailed significance test was not significant at $p < 0.05$.

Table 6.6 **"If the [state legislature/governor/judges in your state] legalized same-sex marriage, would you support the decision?" Breakdown by Judicial Retention Method**

	All States		
	Control	Treatment	TOTAL
Anti-SSM	302 (59.5%)	155 (58.5%)	457 (59.1%)
Pro-SSM	206 (40.6%)	110 (41.5%)	316 (40.0%)
TOTAL	508 (100.0%)	265 (100.0%)	773 (100.0%)
	Contested Election States		
	Control	Treatment	TOTAL
Anti-SSM	160 (58.2%)	100 (63.3%)	260 (60.1%)
Pro-SSM	115 (41.8%)	58 (36.7%)	173 (40.0%)
TOTAL	275 (100.0%)	158 (100.0%)	433 (100.0%)
	Reappointment/Retention Election States		
	Control	Treatment	TOTAL
Anti SSM	142 (60.9%)	55 (51.4%)	197 (57.9%)
Pro SSM	91 (39.1%)	52 (48.6%)	143 (42.1%)
TOTAL	233 (100.0%)	107 (100.0%)	340 (100.0%)

Note: In the treatment group, the legalization of same-sex marriage was attributed to a state court. In the control group, legalization was attributed to another institution (i.e., the state legislature or governor).

legalization of same-sex marriage to a court or another institution, I have not randomly assigned the method of judicial selection in respondents' home states. It is possible, then, that if there are other systematic differences between election states and nonelection states, it is these differences that actually account for variations in public support.

However, a comparison of the control groups in Table 6.6 suggests that these concerns are not warranted. Regardless of whether respondents are from contested election states or from states that use different selection methods, support for policies favoring the legalization of same-sex marriage is at about 40.0 percent among subjects in the control groups, which is consistent with the level of support for the legalization of same-sex marriage across all states. This finding is important because it establishes that the baseline level of support for the legalization of same-sex marriage is the same in contested election states and reappointment/retention election states. In other words, citizens are not simply predisposed to support same-sex marriage in states that use reappointment or retention elections.

There are, however, significant differences among subjects in the treatment groups. In states with contested judicial elections, support for a government policy favoring the legalization of same-sex marriage is five percentage points lower in the treatment group, in which the policy is attributed to a court, than in the control group, in which the policy is attributed to another institution. In states without contested judicial elections, support for a policy favoring legalization is nine percentage points higher in the treatment group. These differences are statistically significant, and therefore provide evidence that judicial elections condition public responses to judicial policies.[35]

To provide a more rigorous test of this hypothesis, I developed a multivariate probit model of public support for the legalization of same-sex marriage. My key independent variable is a dichotomous measure of whether a subject was given a prompt attributing legalization to a court (COURT QUESTION). To assess whether the effect of attributing a policy to a state court is conditional, I interacted this COURT QUESTION variable with an ELECTION variable, which focuses on the method of retention used for high court judges in respondents' home states. My expectation is that partisan or nonpartisan elections will diminish the effect of attributing a decision to a court.

Additionally, I controlled for a number of respondents' background characteristics. I captured the general policy views of respondents by recording their IDEOLOGY, their PARTY ID, and their level of RELIGIOSITY, with the expectation that when respondents identify as more conservative, Republican, or religious, they will be less likely to favor the legalization of same-sex marriage. I measured the IDEOLOGY of respondents on a 100-point scale, with higher values associated with conservative ideologies. The PARTY ID variable is measured on a 7-point scale ranging from "Strong Democrat" to "Strong Republican." For RELIGIOSITY, respondents were asked, "How important is religion in your life?" The responses to the RELIGIOSITY question were "not at all important," "not too important," "important," and "very important."

I controlled for respondents' attitudes about gay rights by measuring their level of support for a federal constitutional AMENDMENT limiting marriage equality.

---

[35] Once again, I establish the significance of the treatment effect using Green and Gerber's Web software for analyzing experimental data, *supra* note 34. In contested election states, the differences between the treatment and control groups are not significant ($p < 0.85$), using a one-tailed test. However, in other states, the differences are significant, at $p < 0.05$, using a one-tailed test.

I expect that citizens who support an amendment prohibiting same-sex marriage will also be less likely to support a government policy favoring the legalization of same-sex marriage. Finally, I included a number of demographic variables measuring respondents' Birth Year, gender (Male), Education Level, race (White, Black, Hispanic, Other), and census division (New England, Middle Atlantic, East North Central, West North Central, Southern Atlantic, East South Central, West South Central, Mountain, and Pacific), and I controlled for within-state correlation.

The results of the probit model are reported in Table 6.7 and affirm, once again, that as a general matter state courts are no more likely than other state institutions to increase public support for the legalization of same-sex marriage. By itself, the Court Question variable does not attain statistical significance. However, the variable does become significant once the method of judicial retention is taken into account. The interaction term (Election*Question) is also significant. The interaction term is signed in the opposite direction from the Court Question variable, which is consistent with my hypothesis that when judges are retained through partisan or nonpartisan elections, they are less likely to increase support for the

Table 6.7 **Probit Model of Public Support for the Legalization of Same-Sex Marriage**

	No Interaction	Election Interaction
Key Variables		
Court Question	−0.006 (0.214)	0.542* (0.248)
Election		0.395 (0.269)
Election*Question		−0.941** (0.337)
Policy Views		
Ideology	−0.013* (0.005)	−0.013** (0.005)
Party ID	−0.138* (0.066)	−0.137* (0.064)
Religiosity	−0.309** (0.104)	−0.327*** (0.096)
Amendment	−2.787*** (0.248)	−2.869*** (0.261)

	No Interaction	*Election Interaction*
Demographics		
Birth Year	0.021***	0.021***
	(0.006)	(0.006)
Male	−0.329	−0.345[a]
	(0.209)	(0.202)
Education Level	0.051	0.057
	(0.062)	(0.063)
White	. −0.574[a]	−0.574[a]
	(0.342)	(0.395)
Black	−0.280	−0.223
	(0.444)	(0.473)
Hispanic	−0.542[a]	−0.619
	(0.328)	(0.380)
Region		
New England	1.386***	1.481***
	(0.339)	(0.345)
Middle Atlantic	0.373	0.389
	(0.234)	(0.255)
East North Central	0.123	0.079
	(0.280)	(0.287)
West North Central	0.270	0.386
	(0.293)	(0.301)
Southern Atlantic	0.024	0.022
	(0.195)	(0.216)
West South Central	0.301	0.257
	(0.282)	(0.288)
Mountain	−0.288	−0.266
	(0.412)	(0.405)
Pacific	0.709***	0.677**
	(0.207)	(0.247)
Constant	−38.080***	−37.634**
	(11.508)	(12.138)
Chi^2	435.310***	748.960***

*$p < 0.05$; **$p < 0.01$; ***$p < 0.001$; [a]$p < 0.10$ N = 674

legalization of same-sex marriage, compared to other institutions.[36] The findings therefore suggest that the capacity of state judges to build support for government policies is diminished in states with contested judicial elections.

One of the difficulties with interpreting interaction effects in nonlinear models is that the magnitude and significance of the interaction may vary across individuals. Interpreting significance levels can be especially misleading, because it is possible that the interaction is only significant for a subset of respondents. I therefore graphed the z-scores for the election interaction model in Figure 1. This figure arranges respondents by their levels of support for same-sex marriage, with those who are predicted to strongly oppose same-sex marriage located at the far left of the graph and those strongly favoring it clustered on the right. Statistically significant interactions are those above or below the three center lines. The trends suggest that the interaction between judicial elections and the attribution of same-sex marriage policy to a court is the strongest among respondents who are not predisposed to support or oppose the legalization of same-sex marriage. The z-scores are not significant at the far left and right of the figure, which represent citizens who have the strongest attitudes. The findings in Figure 6.1 are consistent with public opinion research that has found that individuals who have malleable opinions are more likely to be influenced by elite discourse on public policies.[37]

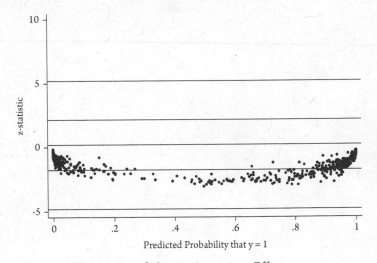

Figure 6.1 Z-Statistics of Election Interaction Effects

[36] One must use caution when interpreting the direction of interaction terms in nonlinear models, so I describe the interaction effect in further detail below. *See* Chunrong Ai & Edward C. Norton, *Interaction Terms in Logit and Probit Models*, 80 ECON. LETTERS 123, 124 (2003) ("the interaction effect may have different signs for different values of covariates. Therefore, the sign does not necessarily indicate the sign of the interaction effect.").

[37] *See* JOHN R. ZALLER, THE NATURE AND ORIGINS OF MASS OPINION (1992); and Valerie J. Hoekstra & Jeffrey A. Segal, *The Shepherding of Local Public Opinion: The Supreme Court and Lamb's Chapel*, 58 J. POL. 1079 (1996).

A number of the other variables in Table 6.7 also attain statistical significance. As expected, Republicans are less likely than Democrats to support same-sex marriage (PARTY ID), as are conservative respondents (IDEOLOGY), religious respondents (RELIGIOSITY), and respondents who support a federal constitutional amendment limiting marriage equality (AMENDMENT). The results also suggest that younger respondents are more likely to be supportive (BIRTH YEAR), and that support is the strongest in the NEW ENGLAND and PACIFIC census divisions. The implication of these findings is that the capacity of judges to build public support for government policies varies with citizen attitudes. Judges are likely to have particular difficulty building public support for decisions legalizing same-sex marriage among religious conservatives, Republicans, and citizens who oppose gay rights.

Conclusion

Overall, the findings of this chapter suggest that state courts can be more effective than other institutions at building public support for government policies. However, this capacity is conditioned by the judges' levels of independence, as reflected by their methods of retention. This finding is consistent with my theoretical expectation that the capacity of state courts to increase public support for morality policies such as same-sex marriage is not universal, but conditional. When judges are retained with partisan or nonpartisan elections, which reduce judicial independence, the public is less likely to extend special deference to courts on issues such as same-sex marriage. In these circumstances, courts are no better than other institutions at building public support.

The findings of this chapter have a number of important substantive implications. The first is that legitimacy theory must be refined when applied to the state judicial context. The capacity of state courts to build support for government policies may be dependent on particular institutional conditions, such as the independence of judges. The evidence here suggests that courthouse democracy reduces the ability of judges to engage in policy leadership. Federal judges, who enjoy life tenure, are in a comparatively better position to build support for policy alternatives. The independence of federal judges from routine politics cultivates a perception that they are above politics, entitling their decisions to special deference in the public eye. Without independence, many state judges find themselves in weaker positions. Instead of appearing as principled interpreters of their constitutions, elected judges more closely resemble other state policy makers.

The second implication is that choices about judicial selection and retention can influence the effectiveness of courts at winning public support for government policies. If, on the one hand, elected judges are more likely to vote consistently with majoritarian values, on the other hand these judges may be less likely to build support for unpopular policies. Elected judges might also be less likely to try, because they need the support of majorities to retain their positions. States with elected judges may therefore be particularly poor venues for minority groups to pursue litigation strategies.

Because this book focuses on a morality policy controversy, it is unclear what the impact of state courts on public opinion might be like in routine cases. My suspicion, however, is that the effects would be stronger. Because same-sex marriage is highly salient, many people have strong opinions about the issue, which means that there is less potential for state courts to influence public opinion. As Figure 6.1 illustrated, the conditioning effects of retention methods are the strongest among individuals who lack well-formed attitudes about same-sex marriage policy. The implication is that in other areas of policy, in which public attitudes are less developed, more individuals might be susceptible to conditioning effects.

On the other hand, in less-salient issue areas there is a strong possibility that the public will not be paying attention to what high courts are doing. Research by Vining and Wilhelm has found that the salience of most state court decisions is very low.[38] Vining and Wilhelm observed that only about 1.5 percent of all state court cases receive front-page newspaper coverage on the day following their decision.[39] Even on issues such as the death penalty, which previous researchers have described as visible,[40] only about 2 percent of cases are salient.[41] It seems likely, then, that only on the most highly visible issues will state courts have a meaningful possibility of influencing public opinion, because it is only on these few issues that the public will possess much, if any, knowledge of what courts have done. The barrier to effective policy leadership for state courts might therefore be very high, requiring the public to be paying attention to what courts are doing but not to have such well-formed opinions that they cannot be persuaded to support the court's position. The casual reader of the news, who pays attention to front-page coverage of high court decisions but has not thought much about them, might be the type of individual whom high court judges can most influence.

Public attitudes about same-sex marriage are probably too well ingrained for courts to completely transform public thinking about the issue. Yet, it is notable that despite the salience of the issue, certain judges do appear to be capable of influencing the public's response. Once again, courthouse democracy accounts for why certain judges come out ahead. Appointed judges are more successful at persuading the public that they are engaged in principled decision making, better enabling them to build support for their decisions.

---

[38] *See* Vining & Wilhelm, *supra* Chapter 5, note 28.

[39] *Id.* at 563.

[40] *See, e.g.,* Hall, *Constituent Influence in State Supreme Courts, supra* Chapter 1, note 7.

[41] Vining & Wilhelm, *supra* Chapter 5, note 28, at 564.

CHAPTER 7

Policy Endurance: The Enactment of State Constitutional Amendments Prohibiting Same-Sex Marriage

The 2008 election was not supposed to be about same-sex marriage. Unlike 2004, when twelve states amended their constitutions on Election Day to limit marriage equality, the focus of media attention in 2008 was on the election of Barack Obama as the nation's first African-American president. The election was supposed to symbolize the progress that the nation was making in its tolerance of diversity, so it was ironic that on the same day California voters approved a ballot initiative amending the state constitution to limit marriage to opposite-sex couples, overturning the California Supreme Court's decision from six months earlier.[1]

Proposition 8 was a major setback for marriage equality in California. Although same-sex couples could still enter into civil unions, they were barred from marriage, reinforcing the second-class status of these relationships. Supporters of same-sex marriage again sought redress in the California Supreme Court, arguing that Proposition 8 was not really a constitutional amendment but a revision, which required a more rigorous approval process than a mere ballot initiative. Their logic was that Proposition 8 changed the character of the state constitution so fundamentally that it went beyond the scope of a typical constitutional amendment. A constitutional convention, requested by two-thirds of the state legislature, was necessary to take away a fundamental right.[2] California law formally distinguishes between amendments and revisions, so supporters of same-sex marriage believed that their case was winnable, especially because the same justices had just ruled in their favor a few months earlier.

---

[1] Proposition 8 did not completely overturn *In re Marriage Cases*, 43 Cal. 4th 757 (2008). As the California Supreme Court observed in *Strauss v. Horton*, 46 Cal.4th 364 (2009), the 2008 decision still required California to provide the same rights and benefits to same-sex couples that opposite-sex couples received.

[2] *See* CAL. CONST. art. XVIII, § 2.

But in oral arguments the California justices seemed wary of frustrating the will of the voters. On May 26, 2009, in *Strauss v. Horton*, the justices ruled that Proposition 8 was a valid amendment and that the court's previous decision was therefore super-seded.[3] The justices did not believe that Proposition 8 qualified as a revision because the amendment did not take away any of the benefits of marriage that were described in *In re Marriage Cases*, nor did it change the heightened standard of review that clas-sifications based on sexual orientation were to receive under the state constitution. The amendment simply reserved the term *marriage* for opposite-sex couples, which was a significant policy change but not sufficient to count as a revision.

"As a qualitative matter," Chief Justice Ronald M. George wrote for the court, "the act of limiting access to the designation of marriage to opposite-sex couples does not have a substantial or, indeed, even a minimal effect on *the government plan or framework of California* that existed prior to the amendment."[4] The justices ruled that the same-sex marriages that had taken place prior to the enactment of Proposition 8 would remain intact, but no further marriages could take place. Supporters of same-sex marriage would have to seek approval of another ballot initiative or take their case to federal court to continue their fight for marriage equality.

Proposition 8 served as an important reminder that state court decisions are not necessarily enduring. Hard-won victories in the state courts might have a short-term impact but fail to have a significant long-term influence on government policy. The focus of this chapter is on *policy endurance*, the process by which courts produce lasting policy change. As with the other stages of judicial policy development, policy endurance can be gauged in a number of ways. It might be reflected in a sustained uptick in popular support for the justices' position or in a refusal by lawmakers to consider policy alternatives. Policy endurance also occurs when lower court judges faithfully apply precedents, when administrators incorporate decisions into their rulemaking, and when judges in other jurisdictions cite precedents as authoritative. All of these actions help to extend the reach of judicial policies.

In the context of same-sex marriage policy, the biggest obstacle to policy endur-ance has been the adoption of state constitutional amendments prohibiting the legalization of same-sex marriage. Table 7.1 provides an overview of the states that had amendments prohibiting same-sex marriage in place at the end of 2008. As the table reports, same-sex marriage amendments spanned the country by the time that California voters approved Proposition 8. The first amendments were enacted in Hawaii and Alaska in 1998, but within ten years the number had expanded to thirty.[5] Nineteen of these states used restrictive language in their amendments prohibiting the creation of alternative institutions to marriage, such as civil unions.

[3] Strauss v. Horton, 46 Cal. 4th 364 (2009).

[4] *Id.* at 388.

[5] In 2012, North Carolina became the thirty-first state to approve a constitutional amendment pro-hibiting same-sex marriage. The amendment was approved too late to be included in the data analysis that follows, but I make note of it here.

Table 7.1 **Dates of Initial Consideration and Adoption of State Constitutional Amendments Prohibiting Same-Sex Marriage, 1990–2008 (with Date of Statutory Prohibition)**

State	Initial Consideration of SSM Amendments	Adoption of SSM Amendments	Statutory Prohibition of SSM
Alabama	2006	2006	1998
Alaska	1998	1998	1996
Arizona	2006	2008	1996
Arkansas	2004	2004	1997
California	2008	2008	pre-1990
Colorado	2006	2006	2000
Delaware	2004		1996
Florida	2008	2008	1997
Georgia	2004	2004	1996
Hawaii	1997	1998	1994
Idaho	2004	2006	pre-1990
Indiana	2004		pre-1990
Iowa	2005		1998
Kansas	2004	2005	1996
Kentucky	2004	2004	1998
Louisiana	2004	2004	pre-1990
Maine	2004		1997
Maryland	2005		pre-1990
Massachusetts	2002		
Michigan	2004	2004	1996
Minnesota	2004		1997
Mississippi	2004	2004	1997
Missouri	2004	2004	1996
Montana	2004	2004	1997
Nebraska	2000	2000	
Nevada	2000	2002	pre-1990
New Hampshire	2006		pre-1990
New Mexico	2008		

(Continued)

Table 7.1 (Continued)

State	Initial Consideration of SSM Amendments	Adoption of SSM Amendments	Statutory Prohibition of SSM
North Carolina	2004		1996
North Dakota	2004	2004	1997
Ohio	2004	2004	2004
Oklahoma	2004	2004	pre-1990
Oregon	2004	2004	
Pennsylvania	2006		1996
South Carolina	2006	2006	1996
South Dakota	2006	2006	1996
Tennessee	2004	2006	1996
Texas	2004	2005	1997
Utah	2004	2004	1993
Virginia	2005	2006	pre-1990
West Virginia	2006		pre-1990
Wisconsin	2004	2006	

Sources: Lambda Legal (for the initial consideration and adoption of amendments); and Scott Barclay & Shauna Fisher, *Said and Unsaid: State Legislative Signaling to State Courts over Same Sex Marriage, 1990–2004*, 30 LAW & POL'Y 254 (2008) (for statutes).

The amendments had two distinct effects on judicial impact. Some of the amendments overturned specific decisions within their states. In Hawaii, California, and Alaska, the amendments halted the progress of gay rights by overturning court decisions endorsing marriage equality. In other states, however, in which courts had not yet ruled on the marriage question, the amendments preempted judicial activity. Judges in these states were expressly prohibited from following the examples of pro-marriage rulings in states such as Massachusetts and Connecticut, thus extinguishing any spark that these earlier rulings might have ignited.

In general, then, the passage of amendments had substantial implications for the impact of courts, making it important to understand their adoption. As in previous chapters, I expect institutional explanations to be at least partially responsible. For example, judges in initiative amendment states might have been particularly vulnerable to having their decisions overturned or preempted by the passage of amendments because it was easier for opponents of same-sex marriage to get amendments on the ballot and to secure their passage. In other states, which had more deliberative amendment procedures, court decisions would have been more insulated.

In states that had yet to consider the marriage question, the adoption of amendments might also have been affected by whether courts were institutionally capable of producing decisions favoring marriage equality. Professionalized courts, which have a greater capacity "to generate and evaluate information,"[6] might have been targeted because of their tendency to issue decisions favoring disadvantaged parties.[7] Appointed judges might also have been targeted because they are more willing to make decisions at odds with public opinion. Opponents of same-sex marriage would have anticipated a greater risk that the judges in these states would endorse marriage equality, making it necessary for the opponents to curb judicial power.

The Politics of State Constitutional Amendments

The literature on state constitutional amendments is largely undeveloped, but the few existing studies on the subject agree that the single most important distinction between federal and state constitutional amendment procedures is the role of the public.[8] As discussed in Chapter 2, states vary widely in their amendment procedures, but virtually all of them submit proposed amendments to the public for a vote. In some states such as California, citizens can propose amendments directly using initiative amendment procedures. Other states do not permit citizens to propose constitutional amendments but let the public vote on amendments proposed by the legislature.

The extent to which public attitudes actually influence the passage of state constitutional amendments depends on the nature and salience of the issue. Tarr suggests that most amendments are low salience and are governed by "political insider" politics, proposed "not in response to a public outcry but because of problems identified in the course of governing."[9] These amendments tend to receive bipartisan support and are easily ratified. When it comes to amendments involving morality policies such as same-sex marriage, however, the role of the public is much more important. In fact, public attitudes, as well as other demographic and environmental characteristics, may be central to their passage. A study by Fleischmann and Moyer found that support for ballot initiatives prohibiting same-sex marriage varied

---

[6] Squire, *Measuring the Professionalization of State Courts of Last Resort, supra* Chapter 1, note 59, at 223.

[7] Brace & Hall, *"Haves" versus "Have Nots" in State Supreme Courts, supra* Chapter 1, note 59.

[8] *See* Janice C. May, *Constitutional Amendment and Revision Revisited*, 17 PUBLIUS 153, 179 (1987) ("The states have established mechanisms for direct popular participation in the amendment and revision of state constitutions on a scale unmatched by the federal government."); and Donald S. Lutz, *Toward a Theory of Constitutional Amendment*, 88 AM. POL. SCI. REV. 355 (1994) (finding that the rate at which states amend their constitutions vary with constitution length and the difficulty of amendment procedures).

[9] G. ALAN TARR, UNDERSTANDING STATE CONSTITUTIONS 142 (1998).

Table 7.2 **Summary of State Constitutional Amendments, by Amendment Procedure**

	Initiative	*No Initiative*	*TOTAL*
Same-Sex Marriage Amendment	16 (88.9%)	15 (46.9%)	31 (60.0%)
No Same-Sex Marriage Amendment	2 (11.1%)	17 (53.1%)	19 (40.0%)
Total	18 (100.0%)	32 (100.0%)	50 (100.0%)

Source: Initiative and Referendum Institute

depending on the size of the evangelical population, the education levels of citizens, and the concentration of gay organizations within particular counties, among other factors.[10]

Although some literature has doubted the extent to which direct democracy threatens minority rights,[11] the emerging consensus is that LGBT interests fare poorly under direct democracy.[12] Table 7.2 summarizes data that I introduced in Chapter 2, illustrating the relationship between state constitutional amendment procedures and the adoption of amendments restricting marriage equality. The data show that 88.9 percent of states that permit citizens to propose amendments using initiative amendment procedures amended their constitutions to forbid same-sex marriage, while just 46.9 percent of the states with no initiative procedures did so. These findings suggest that when amendment procedures become more open and democratic, judges have more difficulty enacting policies that a majority of the public opposes.

Court-Curbing and the Adoption of State Constitutional Amendments

Less clear is whether the same-sex marriage amendments were a deliberate effort to curb judicial power, although research suggests that state constitutions are

[10] Arnold Fleischmann & Laura Moyer, *Competing Social Movements and Local Political Culture: Voting on Ballot Propositions to Ban Same-Sex Marriage in the U.S. States*, 90 Soc. Sci. Q. 134 (2009).

[11] Todd Donovan & Shaun Bowler, *Direct Democracy and Minority Rights: An Extension*, 42 Am. J. Pol. Sci. 1020 (1998).

[12] *See* Gamble, *supra* Chapter 2, note 61; Haider-Markel et al., *supra* Chapter 2, note 61; D. Lewis, *supra* Chapter 2, note 61; Lupia et al., *supra* Chapter 2, note 61; and Mucciaroni, *supra* Chapter 2, note 61.

frequently amended for this purpose.[13] Otherwise, it would be unclear why states would have preferred constitutional amendments to statutory prohibitions of same-sex marriage, or, indeed, why they would have amended their constitutions when they already had statutory prohibitions of same-sex marriage in place. For the most part, the same-sex marriage amendments did little to change the policy status quo in the states in which they were adopted. As Table 7.1 shows, twenty-seven of the thirty states that approved amendments by the end of 2008 had statutory prohibitions of same-sex marriage in place at the time of adoption. The primary effect of the amendments was not to change the legal status of same-sex couples or even to clarify the status of same-sex couples under state law.

Instead, the amendments prevented state institutions from changing the status quo. In states in which courts had already acted, the purpose of the amendments was to overturn the actions of state courts. In other states, the purpose was to preempt this activity. Constitutional amendments constrain the behavior of state legislatures as well as courts, but it is reasonable to assume that the adoption of amendments was primarily a reaction to state court activity. State legislators mostly reinforced the status quo during the years under analysis, enacting statutes clarifying that same-sex marriage was prohibited under state law.[14] Before 2009, the only same-sex marriages to become legal occurred because of court orders.[15]

The adoption of amendments also closely tracked state court activity. The first amendments, in Hawaii and Alaska in 1998, were adopted soon after landmark same-sex marriage decisions in these states and had the effect of directly overturning these decisions. The second wave of constitutional amendments, beginning in 2004, were enacted soon after the Supreme Judicial Court of Massachusetts required full marriage equality for same-sex couples in *Goodridge v. Department of Public Health*[16] and the *Opinion of the Justices*.[17] Except for California's, these later amendments were enacted in states that had not ruled on the issue. The primary effect of the amendments, then, was to prevent judges from following the example of Massachusetts and imposing same-sex marriage on their constituents. Indeed, Rosenberg reports that many opponents of same-sex marriage were concerned "that judges in their states would follow the Massachusetts Supreme Court and force gay

[13] *See* May, *supra* note 8, at 179 ("The record of amendment changes during the past fifteen years or so shows that the voters have approved many restrictive amendments in criminal justice and many expansive amendments in other areas of civil rights law....The ballot proposition tilts the state constitutional tradition toward judicial accountability rather than toward judicial independence with respect to the protection of rights and liberties.").

[14] *See* Scott Barclay, *In Search of Judicial Activism in the Same-Sex Marriage Cases: Sorting the Evidence from Courts, Legislatures, Initiatives and Amendments*, 8 Persp. on Pol. 111 (2010).

[15] Both houses of the California legislature voted to legalize same-sex marriage as early as 2005, but Governor Arnold Schwarzenegger did not sign the bill into law.

[16] Goodridge v. Dep't of Public Health, 798 N.E.2d 941 (Mass. 2003).

[17] Opinion of the Justices to the Senate, 802 N.E.2d 565 (Mass. 2004).

marriage upon them."[18] Barclay and Fisher similarly found that a "substantial minority" of state legislatures between 1990 and 2004 introduced new legislative bills regarding same-sex marriage, even after the practice was clearly prohibited, in order to discourage the intervention of state courts.[19]

For these reasons, I think it is fair to characterize the adoption of the same-sex marriage amendments as primarily a reaction to state courts. The practical effect of the amendments was to halt judicial activity on the issue of same-sex marriage. State supreme court justices in California found their work on the marriage issue immediately undone. Judges in Hawaii and Alaska found their work interrupted before it could be finalized. In other states, judges found themselves incapable of even deciding the question. Nationwide, the effect of the amendments was to blunt the impact of decisions in states such as Hawaii and Massachusetts, ensuring that these precedents did not spill over into other jurisdictions.

The Professionalization of State Supreme Courts

Which state courts were particularly likely to be targeted by amendments? I suggest that at least part of the explanation relates to the institutional capacity of state supreme courts. Judges who appeared capable of voting in favor of marriage equality would have been of particular concern to opponents of same-sex marriage. Quite obviously, judges who had already ruled in favor of marriage equality would have been targeted, but in states in which judges had not acted, opponents of same-sex marriage would have had to have made a prediction about whether their judges were likely to legalize same-sex marriage in the future. When state courts appeared capable of requiring marriage equality, opponents of same-sex marriage would have had incentives to approve amendments curbing judicial power. Amendments have the advantage of limiting the power of judges in certain targeted areas, such as same-sex marriage policy, while leaving judges capable of setting policies in other areas where they have greater public support.

One way of gauging the capability of state courts is with reference to their degree of professionalization. Professionalization is an indicator of institutional quality that is grounded in "attributes of the institution" rather than "personal characteristics and attitudes of individuals who serve in office."[20] Following Squire, I define *judicial professionalization* as "a court's ability to generate and evaluate information."[21]

---

[18] ROSENBERG, *supra* Chapter 1, note 3, at 369; *see also* Debra Rosenberg & Karen Breslau, *Winning the "Values" Vote*, NEWSWEEK, Nov. 15, 2004, at 23.

[19] Scott Barclay & Shauna Fisher, *Said and Unsaid: State Legislative Signaling to State Courts over Same-Sex Marriage*, 30 LAW & POL'Y 254 (2008).

[20] Peverill Squire, *Professionalization and Public Opinion of State Legislatures*, 55 J. POL. 479, 480 (1993).

[21] Squire, *Measuring the Professionalization of State Courts of Last Resort*, *supra* Chapter 1, note 59, at 223.

Professionalization improves the capability of state courts to act on behalf of disadvantaged parties by enabling judges to give litigants full, fair hearings of the legal questions that are presented. Over time, political scientists have used different criteria to identify professionalized courts. The earliest measures tracked how closely state judiciaries followed the American Bar Association's model court system.[22] More recently Squire developed a measure of high court professionalization that focused on the size of judicial salaries, the number of law clerks assigned to high court judges, and the amount of control that judges have over their dockets.[23] The new measure synthesized a measure that was developed by Brace and Hall[24] with Squire's own measure of legislative professionalization.[25]

The movement to professionalize state courts was designed to improve their quality, to make courts more "capable of administering justice equitably and expeditiously."[26] Higher salaries attract higher-quality judges, whereas more clerks and docket control let judges focus their attention on important legal problems.[27] So it is ironic that the public's view of professionalized institutions has frequently been negative. Research has demonstrated that the public views professionalized institutions as complex, inefficient, and out of touch with the public's values. As Hibbing and Theiss-Morse explain, "Most citizens of today are not at all fond of either professional politicians or big, professional political institutions, and both contribute to a hatred of politics."[28] For opponents of same-sex marriage, the more specific problem with professionalized courts is their tendency to support disadvantaged parties. Brace and Hall demonstrated that the capacity of high court judges "to protect the disadvantaged" and to stand "as a barrier against majority tyranny" varies with their level of professionalization.[29] They found that professionalized courts devote a greater proportion of their docket to have/have-not disputes and are more likely to side with underdog parties on the merits.[30] It would have been reasonable, then, for

---

[22] *See* GLICK & VINES, *supra* Chapter 1, note 59.

[23] Squire, *Measuring the Professionalization of State Courts of Last Resort, supra* Chapter 1, note 59.

[24] Brace & Hall, *"Haves" versus "Have Nots" in State Supreme Courts, supra* Chapter 1, note 59; *see also* Atkins & Glick, *supra* Chapter 1, note 59.

[25] Squire, *Professionalization and Public Opinion of State Legislatures, supra* note 20; and Peverill Squire, *Measuring Legislative Professionalism: The Squire Index,* 7 ST. POL. & POL'Y Q. 211 (2007).

[26] S. KENNETH HOWARD & DAVID B. WALKER, THE QUESTION OF STATE GOVERNMENT CAPABILITY 183 (1985).

[27] *See* Squire, *Measuring the Professionalization of State Courts of Last Resort, supra* Chapter 1, note 59, at 226 ("Appellate courts that can largely determine which cases they hear have a greater ability to craft their decisions compared with appellate courts that cannot pick and choose.").

[28] HIBBING & THEISS-MORSE, CONGRESS AS PUBLIC ENEMY, *supra* Chapter 2, note 37, at 10.

[29] Brace & Hall, *"Haves" versus "Have Nots" in State Supreme Courts, supra* Chapter 1, note 59, at 395.

[30] *Id.* at 402 ("Generally speaking, supreme court professionalism should give state supreme courts greater latitude in shaping their dockets and in reviewing the information related to the cases before them. More highly professionalized state supreme courts will have greater liberty to consider have/have-not cases than courts with fewer staff resources or other support.").

opponents of gay marriage in states with professionalized judiciaries to expect their judges to be more likely to rule in favor of the legalization of same-sex marriage.

Judicial Selection and Retention Methods

A second way of gauging the capability of state institutions is with reference to their degree of independence from electoral processes. As I discussed in previous chapters, the literature is generally in agreement that elected judges are less likely to vote against the public in salient issue areas, making elected judges less capable of producing decisions favoring marriage equality.[31] Particularly in controversial areas of public policy, such as death penalty cases and same-sex marriage cases, electoral incentives encourage state supreme court justices to vote consistently with the preferences of their constituents. With elected judges less capable of producing decisions favoring the legalization of same-sex marriage, the adoption of state constitutional amendments would become less necessary. I therefore expect opponents of same-sex marriage to have been less likely to push for constitutional amendments in states with elected supreme courts.

Additional Considerations

A general problem with institutional explanations for the enactment of public policies is that government institutions are, for the most part, static. Although of course there have been changes in the methods of selection and retention used for high court judges and in their levels of professionalization, among other institutional characteristics, these institutional features have generally been slow to change and are therefore best characterized as latent features of a state's political system. The challenge, then, is to explain why latent features of political systems might account for the adoption of same-sex marriage amendments in particular years.

The most likely explanation is that latent public attitudes about state institutions become activated once other, more routine policy considerations put constitutional amendments on the policy agenda. In other words, institutional explanations might be less relevant to policy initiation than to adoption. These theoretical expectations are consistent with the findings of Chapter 5, which found that environmental considerations have primarily influenced which courts have been asked by LGBT litigants to consider the marriage question, whereas institutional considerations have determined which state courts have actually ruled in favor of same-sex couples.

Because institutional features are slow to change and implicate a broad range of specific public policies, they are too diffuse to account for why particular

---

[31] For a comprehensive list of citations, see *supra* Chapter 1, note 7.

constitutional amendments are under consideration at a particular point in time. Instead, policy initiation is driven by more variable, policy-based explanations, such as public attitudes about a policy, party control of state government, and so forth. Once constitutional amendments are on the agenda, however, institutional features become more relevant to determining whether the amendments actually pass. For this reason, in the analysis below, I develop separate models for the initial consideration and adoption of amendments. My expectation is that the initial consideration of amendments will be primarily driven by policy considerations, whereas institutional considerations will influence whether particular amendments are adopted.

Research Design

To analyze the patterns of adoption of state constitutional amendments prohibiting same-sex marriage, I once again used event history analysis.[32] I developed two models, one focusing on the initial consideration of amendments and the other modeling the adoption of amendments. For the initial consideration model, the dependent variable records whether a state in a given year considered an amendment prohibiting same-sex marriage. For policy adoption, the dependent variable records whether a state in a given year passed an amendment.

Following the format of dependent variables used in other policy diffusion studies, the dependent variables are coded 0 for every year in which a state has not acted and 1 when it does, with no further observations recorded. Alabama, for example, enacted a constitutional amendment prohibiting same-sex marriages in 2006, so for the policy adoption model, the dependent variable for Alabama is coded 0 from 1998 to 2005, and 1 in 2006, with no observations recorded after that year. Because Hawaii was the first state to consider an amendment, I excluded it from the analysis, setting the year of entry into the risk set for other states at 1998, the year after Hawaii's amendment was introduced in the state legislature. I assume that no state was at risk of considering or adopting an amendment before that time.

Measuring initial consideration varied depending on whether states permit initiative amendments. For states that do not use initiative amendments, I followed Haider-Markel in defining consideration as the introduction of an amendment in the state legislature.[33] When states do permit initiative amendments, the date of introduction could also be the year that the threshold number of signatures was collected. For all states, I used Lexis to scan regional and national news sources to find the first mention that an amendment had been introduced in the state legislature or that the required number of signatures had been collected.

[32] See Chapter 5 for a fuller discussion of event history analysis.
[33] *See* Haider-Markel, *supra* Chapter 2, note 79.

A. COURT ATTRIBUTES

My first hypothesis predicts that the adoption of state constitutional amendments will vary depending on the capacity of state courts to produce decisions requiring marriage equality. To test this hypothesis, I developed variables measuring several different dimensions of judicial capacity. First, I included Squire's measure of the level of professionalization of state high courts, based on judicial salaries, the size of their staffs, and their levels of docket control.[34] As discussed above, I expect the public to be more likely to support amendments when courts are professionalized because these courts are more likely to side with disadvantaged parties.

I also expect the independence of state courts to influence the passage of same-sex marriage amendments. Specifically, I expect the public to be less likely to support amendments in judicial election states because electoral incentives make judges less capable of voting in favor of marriage equality. To test this hypothesis, I included dummy variables measuring whether states used either PARTISAN ELECTIONS or NONPARTISAN ELECTIONS for the initial selection[35] of high court judges.[36] I also included a direct measure of independence, developed by Choi et al.,[37] which measures the percentage of the time that state judges on a court vote with judges from the opposite party. State high courts ranked closer to +1 are highly independent, whereas courts ranked closer to -1 are less independent. I expect that as the INDEPENDENCE of state high courts increases, the adoption of same-sex marriage amendments will be more likely.

B. JUDICIAL BEHAVIOR

In addition to considering institutional characteristics of state courts, I also expect the behavior of state court judges to influence the decision to adopt an amendment. For example, I expect that citizens will be more likely to support amendments when their high court judges have already ruled in favor of marriage equality (PRO-SSM HIGH COURT DECISION). I also measured whether a lower court ruling was in effect favoring the legalization of same-sex marriage (PRO-SSM LOWER COURT DECISION), using the same methodology. On the other hand, when judges in the state, at any level, have ruled against the legalization of same-sex marriage,

---

[34] *See* Squire, *Measuring the Professionalization of State Courts of Last Resort, supra* Chapter 1, note 59.

[35] I chose initial selection because it includes judges who are selected, but not retained, in contested elections. The electoral connection may be somewhat weaker in these states, but judges are still more likely to reflect public values, making them less capable of producing decisions that are at odds with public opinion.

[36] The baseline category includes appointment and merit systems. Classifications of judicial selection procedures are consistent with Table 2.1 and reflect the fact that methods of selection have changed over time. For example, Arkansas switched from partisan to nonpartisan elections in 2000, whereas North Carolina made this switch in 2002.

[37] *See* Choi et al., *supra* Chapter 5, note 23.

amendments should be less likely (ANTI-SSM COURT DECISION). As with the PRO-SSM HIGH COURT DECISION variable, I recorded 1 for every state year in which a court decision was in effect opposing the legalization of same-sex marriage. I also controlled for MEDIAN HIGH COURT IDEOLOGY, using a measure taken from the Lindquist database,[38] with the expectation that liberal courts will be more likely to favor marriage equality and will therefore be the target of constitutional amendments.

Next I tested for whether the adoption of amendments is less likely when judges have prestigious reputations. As Choi et al. discuss, judges who are prestigious, who are cited frequently by their peers in other states, tend to produce high quality opinions, which benefit their own states' citizens.[39] Even if citizens are not directly knowledgeable about the reputations of their judges, they are likely to be aware of whether their judges are adequately serving them, and these considerations might influence the passage of amendments. I therefore hypothesized that when state supreme court justices are prestigious, the enactment of state constitutional amendments is less likely. I measured state court reputation using a measure of opinion quality created by Choi et al.[40] Like other measures of judicial prestige,[41] it is based on the number of citations to a state high court's opinions by out-of-state judges, including judges on other state courts, the U.S. Supreme Court, and other federal courts outside the home circuit.[42]

C. CONSTITUTIONAL FEATURES

I also controlled for variations in state constitutional systems that might influence the enactment of amendments. Arguably the most important of these differences are variations in state constitutional amendment procedures. The potential for state supreme courts to influence same-sex marriage policy is likely to be diminished in initiative amendment states because citizens can more easily revise their constitutions to ensure that the justices interpret state marriage law consistently with their values. The INITIATIVE AMENDMENT variable is coded 1 when a state

---

[38] LINDQUIST, *supra* Chapter 5, note 18.

[39] *See* Choi et al., *supra* Chapter 5, note 23, at 1321 ("A high quality opinion benefits the litigants themselves and everyone in the state whose activities might bring them under the law at issue.").

[40] *Id.*

[41] *See* Caldeira, *On the Reputation of State Supreme Courts*, *supra* Chapter 5, note 23; and Klein & Morrisroe, *supra* Chapter 5, note 23.

[42] Although it is true that this variable most directly measures a state court's out-of-state influence, Choi et al. treat it as a general measure of judicial quality. *See* Choi et al., *supra* Chapter 5, note 23, at 1321–322 ("[I]nfluence and high quality opinions are highly correlated. Focusing on influence…will likely measure an attribute…that benefits litigants and in-state residents."). A major advantage of their measure over previous measures of prestige is that it is based on data from 1998 through 2006, so the data are contemporaneous with the study period.

permits either direct or indirect initiatives to propose constitutional amendments, and 0 otherwise.

Aside from looking at amendment procedures, I controlled for the rate at which state constitutions are amended. When constitutions are amended with greater frequency, the text is likely to seem more malleable and less sacred, which can make citizens and public officials more willing to change it. To capture this effect, I included a variable developed by Lutz[43] and featured in the State Politics and the Judiciary Database,[44] measuring the rate at which each state's constitution has been amended. I expect that as the AMENDMENT RATE increases, the likelihood of a same-sex marriage amendment will also increase.

D. LEGISLATIVE ATTRIBUTES AND BEHAVIOR

Although I expect the adoption of state constitutional amendments to be associated primarily with attributes of state courts, I controlled for two attributes of state legislatures that might be associated with the adoption of amendments. I controlled for LEGISLATIVE PROFESSIONALIZATION, using Squire's measure, to test whether amendments are related to state legislative capacity.[45] I also examined whether the public is less likely to support amendments when a statute is already in place prohibiting same-sex marriage (ANTI-SSM STATUTE). I included these variables primarily as controls, to affirm that the adoption of amendments is primarily related to the behavior and attributes of state courts. I do not expect these variables to be statistically significant.

E. ENVIRONMENTAL EXPLANATIONS

The next variables test environmental explanations for the adoption of state constitutional amendments. Because same-sex marriage is a morality policy, its politics should be driven mostly by citizen attitudes about the issue. The first variable measures citizen attitudes about same-sex marriage (PRO-SSM CITIZEN ATTITUDES), using Lax and Phillips's issue-specific same-sex marriage scores.[46] I hypothesize that when a state's citizens are more supportive of same-sex marriage, they will be less likely to approve constitutional amendments prohibiting the practice.

Additionally, I expect elite attitudes about same-sex marriage to influence the enactment of amendments. In particular, I expect amendments prohibiting

---

[43] See Lutz, supra note 8.

[44] LINDQUIST, supra Chapter 5, note 18.

[45] Squire, Professionalization and Public Opinion of State Legislatures, supra note 20; and Squire, Measuring Legislative Professionalism, supra note 25.

[46] See Lax & Phillips, supra Chapter 2, note 77.

same-sex marriage to be less likely the more institutions of state government that the Democratic Party controls. I coded the DEMOCRATIC CONTROL variable on a scale of 0 to 3, based on the number of state institutions the Democratic Party controlled in a given state year.[47] Consistently with other research on same-sex marriage policy,[48] I controlled for whether it was an election year for the governor (ELECTION YEAR—GOVERNOR) or the lower house of the state legislature (ELECTION YEAR—LEGISLATURE), with the expectation that amendments will be more common in election years. I also controlled for whether it was a presidential election year (ELECTION YEAR—PRESIDENT), because reports suggest that some amendments were introduced by interest groups to mobilize the conservative base of the Republican Party to vote for Republican presidential candidates.[49]

Finally, I included a variable measuring the level of party competition in a given state year.[50] Research has found that states with high levels of party competition have more competitive elections, which influence the behavior of office holders.[51] Haider-Markel found that states with high levels of party competition were less likely to consider laws prohibiting same-sex marriage because of the political risks involved with taking a position on such a high-profile and controversial issue.[52] For similar reasons, I expect higher levels of party competition to be negatively associated with the enactment of state constitutional amendments prohibiting same-sex

[47] Included institutions were the governor's office, the lower house of the state legislature, and the upper house. For Nebraska, which has a unicameral legislature, the DEMOCRATIC CONTROL variable was coded 3 when Democrats controlled both the legislature and the governor's office.

[48] *See* Barclay & Fisher, *The States and the Differing Impetus for Divergent Paths on Same-Sex Marriage*, *supra* Chapter 2, note 79.

[49] *See* Alan Cooperman & Thomas Edsall, *Evangelicals Say They Led Charge for the GOP*, WASH. POST, Nov. 8, 2004, at A1; and Daniel A. Smith, Matthew DeSantis & Jason Kessel, *Same-Sex Marriage Ballot Measures and the 2004 Presidential Election*, 38 ST. & LOC. GOV'T REV. 78 (2006).

[50] Originally, I included variables measuring the size of the evangelical population in each state as well as the visibility of the gay population. However, I found that the measures were highly correlated with PRO-SSM CITIZEN ATTITUDES, leading me to conclude that they were simply proxies for citizen attitudes about same-sex marriage. Because I already have a direct measure of citizen attitudes in the models, I excluded these variables. For similar reasons, I excluded variables measuring the median household income, the percentage of the population living in an urban area, and the percentage of the population with a high school diploma.

[51] *See* DUBOIS, *supra* Chapter 2, note 46; Samuel C. Patterson & Gregory A. Caldeira, *The Mobilization of Voters in Congressional Elections*, 47 J. POL. 490 (1985); Henry R. Gick & George W. Pruet, Jr., *Dissent in State Supreme Courts: Patterns and Correlates of Conflict, in* JUDICIAL CONFLICTS AND CONSENSUS: BEHAVIORAL STUDIES OF AMERICAN APPELLATE COURTS (Sheldon Goldman & Charles M. Lamb eds., 1986); Brace & Hall, *Neo-Institutionalism and Dissent in State Supreme Courts*, *supra* Chapter 1, note 7; Brace & Hall, *Integrated Models of Judicial Dissent*, *supra* Chapter 1, note 7; Hall, *State Supreme Courts in American Democracy*, *supra* Chapter 2, note 47; and Chris W. Bonneau & Melinda Gann Hall, *Predicting Challengers in State Supreme Court Elections: Context and the Politics of Institutional Design*, 56 POL. RES. Q. 337 (2003).

[52] Haider-Markel, *supra* Chapter 2, note 79; *see also* Mooney & Lee, *supra* Chapter 1, note 63.

marriage. To measure PARTY COMPETITION, I use the political competition index developed by Holbrook and Van Dunk,[53] recalculated from the original Ranney Index.[54]

F. REGIONAL EFFECTS

State policy research has long emphasized the importance of regional effects on policy diffusion,[55] finding that states are more likely to adopt policies that have already been adopted by bordering states or other states in the same region. This research has measured regional effects using a variety of indicators, including the number of border states to have adopted a policy[56] and the number of states in a census division to have adopted it.[57] Neither method is perfect because each risks underreporting regional effects. Using the census division excludes border states that have been classified into different census divisions, but using border states excludes regional states that are similar but not on the border. A way of overcoming this problem is by using both measures; however previous research on gay rights policy[58] and morality policy in general[59] has suggested that the census division is the better measure because it captures the types of regional cultural values that may influence same-sex marriage policy diffusion. To keep the model parsimonious, this analysis uses the census division. Specifically, I included two variables, following procedures developed by Mooney.[60] The REGIONAL EFFECTS variable is a count of the number of states in a particular state's census division to have adopted an amendment prohibiting same-sex marriage in each state year. The second variable, PIECEWISE, is a piecewise interaction term that assesses whether the regional effect changed after 2004, the breakpoint year.[61] The PIECEWISE variable assumes a value

---

[53] Thomas Holbrook & Emily Van Dunk, *Electoral Competition in the American States*, 87 AM. POL. SCI. REV. 955 (1993).

[54] Austin Ranney, *Parties in State Politics*, in POLITICS IN THE AMERICAN STATES (Herbert Jacob & Kenneth Vines, eds., 1976).

[55] See Berry & Berry, *State Lottery Adoptions as Policy Innovations, supra* Chapter 5, note 56; Berry & Berry, *Tax Innovation in the States, supra* Chapter 5, note 56; Mooney & Lee, *supra* Chapter 1, note 63; and Mooney, *supra* Chapter 5, note 56.

[56] See Berry & Berry, *State Lottery Adoptions as Policy Innovations, supra* Chapter 5, note 56; and Mintrom, *supra* Chapter 5, note 56.

[57] See Mooney & Lee, *supra* Chapter 1, note 63.

[58] See Haider-Markel, *supra* Chapter 2, note 79.

[59] See Frances Stokes Berry & William D. Berry, *Innovation and Diffusion Models in Policy Research*, in THEORIES OF THE POLICY PROCESS (Paul E. Sabatier, ed., 1999).

[60] Mooney, *supra* Chapter 5, note 56.

[61] I set the breakpoint year at 2004, when thirteen states amended their constitutions to prohibit same-sex marriage. Twelve of these states amended their constitutions on the same day, November 2, 2004, the date of the 2004 presidential election. The sudden increase in the number of amendments appears to have had an impact on adoptions in regions throughout the country. Through 2004, the

of 0 through 2004, but after 2004 counts the number of states that enacted an amendment since the breakpoint. Together, these variables permit an evaluation of whether the enactment of amendments has been influenced by the activities of other states in the region and whether regional effects have changed over time.[62]

Results

The results, presented in Table 7.3, affirm that both institutional and environmental conditions have influenced the adoption of state constitutional amendments prohibiting the legalization of same-sex marriage. The initial consideration and adoption models are each presented in full and reduced formats, with the reduced

Table 7.3 **Event History Analysis of the Enactment of State Constitutional Amendments Prohibiting Same-Sex Marriage, 1997–2008 (Logistic Regression Coefficients, Standard Errors in Parentheses)**

	Consideration (Full Model)	Consideration (Reduced Model)	Adoption (Full Model)	Adoption (Reduced Model)
Court Attributes				
High Court Professionalization	0.478 (2.235)		5.783* (2.536)	3.229* (1.664)
Partisan Elections	−0.545 (0.709)		−0.350 (0.919)	
Nonpartisan Elections	0.840 (0.617)		1.002 (0.648)	
Independence	−0.978 (2.720)		−0.273 (3.783)	
Judicial Behavior				
Pro-SSM High Court Decision	2.504* (1.149)	2.000* (0.981)	4.956** (1.664)	4.276** (1.359)
Pro-SSM Lower Court Decision	−0.473 (1.503)		3.353** (1.318)	2.952** (1.133)

(Continued)

average proportion of adjacent adopters (APAA) did not exceed 10 percent, but by the twenty-eighth adoption four years later, in 2008, the APAA doubled to 23.0 percent. The trends suggest that 2004 was the break-point year, after which the diffusion of amendments became more rapid.

[62] *See* Mooney, *supra* Chapter 5, note 56, for more about the calculation procedure. For each year and unit, the interaction term is the multiple of (a) a dummy variable coded 0 before the break point and 1 after the break point; and (b) a count of the number of states in the region to have adopted the

Table 7.3 (Continued)

	Consideration (Full Model)	Consideration (Reduced Model)	Adoption (Full Model)	Adoption (Reduced Model)
Anti-SSM Court Decision	−0.475 (0.693)		−1.045 (0.904)	
Median High Court Ideology	0.006 (0.015)		−0.005 (0.018)	
High Court Reputation	−0.025 (0.053)		−0.154** (0.060)	−0.149** (0.055)
Constitutional Features				
Initiative Amendment	0.259 (0.555)		2.215** (0.731)	2.009*** (0.571)
Amendment Rate	−0.104 (0.187)		0.071 (0.188)	
Legislative Attributes/ Behavior				
Legislative Professionalization	0.127 (3.224)		−3.941 (4.251)	
Anti-SSM Statute	−0.296 (0.745)		−1.253 (1.027)	
Policy Considerations				
Pro-SSM Citizen Attitudes	−0.088* (0.043)	−0.069** (0.025)	−0.211*** (0.061)	−0.188*** (0.047)
Democratic Control	−0.000 (0.264)		−0.465 (0.307)	−0.546* (0.250)
Party Competition	0.005 (0.030)		0.001 (0.031)	
Election Year—Governor	1.067 (0.570)	0.867 (0.506)	1.316* (0.688)	1.586** (0.525)
Election Year—Legislature	1.527* (0.709)	1.497* (0.661)	0.844 (0.838)	
Election Year—President	1.010 (0.600)	1.066* (0.528)	1.570* (0.764)	1.997** (0.593)

	Consideration (Full Model)	Consideration (Reduced Model)	Adoption (Full Model)	Adoption (Reduced Model)
Regional Effects				
Regional Effects	0.182 (0.285)		1.114*** (0.337)	0.957*** (0.298)
Piecewise	0.719 (0.718)		−1.434* (0.718)	−1.435* (0.677)
Spline	1.315*** (0.247)	1.181*** (0.207)	0.989** (0.312)	0.864** (0.276)
Constant	1.449 (2.134)	0.923 (1.094)	4.539 (2.684)	3.917* (1.721)
Wald Chi²	47.020**	47.030***	40.690**	40.670***
N	382	382	442	442

$^*p < 0.05$; $^{**}p < 0.01$; $^{***}p < 0.001$ (2-tailed)

models including only variables that were statistically significant at $p < 0.10$ or better in the full models.[63] Consistent with expectations, the adoption of amendments is associated with HIGH COURT PROFESSIONALIZATION. The positive,

policy since the break point. To clarify the coding procedure, consider the patterns of regional diffusion that occurred in Division 8, a census region that includes Arizona, Colorado, Idaho, Montana, New Mexico, Nevada, Utah, and Wyoming. By 2008, six of the eight states in this region had enacted constitutional amendments prohibiting same-sex marriage, with only New Mexico and Wyoming declining to enact amendments in this period. The first state to approve an amendment was Nevada in 2002, followed by Montana and Utah in 2004, Colorado and Idaho in 2006, and Arizona in 2008. Counting the number of regional states to have previously adopted an amendment prohibiting same-sex marriage (REGIONAL EFFECT) is fairly straightforward. In 2002, no states in the region had enacted a same-sex marriage amendment. After 2002, until 2004, only one state had enacted an amendment, after which three states had previously approved amendments through 2006. The PIECEWISE variable measures whether the regional effect changed after the break-point year, which is hypothesized to be 2004. The variable assumes a value of 0 for each year through 2004 and then beginning in 2005 it is equivalent to the number of regional states since 2004 to have enacted a constitutional amendment. In Division 8, when both Colorado and Idaho enacted same-sex marriage amendments on the same day in 2006, no other states in the region had enacted similar amendments since the break-point year, so the PIECEWISE variable is coded as 0. After 2006, however, the PIECEWISE variable is assigned a value of 2 through 2008, when Arizona became the third state in the region after the break-point year to enact an amendment.

[63] To control for duration dependence, I developed cubic spline terms for each model, using a "spline" macro for Stata developed by Sasieni, *supra* Chapter 5, note 59. *See also* Buckley & Westerland, *supra* Chapter 5, note 59.

statistically significant relationships in both adoption columns affirm that as the professionalization of state high courts increases, the likelihood that states will adopt amendments prohibiting same-sex marriage also increases. This finding is consistent with my hypothesis that professionalized courts are more likely to be targeted by amendments because of their tendency to side with disadvantaged parties.

Although professionalization influences the adoption of amendments, it has no influence on their initial consideration. This finding is also consistent with expectations. As I discussed above, professionalization is a relatively stable feature of a state's political system that is unlikely to account for why particular types of amendments are on the agenda in given state years. Instead, the initial consideration of amendments is driven primarily by policy considerations. The more that the public favors the legalization of same-sex marriage (PRO-SSM CITIZEN ATTITUDES), the less likely that states are to consider amendments. Initial consideration is also affected by whether it is a legislative election year (ELECTION YEAR—LEGISLATURE), and whether it is a presidential election year (ELECTION YEAR—PRESIDENT). The latter finding corroborates reports that conservative interest groups sought to introduce the amendments during presidential election years to mobilize the conservative base of the Republican Party.

Additionally, Table 7.3 reports that the initial consideration of amendments has been more likely when state high courts have ruled in favor of the legalization of same-sex marriage (PRO-SSM HIGH COURT DECISION). As expected, this state court activity has also influenced adoption. Table 7.3 reports that adoption has been more likely when state high courts have ruled in favor of same-sex marriage (PRO-SSM HIGH COURT DECISION), as well as when lower courts have favored marriage equality (PRO-SSM LOWER COURT DECISION), but that adoption is not associated with court decisions opposing the legalization of same-sex marriage (ANTI-SSM COURT DECISION). The implication of this finding is that efforts by state high courts to change the policy status quo have encouraged the adoption of amendments, but that adoption has not been influenced by state court decisions that have maintained current policy. Adoption is also unrelated to LEGISLATIVE PROFESSIONALIZATION and the presence of an ANTI-SSM STATUTE, consistent with my expectation that the adoption of same-sex marriage amendments has been a response primarily to state courts.

Contrary to expectations, the independence of courts has no systematic influence on the adoption of amendments. Neither the method of selection used for high court judges (PARTISAN ELECTIONS, NONPARTISAN ELECTIONS) nor their tendency to vote with judges from the opposing party (INDEPENDENCE) is associated with the adoption of amendments. Opponents of same-sex marriage therefore do not appear to take judicial selection methods into account when deciding whether to adopt amendments. The explanation for this finding is not immediately clear. It could be that appointed judges are not the special target of amendments, as hypothesized, because the public also has incentives to curb the power of elected judges. As the previous chapter demonstrated, the public is less likely to trust elected judges to resolve the marriage question, as elected judges are less likely to appear to be principled decision makers who are above politics.

On the other hand, Table 7.3 reports that amendments are more likely in states that permit initiative amendments (INITIATIVE AMENDMENT), corroborating research that has found that gay rights groups and other political minorities fare less well under systems of direct democracy.[64] Courthouse democracy therefore does appear to limit the capacity of judges to have a lasting impact on government policy, at least in this one respect. The democratization of state constitutional amendment procedures has made it difficult for judges in states such as California to exercise policy leadership on salient issues such as same-sex marriage. Unlike federal judges, or judges from states that lack initiative amendment procedures, judges in initiative states can have unpopular rulings overturned relatively easily.

Other trends in Table 7.3 are also worth noting. Consistent with expectations, Table 7.3 reports that elite attitudes influence the adoption of amendments prohibiting same-sex marriage. In the reduced model, adoption is related to the number of institutions of state government that the Democratic Party controls (DEMOCRATIC CONTROL). Table 7.3 also indicates that amendments are less likely to be adopted when high court judges have prestigious reputations (HIGH COURT REPUTATION), suggesting that amendments are less likely when judges are serving their constituents well. Finally, Table 7.3 reports that the adoption of state constitutional amendments has been influenced by regional effects. Amendments have been more likely as the number of states enacting constitutional amendments in the same census division has increased (REGIONAL EFFECTS), but these effects became attenuated after 2004 (PIECEWISE).

What, then, can we conclude about when states have been more likely to enact constitutional amendments prohibiting same-sex marriage? Overall, it would appear that amendments have been more likely to get on the agenda in states in which high courts have ruled in favor of same-sex marriage and in which public support for same-sex marriage is low. Amendments have also been introduced during presidential election years to mobilize conservative voters to come to the polls and vote for Republican candidates. The adoption of amendments, however, is a more deliberative process. It matters not only whether courts have ruled in favor of the legalization of same-sex marriage, but whether judges are serving the public well. It also matters whether courts appear capable of voting in favor of same-sex marriage in the future. When state high courts are professionalized, adoption is more likely. Adoption also occurs more commonly in initiative states, in which citizens play a greater role in the amendment process, but adoption is less likely when the Democratic Party controls state government.

[64] Interestingly, and contrary to expectations, the findings suggest that amendment procedures are related to adoption but not initial consideration. To explain these trends, it should be noted that it is very easy for opponents of same-sex marriage to propose amendments, requiring only that a legislator sponsor an amendment. With the barrier to entry so low, there is little reason to think that proposing amendments should be easier in initiative states. On the other hand, adoption should be easier in initiative states, particularly direct initiative states, because the support of the legislature is not required to secure passage.

Conclusion

The results provide important insights into the factors that influence the capacity of state courts to have an enduring impact on government policy. First, the results suggest that the passage of constitutional amendments prohibiting same-sex marriage has been a response to state court activity, as courts have been targeted based on their capacity to produce rulings favoring marriage equality. As Rosenberg and others have suggested, the goal of the amendments was to prevent state courts from following judges in Hawaii and Massachusetts and imposing same-sex marriage on unwilling publics.[65] It makes sense, then, that among the states that were more likely to adopt amendments were those in which judges had already produced rulings in favor of same-sex marriage and those in which judges appeared capable of producing decisions requiring marriage equality at some point in the future.

A second important finding is that amendments are more likely to be adopted in states that employ initiative amendment procedures. As the amendment process becomes more democratized, the likelihood that judicial power will be curbed or preempted increases. The implication of this finding may be troubling to reform groups, such as supporters of same-sex marriage, who would use courts as instruments of social change. The logic of a litigation strategy is that minority groups can turn to courts for relief when majorities impose on their rights. When state judicial outlets are closed off through the amendment process, important checks on majority tyranny are lost. State constitutional amendments leave minority groups with few options but to appeal to the federal courts.

What, then, can account for the fact that the California Supreme Court's 2008 same-sex marriage decision was overturned when a decision from the same year in Connecticut was not? To begin with, the California court was probably not aided by the fact that it ranks highly in its level of professionalization. California ranks first in professionalization, compared to Connecticut, which ranks twenty-seventh. Based on the findings of the event history analysis, one would expect a state court that ranks so highly in professionalization to be targeted because of the tendency of professionalized courts to rule in favor of disadvantaged litigants. My suspicion, however, is that professionalization is not sufficient to explain the different outcomes here because both courts had already acted on the marriage question by the time that constitutional amendments were being considered in 2008. Both courts had already proven themselves capable of legalizing same-sex marriage.

Instead, the reason for the differing outcomes in Connecticut and California is most likely grounded in the ease with which the state constitution in California can be overturned. In Connecticut a proposed amendment requires the approval of three-quarters of both houses of the state legislature convening in two successive sessions before it is submitted to the voters. In California, the citizens can pass

---

[65] ROSENBERG, *supra* Chapter 1, note 3; *see also* Rosenberg & Breslau, *supra* note 18.

over the heads of their legislators and put amendments directly on the ballot. State supreme court decisions that rule in favor of minority interests can therefore be overturned relatively easily by majorities who disapprove of those decisions.

Comparisons to Massachusetts are instructive. The immediate public reaction to *Goodridge v. Department of Public Health* was not favorable, and in fact the state legislature twice approved constitutional amendments that would have overturned the decision. One of these amendments, initially approved by the legislature in 2007, was the result of a citizen initiative. Yet, the Massachusetts constitution cannot be amended so easily. Each of the proposed amendments had to be approved by the state legislature in two consecutive legislative sessions, but neither amendment had enough support the second time around to be placed on the ballot for a public vote. The deliberation built into the amendment process in Massachusetts permits time for public and elite indignation at a state supreme court decision to diffuse, giving judges more opportunity for influence over controversial public policies.

Surely if the amendment process had been more deliberative in California in 2008, same-sex marriage would have survived the year and perhaps much longer. There was little interest in the California legislature in overturning the state supreme court's decision. The legislature had even tried to legalize same-sex marriage in 2005, but Governor Arnold Schwarzenegger had vetoed the measure.[66] By 2008 the governor was more supportive of same-sex marriage and announced his opposition to Proposition 8.[67] If the legislature had been required to approve Proposition 8 before it had been placed on the ballot, there is a good chance it never would have gone to the voters. Initiative amendment procedures limited the impact of the California Supreme Court, just as different amendment procedures enhanced the impact of the Supreme Judicial Court of Massachusetts.

In explaining the different reactions to the same-sex marriage decisions in California, Connecticut, and Massachusetts, it appears that institutional variations among the states made all of the difference. *Goodridge* survived because it was protected by more restrictive amendment procedures, just as California's decision fell to an amendment process that was much less burdensome. The California Supreme Court failed to have an enduring impact on state policy, not because of what it ruled or how it defended its judgment in its opinion, but because of forces beyond its control. State supreme court decisions are only as enduring as institutional conditions permit them to be.

[66] See Lynda Gledhill, *Governor's Gay-Rights Moves Please No One; Marriage Bill Vetoed, Partner Benefits Preserved*, S.F. CHRON., Sept. 30, 2005, at A1; Nancy Vogel & Jordan Rau, *Gov. Vetoes Same-Sex Marriage Bill; Schwarzenegger Rejects 52 Bills, Including Ones to Raise the Minimum Wage and Give Residents Access to Cheaper Prescriptions in Canada*, L.A. TIMES, Sept. 30, 2005, at B3.

[67] See Michael Rothfeld & Tony Barboza, *Governor Backs Gay Marriage; Schwarzenegger Voices Hope That Proposition 8 Will Be Overturned by Courts as Crowds Continue to Protest*, L.A. TIMES, Nov. 10, 2008, at B1.

CHAPTER 8

The Promise of State Courts

The celebrations were restrained on the first anniversary of same-sex marriage in California. "Had we not have lost Prop. 8, I think there would be a lot more celebrating on the one-year anniversary," said Tom Felkner, who married his husband, Bob Lehman, in June 2008. "Unfortunately, all of our energies have gone into our disappointment and not celebrating people gaining their civil rights and gaining their equality."[1] Eighteen thousand same-sex couples had married before Proposition 8 overturned the California Supreme Court's decision, *In re Marriage Cases*,[2] and these marriages were still intact. But other same-sex couples in California would have to seek marriage elsewhere, in states such as Massachusetts and Connecticut, where court decisions favoring same-sex marriage had not yet been overturned.

I began this book with the question of why some state supreme courts have a greater impact on salient morality policies than others. Based on the findings in the previous chapters, which are summarized in Table 8.1, it is possible to formulate a response. In general, the results suggest that the impact of courts is not constant but

Table 8.1 **Factors Influencing Judicial Policy Development**

	Initiation	→	*Legitimation*	→	*Endurance*
Institutional Differences	• Judicial Selection • Professionalization		• Judicial Selection		• Professionalization • Judicial Reputation
Constitutional Differences	• ERA				• Initiative Procedures
Environmental Differences	• Citizen Ideology • Institution Ideology • Interest Groups		• Citizen Ideology		• Citizen Ideology • Institution Ideology

[1] Jared Grigsby, *Jubilation Muted on Calif Gay Marriage Anniversary*, THE ASSOCIATED PRESS, June 16, 2009.

[2] In re Marriage Cases, 43 Cal. 4th 757 (2008).

188

variable, depending on institutional and environmental conditions that vary from state to state. The potential for state courts to influence government policy can be affected by their institutional design, the nature of a state's constitutional system, and the political and cultural environments in which state supreme court justices operate. In the area of same-sex marriage policy, these conditions have influenced the transmission of judicial policy innovations to other states, public reactions to state court decisions, and the passage of state constitutional amendments curbing judicial power.

The particular institutional and environmental factors that influence the impact of state supreme courts depend on the stage of judicial policy development that one is studying. With regards to policy initiation, the findings suggest that different factors influence whether judges are willing to innovate in same-sex marriage policy and whether they have the opportunity to do so. Judges are less likely to have the opportunity to innovate on the marriage question in states with conservative citizens and institutions because these states are less likely to produce appropriate test cases that would permit judges to legalize same-sex marriage. But even when judges have the opportunity to act, they might be unwilling to do so depending on their ideological preferences and their manner of selection. Elected judges, who are accountable to the voting public, have more to risk than judges who have life tenure or are reappointed.

Policy legitimation, specifically the capacity for state judges to influence public opinion, has also depended on the method of judicial selection. The findings from my survey experiment in Chapter 6 indicate that citizens are less likely to support state court decisions favoring the legalization of same-sex marriage when judges in their states are retained in contested partisan or nonpartisan elections. These findings are corroborated by my analysis of a second poll conducted by the *Washington Post*/ABC News, which found that citizens in states with appointed courts are more likely to trust their judges to deal with the issues of gay marriage, abortion, and the death penalty. The explanation for these findings is grounded in how different selection and retention systems influence public perceptions of judicial independence. Because elected judges are less independent than judges in appointment and merit systems, they are less likely to appear as principled decision makers who are above politics, thereby losing the institutional mechanism that permits them to build public support for government policies.

As with policy initiation and legitimation, policy endurance has been influenced by attributes of courts, but in this case I found that the degree of high court professionalization mattered more than the methods of selection and retention. The findings of the event history analysis in Chapter 7 indicate that professionalized courts, which are more capable of providing full, fair hearings to disadvantaged parties, have been more likely to be the targets of amendments curbing their power. The findings also indicate that variations in state constitutional amendment procedures have influenced when same-sex marriage amendments have been adopted. The ability of citizens to propose amendments directly through the initiative process has made it easier for opponents of same-sex marriage to overturn state court decisions they dislike, as demonstrated by the passage of Proposition 8 in California in 2008. Opponents of same-sex marriage have also been able to use initiative amendment procedures to preempt the activities of state judges who have not yet considered the marriage question. States that lack initiative amendment procedures, which require instead that their legislatures propose constitutional amendments, have been less likely to approve amendments.

The portrait of state judicial impact that emerges from these accounts may be disheartening to supporters of same-sex marriage and other reform groups who would use state courts as instruments of social change. Collectively, the findings suggest that when state judiciaries and state constitutional systems increase in their levels of democratization, their capacity to check democratic processes is diminished. Court decisions on salient morality policies such as same-sex marriage are less likely to have a lasting impact, or even to be produced, when judges are accountable to the voting public and when state constitutions are relatively easy to amend. Courthouse democracy makes judges less trusted to resolve these types of controversies, and it makes their decisions on these issues less resilient.

The normative implications of these findings are complicated. On the one hand, it would seem to be unquestionably good for citizens to have more democratically accountable institutions. The movement toward judicial elections and initiative amendment procedures was designed to increase citizen participation in government, to ensure that state judiciaries and constitutional systems reflect public values instead of the values of elites; in fact, research indicates that the democratization of judicial institutions has increased voter participation and knowledge of judicial candidates.[3] Surely it is good for a democracy to have representative institutions and informed citizens. On the other hand, it is also important for a democracy to have institutions that are capable of resisting majoritarian sentiment and of preserving the rights of minorities. The problem with democratizing state constitutions and judicial institutions is that courts become less capable of serving in this capacity. The data in this book suggest that elected judges have been reluctant to innovate and are less likely to have the public's trust when they do act. States with initiative amendment procedures have been more likely to overturn court decisions legalizing same-sex marriage and to preempt state court activity on this issue. It would seem, then, that democratization risks further marginalizing the interests of minorities. A more insulated constitutional system would not bend so easily to majority will, ensuring that minority interests are also heard and reflected in government policies.

Of course, there is no guarantee that independent judges will advance minority interests in place of their own personal values. Quite often, in fact, judges reflect

---

[3] See Melinda Gann Hall, *Voting in State Supreme Court Elections: Competition and Context as Democratic Incentives*, 69 J. POL. 1147 (2007); and BONNEAU & HALL, *supra* Chapter 1, note 67.

majoritarian sentiment regardless of how they are selected or retained.[4] It should be remembered that, at the federal level, the same U.S. Supreme Court that produced *Brown v. Board of Education*[5] and *Lawrence v. Texas*[6] also produced, in earlier times, *Plessy v. Ferguson*[7] and *Bowers v. Hardwick*,[8] decisions that disregarded minority rights in favor of popular prejudices. Critics of an independent judiciary are right to point to these decisions and to question how frequently independent judges will actually seek to act as checks on majoritarian processes. At the same time, increasing judicial accountability risks eliminating altogether the possibility that state supreme courts can act as transformative agents of social change.

The same-sex marriage movement may or may not be successful at achieving marriage equality nationwide. At the time of this writing, the issue has yet to make its way to the U.S. Supreme Court, although the issue was set to appear before the justices in the spring of 2013. If the movement is successful, then state courts will surely have been instrumental to that success. It is worth considering, however, what the success of the same-sex marriage movement would have been like if state supreme court justices in Hawaii, Massachusetts, Connecticut, and Vermont were selected or retained in contested elections. Not a single judge in a contested election state has ruled in favor of same-sex marriage. Most of these judges were not even asked to do so, no doubt because LGBT advocates understood how reluctant elected judges would be to issue controversial pro-marriage rulings.

It is also worth considering how differently marriage equality would have progressed if initiative amendment procedures were more widely adopted. The deliberation built into the amendment process in Massachusetts insulated the *Goodridge* decision from an immediate public backlash, insuring that the impact of this decision would not be as short-lived as the decision in California proved to be. It is hard to imagine that *Goodridge* would have had a comparable impact if Massachusetts had implemented democratic reforms to its state judiciary and amendment process. Time and again, the marriage equality movement has found its efforts frustrated by these types of accountability mechanisms. Although such mechanisms are appropriate in a democracy, it is also true that when constitutional systems are too democratically responsive, the capacity for minorities to influence policy is substantially reduced.

These points have not been lost on the judges who have been at the heart of the same-sex marriage cases. The Honorable Marsha Ternus, who lost her job as Chief Justice of the Iowa Supreme Court following the *Varnum* decision, commented in 2011 at a symposium at Albany Law School that judicial independence was essential

---

[4] See, for example, Dahl, *supra* Chapter 2, note 6.
[5] Brown v. Board of Education, 347 U.S. 483 (1954).
[6] Lawrence v. Texas, 539 U.S. 558 (2003).
[7] Plessy v. Ferguson, 163 U.S. 537 (1896).
[8] Bowers v. Hardwick, 478 U.S. 186 (1986).

if the rule of law was to prevail over popular prejudices. "When citizens fail to value a strong judiciary," she said, "that will make decisions free from intimidation and free from the influence of special interest groups and campaign contributors, we are all at risk of losing our liberties and rights."[9] At the same symposium, Chief Justice Margaret H. Marshall of Massachusetts—who authored the *Goodridge* decision— agreed, advocating that all judges should be retained for a single lengthy term. "That is the federal system; in my view that should be the system for all judges," she said. "If that system had been in place in Iowa, Chief Justice Ternus would still be the Chief Justice of Iowa. If we had that system in other states where the political battles are occurring, judges would not need to look over their shoulders when they have to rule in a case or make a judicial decision."[10]

Broken Promises?

State supreme courts are not necessarily dependable agents of social change. Unless state judiciaries and state constitutional systems are structured in ways that promote judicial independence, judges will be unable to range very far from what the public is willing to accept. Very few state judicial systems actually meet these requirements. Minority groups who would use state courts as instruments of social change would do well to recognize the limitations of a litigation strategy in most state courts. Many of these courts simply do not have the same capacity that federal judges have to issue decisions that are politically unpopular.

Some prominent commentators have criticized the same-sex marriage movement for this reason, for pursuing a litigation strategy in the states without an adequate foundation of public support.[11] Litigants secured victories in a handful of state courts before citizens in these states and the nation as a whole were ready to accept them. Instead of inspiring social change, the decisions led citizens across the country to amend their state constitutions, harming the long-term interests of the same-sex marriage movement by making it more difficult for litigation strategies to succeed at a later point in time, when public opinion was more open to it. According to Rosenberg, a better strategy would have been for supporters of same-sex marriage to wait until there was a clearer national shift in favor of same-sex marriage.

This characterization of the same-sex marriage decisions as a series of broken promises is, to some extent, accurate. In Hawaii and California, state supreme court justices were not able to provide same-sex couples with relief because the courts' decisions were overturned by state constitutional amendments. In Massachusetts,

---

[9] Ternus, *supra* Chapter 5, note 8, at 1576.

[10] See Margaret H. Marshall, *Remarks*, 74 ALB. L. REV. 1595, 1603 (2011).

[11] See Klarman, Brown *and* Lawrence *(and* Goodridge*), supra* Chapter 1, note 6; and ROSENBERG, *supra* Chapter 1, note 3.

Connecticut, and Iowa, the justices were able to fulfill the promises to their own citizens, but they were not able to bring change to citizens located outside of their jurisdictions because constitutional amendments in other states made it impossible for the decisions to transmit. Supporters of same-sex marriage who looked to the *Goodridge* decision as the beginning of a larger movement would be correct to observe that, in at least some respects, the decision has failed to live up to its promise.

On the other hand, this assessment is probably too pessimistic. It is hard to imagine that state legislatures would have begun legalizing same-sex marriage in 2009 if state courts had not kicked off a national conversation about marriage equality, transforming same-sex marriage from a pipe dream into a thinkable policy alternative. Support for civil unions has become even more widespread. By the beginning of 2009, most Americans indicated that they supported civil unions, even though a majority of Americans still opposed same-sex marriage itself. In a Quinnipiac University poll conducted April 21–27, 2009, 38 percent of Americans indicated that they would support a state law permitting same-sex marriage, while 55 percent of national survey respondents opposed it.[12] However, the same poll found much more support for civil unions, with 57 percent of respondents indicating that they would support a law permitting civil unions for same-sex couples, and just 38 percent opposing such a law. A *Newsweek* poll that was conducted the previous December similarly found that 55 percent of Americans supported "legally-sanctioned gay and lesbian unions or partnerships," even though only 39 percent supported "legally-sanctioned gay and lesbian marriages."[13]

Figure 8.1 reports national trends in support for same-sex marriages and civil unions between 2003 and 2009, based on a series of polls conducted by the Pew Research Center for People & the Press. Consistent with the findings of other polls, the data show that public support for civil unions was consistently above 50 percent by 2009, and that these high levels of support had come relatively recently. In 2003, when the Supreme Judicial Court of Massachusetts issued its decision in *Goodridge v. Department of Public Health*, support for civil unions was at about 40 percent. It would appear, then, that majority support for civil unions occurred only after state supreme courts began requiring full marriage equality for same-sex couples.

Civil unions also received support from unexpected places. President George W. Bush, who favored a federal constitutional amendment limiting marriage to opposite-sex couples, in 2004 came out as a supporter of civil unions. "I don't think we should deny people rights to a civil union, a legal arrangement, if that's what a

---

[12] The poll is based on a national sample of 2,041 registered voters, with a margin of error ± 2.2%. See *Quinnipiac University Poll*, POLLINGREPORT.COM (April 21–27, 2009), http://www.pollingreport.com/civil.htm.

[13] The poll was based on a national sample of 1,006 adults with a margin of error of 3.7%. See Princeton Survey Research Associates International, *Newsweek Poll* (December 3–4, 2008), http://www.pollingreport.com/civil.htm.

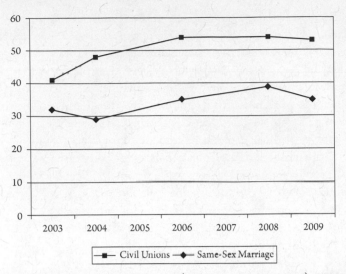

Figure 8.1 Public Support for Civil Unions (and Same-Sex Marriage), 2003–2009

Note: Surveys were based on national samples of adults, ranging from about 1,500 to 3,000 respondents, depending on the survey. For the first question, respondents were asked, "Do you strongly favor, favor, oppose, or strongly oppose allowing gay and lesbian couples to enter into legal agreements with each other that would give them many of the same rights as married couples?" For the second, respondents were asked, "Do you strongly favor, favor, oppose, or strongly oppose allowing gay and lesbian couples to marry legally?" Results above combine "favor" and "strongly favor" responses.

Source: Pew Research Center for People & the Press.

state chooses to do so," Bush said. "I view the definition of marriage different from legal arrangements that enable people to have rights. And I strongly believe that marriage ought to be defined as between, a union between a man and a woman. Now, having said that, states ought to be able to have the right to pass laws that enable people to be able to have rights like others."[14] In the conservative state of Utah, Republican (and Mormon) Governor Jon Huntsman, Jr., also expressed support for civil unions in February 2009, even though 70 percent of Utah residents opposed them.[15] "I'm a firm believer in the traditional construct of marriage, a man and a woman," he said. "But I also think that we can go a greater distance in enhancing equal rights for others in nontraditional relationships."[16] Although most residents of Utah disagreed with Huntsman's position on the issue, the governor's

[14] Elizabeth Bumiller, *Bush Says His Party is Wrong to Oppose Gay Civil Unions*, N.Y. TIMES, October 26, 2004, at A21.

[15] Rosemary Winters, *Guv, at Odds with Most Utahns, Backs Civil Unions for Gays*, SALT LAKE TRIB., February 9, 2009.

[16] Lisa Riley, *Guv Calls Self "Moderating Voice" on Many Issues*, DESERET MORNING NEWS, February 11, 2009.

support for civil unions did not cause a backlash against him. Public opinion polls conducted the next month indicated that two-thirds of citizens in the state had not changed their opinion about the governor because of his stance, and 80 percent still approved of the job that he was doing.[17]

It is hard to imagine that civil unions would have generated this kind of mainstream support if supreme courts in other states had not been authorizing marriages at the time. By setting the bar so high with their requirement of marriage, judges in states such as Massachusetts and Connecticut moved the center of politics on the issue to the left. By 2008, in much of the country, the debate had become not so much about whether same-sex couples should receive the same rights and benefits as opposite-sex couples, but what their relationships should be called. Civil unions, which in the 1990s might have seemed too radical, were established as moderate compromises for Americans who were uncomfortable with same-sex marriage. As a result, same-sex couples in many states were provided with access to a variety of benefits that were unavailable to them before state supreme courts had acted, including rights of inheritance and hospital visitation, healthcare coverage, and stepparent adoption. Some of the states, such as Vermont and New Jersey, provided these benefits as the result of court orders, but most established civil unions or domestic partnerships voluntarily, including Hawaii (1997), California (1999), Maine (2004), Connecticut (2005), New Hampshire (2007), Washington (2007), Oregon (2008), Nevada (2009), Wisconsin (2009), Delaware (2011), and Rhode Island (2011).[18]

Some commentators have maintained that the activity of state courts was not so instrumental, but instead part of a larger cultural movement that was becoming more tolerant of gay people. Rosenberg has observed that at the same time that state supreme court justices were ruling in favor of same-sex marriage, popular television programs such as *Ellen* and *Will & Grace* were bringing the LGBT community into the cultural mainstream.[19] Gay people were featured regularly on *The Real World* and other MTV programs, which helped to familiarize young Americans with their relationships. LGBT issues also became the subjects of high-profile Hollywood films such as *Boys Don't Cry* (1999), *Brokeback Mountain* (2005), and *Bruno* (2009). It is possible, then, that American culture was already moving inexorably in the direction of expanding gay rights, and the legalization of same-sex marriage is something that would have developed without the intervention of state supreme courts.

[17] Kirk Johnson, *G.O.P. Governor Challenges Utah's Conservative Verities*, N.Y. Times, March 14, 2009, at A12.

[18] For a list of states with civil unions and domestic partner laws, see *Civil Unions & Domestic Partnership Statutes*, National Conference on State Legislatures (February 2012), http://www.ncsl.org/issues-research/human-services/civil-unions-and-domestic-partnership-statutes.aspx.

[19] Rosenberg, *supra* Chapter 1, note 3, at 413.

It is beyond question that society was liberalizing in its attitudes about gay rights, and no doubt these trends created a climate that helped to make same-sex marriage a viable policy alternative. Yet, this fact does not mean that the intervention of state courts was not necessary or indeed essential to achieving marriage equality. Supporters of this contrary position would do well to identify any same-sex marriages that occurred without judicial compulsion before 2009, when the Vermont legislature overrode a gubernatorial veto to approve same-sex marriage in the state. Same-sex marriage was simply not on the agenda in most state legislatures,[20] and from the vantage point of the 1990s, the prospects for legislative action seemed dim.

State courts were the catalysts that made same-sex marriage possible. More specifically, same-sex marriage resulted from the actions of unelected, professional judges who presided over state constitutional systems that were relatively insulated from potential democratic counterreactions to decisions favoring minority interests. These judges had the institutional resources to compel majorities to acknowledge gay rights. Citizens in Massachusetts discovered that they would have to live with the *Goodridge* decision, at least for a time, because they could not easily remove the judges or amend the state constitution. In other states, such as California and Iowa, in which state supreme court justices had fewer protections, majorities fought back.

Sometimes it takes an undemocratic institution to get majorities to consider necessary reforms, particularly when these reforms do not operate to the immediate or obvious benefit of the citizenry as a whole. Judges in Massachusetts were capable of getting citizens to acknowledge gay relationships, to grow more familiar with these relationships, and ultimately to become more accepting of them. In this way, judges "refined and enlarged" public opinion in the noblest sense of the phrase, engaging in policy leadership that did not just force citizens down a path but enabled them to see its virtues. If the *Goodridge* decision had proven to be truly untenable to the people of Massachusetts, they could have overturned it. Although the amendment process in the state is difficult, it is not impossible. It simply takes time, requiring proposed amendments to be approved in two successive legislative sessions. Because they had a cooling-off period for the decision to sink in, citizens in Massachusetts could deliberate about whether to accept the change that the judges were imposing. Initial public anger at *Goodridge* could subside, so that tolerance of the newly celebrated marriages could grow. Were these mechanisms not in place, *Goodridge* surely would have been overturned as easily as California's decision was, assuming that the justices had even risked handing down the decision in the first place. Then there would have been no model for other states to follow, and no examples of same-sex marriages to discredit the persistent myths about these relationships.

---

[20] The California legislature did vote to legalize same-sex marriage in 2005, but this bill was not signed into law.

Conclusion

If state supreme courts did not fully realize their potential to transform the nation's laws regarding same-sex marriage, they remain capable of becoming effective agents of social change, at least when certain institutional and environmental conditions are met. Efforts to improve the democratic accountability of state courts and state constitutional systems risk eroding this potential, but for now judges in at least a few states have the institutional cover that they need for them to be successful policy innovators, interpreting their state constitutions to provide a more generous collection of rights than the federal constitution guarantees. Courts in these jurisdictions can serve as examples to other states, laboratories of innovation that other states can observe and perhaps learn from when making their own policy choices.

It is possible that in other issue areas the potential for state courts to be transformative agents of change will be greater than it has been here. This book has considered only the impact of state supreme courts on same-sex marriage policy, and it is unclear whether the accountability mechanisms that I have found to be so important in the same-sex marriage context, specifically contested judicial elections and initiative amendment procedures, would constrain judicial power to the same degree in less-salient issue areas. My suspicion is that they would not. The distinguishing characteristics of morality policies such as same-sex marriage are their visibility and their engagement of the public. It seems unlikely that accountability mechanisms would influence the impact of courts as strongly when the public is less engaged in particular areas of law. In most legal matters, there are unlikely to be strong public reactions to state supreme court decisions, regardless of how the courts are structured, nor do I expect the public to push for state constitutional amendments to overturn most state supreme court decisions.

Judges are unlikely to feel electoral pressures from their constituents in less-salient issue areas, giving them more flexibility to act.[21] Judges might also feel more empowered to push back against initiative amendments in less-salient areas of law. Manweller reports that judges frequently find ways to overturn the results of direct democracy on procedural grounds, usually because organizers "fail to meet procedural hurdles such as single subject and separate vote procedures, title hearing standards, and restrictions against revising, rather than amending the constitution."[22] In fact, the California Supreme Court had the opportunity in *Strauss v. Horton* (2009) to strike down Proposition 8 on procedural grounds, but chose not to do so. With less public scrutiny around the issue, the justices might have been more willing to strike it down.

[21] See Cann & Wilhelm, *supra* Chapter 5, note 27.
[22] MATHEW MANWELLER, THE PEOPLE VERSUS THE COURTS: JUDICIAL REVIEW AND DIRECT DEMOCRACY IN THE AMERICAN LEGAL SYSTEM 92–93 (2005).

For these reasons, accountability mechanisms are more likely to matter in high profile cases, such as those involving abortion, gay rights, and other civil liberties issues. Ironically, the impact of state supreme courts might be the most limited in circumstances in which judicial intervention is most needed, such as when majorities are systematically discriminating against minority rights. When minorities cannot get fair hearings in state legislatures, it is courts that have traditionally offered these groups the promise of relief. Without the protections of life tenure and a rigorous constitutional amendment procedure, state judges are likely to find that their capacity to run against the grain of public opinion on controversial morality policies is not much different from that of other elected officials. The public will not defer to elected judges simply because they are judges. The public will hold them accountable at the ballot box and overturn unpopular decisions with state constitutional amendments.

There are limits to what one can expect from a litigation strategy in the states. But it would be a mistake to underestimate the impact of those state courts that possess the necessary institutional resources to act. The findings in this book suggest that, under the right conditions, state supreme court justices can have a transformative impact on even the most controversial areas of policy. When state supreme court justices are insulated from the public, when their decisions are safe from being overturned by initiative amendments, and when the political and cultural environments are receptive to their decisions, state supreme court justices can move public policy in new, more innovative directions. State supreme courts can act as checks on majoritarian institutions and provide relief for disadvantaged minorities.

BIBLIOGRAPHY

ABC News and *The Washington Post*. 2005. ABC/Washington Post Poll #2005-983: Congress/Social Security/War in Iraq/Stem Cell Research. Storrs, CT: The Roper Center, University of Connecticut [distributor].

Ai, Chunrong, and Edward C. Norton. 2003. "Interaction Terms in Logit and Probit Models." *Economics Letters 80*: 123–29.

Amestoy, Jeffrey L. 2004. "Pragmatic Constitutionalism: Reflections on State Constitutional Theory and Same-Sex Marriage Claims." *Rutgers Law Journal 35*: 1249–66.

Andersen, Ellen Ann. 2005. *Out of the Closets & Into the Courts: Legal Opportunity Structure and Gay Rights Litigation*. Ann Arbor: University of Michigan Press.

Atkins, Burton M., and Henry R. Glick. 1974. "Formal Judicial Recruitment and State Supreme Court Decisions." *American Politics Quarterly 2*: 427–49.

Baas, Larry R., and Dan Thomas. 1984. "The Supreme Court and Policy Legitimation: Experimental Tests." *American Politics Quarterly 12*: 335–60.

Baker, Lynn A. 1995. "Governing by Initiative: Constitutional Change and Direct Democracy." *University of Colorado Law Review 66*: 143–58.

Baker, Reg, et al. 2010. "AAPOR Report on Online Panels." The American Association for Public Opinion Research. *Available at* http://www.aapor.org.

Barclay, Scott. 2010. "In Search of Judicial Activism in the Same-Sex Marriage Cases: Sorting the Evidence from Courts, Legislatures, Initiatives and Amendments." *Perspectives on Politics 8*: 111–26.

Barclay, Scott, and Shauna Fisher. 2008. "Said and Unsaid: State Legislative Signaling to State Courts over Same Sex Marriage, 1990–2004." *Law & Policy 30*: 254–75.

——. 2003. "The States and the Differing Impetus for Divergent Paths on Same-Sex Marriage, 1990–2001." *The Policy Studies Journal 31*: 331–52.

Barth, Jay, and L. Marvin Overby. 2003. "Are Gay Men and Lesbians in the South the New 'Threat'? Regional Comparisons of the Contact Theory." *Politics and Policy 31*: 1–19.

Beck, Nathanial, and Simon Jackman. 1998. "Beyond Linearity by Default: Generalized Additive Models." *American Journal of Political Science 42*: 596–627.

Beck, Nathaniel, Jonathan N. Katz, and Richard Tucker. 1998. "Taking Time Seriously: Time-Series-Cross-Section Analysis with a Binary Dependent Variable." *American Journal of Political Science 42*: 1260–88.

Belluck, Pam. 2006. "Massachusetts Effort to End Same-Sex Marriage Is Dead for Now." *The New York Times*. November 10: A16.

——. 2007. "Same-Sex Marriage Vote Advances in Massachusetts." *The New York Times*. January 3: A12.

Benesh, Sara C. 2006. "Understanding Public Confidence in American Courts." *The Journal of Politics* 68: 697–707.

Benesh, Sara C., and Susan E. Howell. 2001. "Confidence in the Courts: A Comparison of Users and Non-users." *Behavioral Sciences and the Law* 19: 199–214.

Berkson, Larry C., Rachel Caufield, and Malia Reddick. 2004. "Judicial Selection in the United States: A Special Report." The American Judicature Society. *Available at* www.ajs.org/selection/docs/Berkson.pdf.

Berry, Frances Stokes, and William D. Berry. 1990. "State Lottery Adoptions as Policy Innovations: An Event History Analysis." *American Political Science Review* 84: 395–416.

———. 1992. "Tax Innovation in the States: Capitalizing on Political Opportunity." *American Journal of Political Science* 36: 715–42.

———. 1999. "Innovation and Diffusion Models in Policy Research." In *Theories of the Policy Process*, ed. Paul E. Sabatier. Boulder, CO: Westview Press.

Berry, William D., Evan J. Ringquist, Richard C. Fording, and Russell L. Hanson. 1998. "Measuring Citizen and Government Ideology in the American States, 1960–93." *American Journal of Political Science* 42: 327–48.

Berry, William D., Richard C. Fording, Evan J. Ringquist, Russell L. Hanson, and Carl Klarner. 2010. "Measuring Citizen and Government Ideology in the American States: A Re-Appraisal." *State Politics and Policy Quarterly* 10: 117–35.

Bierman, Luke. 2002. "Judicial Independence: beyond Merit Selection." *Fordham Urban Law Journal* 29: 851–72.

Bonneau, Chris W. 2005. "What Price Justice(s)? Understanding Campaign Spending in State Supreme Court Elections." *State Politics and Policy Quarterly* 5: 107–25.

Bonneau, Chris W., and Melinda Gann Hall. 2009. *In Defense of Judicial Elections*. New York: Routledge Press.

———. 2003. "Predicting Challengers in State Supreme Court Elections: Context and the Politics of Institutional Design." *Political Research Quarterly* 56: 337–49.

Box-Steffensmeier, Janet M., and Bradford S. Jones. 2004. *Event History Analysis: A Guide for Social Scientists*. New York: Cambridge University Press.

Brace, Paul, and Melinda Gann Hall. 2001. "'Haves' v. 'Have Nots' in State Supreme Courts: Allocating Docket Space and Wins in Power Asymmetric Cases." *Law & Society Review* 35: 393–417.

———. 1993. "Integrated Models of Judicial Dissent." *The Journal of Politics* 55: 914–35.

———. 1997. "The Interplay of Preferences, Case Facts, Context, and Rules in the Politics of Judicial Choice." *The Journal of Politics* 59: 1206–31.

———. 1990. "Neo-Institutionalism and Dissent in State Supreme Courts." *The Journal of Politics* 52: 54–70.

———. 1995. "Studying Courts Comparatively: The View from the American States." *Political Research Quarterly* 48: 5–29.

Brace, Paul, Laura Langer, and Melinda Gann Hall. 2000. "Measuring the Preferences of State Supreme Court Judges." *Journal of Politics* 62: 387–413.

Bradford, Judith, Kirsten Barrett, and Julie A. Honnold. 2002. "The 2000 Census and Same-Sex Households: A User's Guide." The National Gay and Lesbian Task Force Policy Institute. *Available at* http://www.ngltf.org.

Bradley, M.B., Norman M. Green, Jr., Dale E. Jones, Mac Lynn and Lou McNeil. 1992. *Churches and Church Membership in the United States, 1990*. Washington, DC: Glenmary Research Center.

Brennan, William J., Jr. 1977. "State Constitutions and the Protection of Individual Rights." *Harvard Law Review* 90: 489–504.

Bruch, Gregory S. 1984. "*Michigan v. Long*: Presumptive Federal Appellate Jurisdiction over State Cases Containing Ambiguous Grounds of Decision." *Iowa Law Review* 69: 1081–101.

Buckley, Jack, and Chad Westerland. 2004. "Duration Dependence, Functional Form, and Corrected Standard Errors: Improving EHA Models of State Policy Diffusion." *State Politics and Policy Quarterly* 4: 94–113.

Bumiller, Elisabeth. 2004. "Bush Says His Party Is Wrong to Oppose Gay Civil Unions." *The New York Times*. October 26: A21.

Burge, Kathleen. 2003. "SJC Peppers Lawyers on Same-Sex Marriage." *The Boston Globe*. March 5: A1.

Cain, Patricia A. 2000. *Rainbow Rights: The Role of Lawyers and Courts in the Lesbian and Gay Civil Rights Movement*. Boulder, CO: Westview Press.

Caldeira, Gregory A. 1983. "On the Reputation of State Supreme Courts." *Political Behavior* 5: 83–108.

———. 1985. "The Transmission of Legal Precedents: A Study of State Supreme Courts." *American Political Science Review* 79: 178–94.

Caldeira, Gregory A., and James L. Gibson. 1992. "The Etiology of Public Support for the Supreme Court." *American Journal of Political Science* 36: 635–64.

Cameron, Charles M., Jeffrey A. Segal, and Donald Songer. 2000. "Strategic Auditing in a Political Hierarchy: An Informational Model of the Supreme Court's Certiorari Decisions." *American Political Science Review* 94: 101–16.

Cann, Damon. 2002. "Campaign Contributions and Judicial Behavior." *American Review of Politics* 23: 261–74.

Cann, Damon M., and Teena Wilhelm. 2011. "Case Visibility and the Electoral Connection in State Supreme Courts." *American Politics Research* 39: 557–81.

Cann, Damon M., and Jeff Yates. 2008. "Homegrown Institutional Legitimacy: Assessing Citizens' Diffuse Support for State Courts." *American Politics Research* 36: 297–329.

Canon, Bradley C., and Lawrence Baum. 1981. "Patterns of Adoption of Tort Law Innovations: An Application of Diffusion Theory to Judicial Doctrines." *American Political Science Review* 75: 975–87.

Canon, Bradley C., and Charles A. Johnson. 1999. *Judicial Policies: Implementation and Impact*. Second Edition. Washington, DC: CQ Press.

Casey, Gregory. 1974. "The Supreme Court and Myth: An Empirical Investigation." *Law & Society Review* 8: 385–420.

Chertoff, Meryl J. 2010. "At Home and Abroad: Trends in Judicial Selection in the States." *McGeorge Law Review* 42: 47–64.

Choi, Stephen J., Mitu Gulati, and Eric A. Posner. 2009. "Judicial Evaluations and Information Forcing: Ranking State High Courts and Their Judges." *Duke Law Journal* 58: 1313–81.

Clawson, Rosalee A., Elizabeth R. Kegler, and Eric N. Waltenberg. 2001. "The Legitimacy-Conferring Authority of the U.S. Supreme Court: An Experimental Design." *American Politics Research* 29: 566–91.

Cohn, D'Vera. 2001. "Count of Gay Couples Up 300%; 2000 Census Ranks D.C., Arlington, Alexandria among Top Locales." *The Washington Post*. August 22: A3.

Cooperman, Alan, and Thomas Edsall. 2004. "Evangelicals Say They Led Charge for the GOP." *Washington Post*. November 8: A1.

Corvino, John. 2008. "Happily Ever After, Delayed." *Los Angeles Times*. November 6: A29.

Cross, Frank B. 2003. "Thoughts on Goldilocks and Judicial Independence." *Ohio State Law Journal* 64: 195–219.

Cyert, Richard M., and James G. March. 1963. *A Behavioral Theory of the Firm*. Englewood Cliffs, NJ: Prentice-Hall.

Czarnezki, Jason J. 2005. "A Call for Change: Improving Judicial Selection Methods." *Marquette Law Review* 89: 169–78.

Dahl, Robert A. 1957. "Decision-Making in a Democracy: The Supreme Court as a National Policy-Maker." *Journal of Public Law* 6: 279.

Davey, Monica. 2009. "A Quiet Day in Iowa as the State Begins Allowing Same-Sex Couples to Marry." *The New York Times*. April 28: A12.

DiSarro, Brian. 2007. "Judicial Accountability of Majority Tyranny? Judicial Selection Methods and State Gay Rights Rulings." Paper presented at the annual State Politics & Policy Conference, University of Texas-Austin. February 22–24, 2007.

Donovan, Todd, and Shaun Bowler. 1998. "Direct Democracy and Minority Rights: An Extension." *American Journal of Political Science* 42: 1020–24.

Dougherty, George W., Stefanie A. Lindquist, and Mark D. Bradbury. 2006. "Evaluating Performance in State Judicial Institutions: Trust and Confidence in the Georgia Judiciary." *State and Local Government Review* 38: 176–90.

Dubois, Philip L. 1980. *From Ballot to Bench: Judicial Elections and the Quest for Accountability.* Austin: University of Texas Press.

Dworkin, Ronald. 2006. "Three Questions for America." *N.Y. Review of Books.* September 21: 28.

Egan, Patrick J., Nathaniel Persily, and Kevin Wallsten. 2008. "Gay Rights." In *Public Opinion and Constitutional Controversy.* Nathaniel Persily, Jack Citrin, and Patrick J. Egan, eds. New York: Oxford University Press.

Eisenberg, Theodore, and Geoffrey Miller. 2008. "Reversal, Dissent, and Variability in State Supreme Courts: The Centrality of Jurisdictional Source." Public Law & Legal Theory Research Paper Series. Working Paper No. 08–01.

Epstein, Lee, and Jack Knight. 1998. *The Choices Justices Make.* Washington, DC: CQ Press.

Epstein, Lee, Andrew D. Martin, Jeffrey A. Segal, and Chad Westerland. 2007. "The Judicial Common Space." *Journal of Law, Economics, and Organization* 23: 303–25.

Eskridge, William N., Jr. 1999. *Gaylaw: Challenging the Apartheid of the Closet.* Cambridge, MA: Harvard University Press.

Ettelbrick, Paula. 1989. "Since When Is Marriage a Path to Liberation?" *OUT/LOOK: National Gay and Lesbian Quarterly* 6: 8.

Faber, Michael J. 2007. "Defense of Marriage Acts: A Policy Diffusion Study." Paper presented at the Annual Meeting of the Western Political Science Association. Las Vegas, Nevada, March 2007.

Fahlbusch, Patricia, and Daniel Gonzalez. 1987. "*Michigan v. Long*: The Inadequacies of Independent and Adequate State Grounds." *University of Miami Law Review* 42: 159–202.

Failinger, Marie A. 2005. "Can a Good Judge be a Good Politician? Judicial Elections from a Virtue Ethics Approach." *Missouri Law Review* 70: 433–518.

Fleischmann, Arnold, and Laura Moyer. 2009. "Competing Social Movements and Local Political Culture: Voting on Ballot Propositions to Ban Same-Sex Marriage in the U.S. States." *Social Science Quarterly* 90: 134–49.

Franklin, Charles H., and Liane C. Kosaki. 1989. "Republican Schoolmaster: The U.S. Supreme Court, Public Opinion, and Abortion." *The American Political Science Review* 83: 751–77.

Gamble, Barbara S. 1997. "Putting Civil Rights to a Popular Vote." *American Journal of Political Science* 42: 1343–48.

Garrison, Jessica. 2009. "Lawmakers Override the Governor's Veto of Their Legislation. Foes Plan to Respond with a TV Ad Campaign." *Los Angeles Times.* April 8: A14.

Garrow, David J. 1994. "Hopelessly Hollow History: Revisionist Devaluing of *Brown v. Board of Education.*" *Virginia Law Review* 80: 151–60.

———. 2004. "Toward a More Perfect Union." *The New York Times Magazine.* May 9: 52.

Gates, Gary J. 2001. "Gay and Lesbian Families in the United States: Same-Sex Unmarried Partner Households." The Human Rights Campaign. *Available at* http://www.urban.org/UploadedPDF/1000491_gl_partner_households.pdf.

George, Susan, William J. Snape, III, and Rina Rodriguez. 1997. "The Public in Action: Using State Citizen Suit Statutes to Protect Biodiversity." *University of Baltimore Journal of Environmental Law* 6: 1–41.

Gibson, James L. 2008. "Challenges to the Impartiality of State Supreme Courts: Legitimacy Theory and 'New-Style' Judicial Campaigns." *The American Political Science Review* 102: 59–75.

———. 1987. "Homosexuals and the Ku Klux Klan: A Contextual Analysis of Political Tolerance." *Western Political Quarterly* 40: 427–48.

———. 2009. "'New-Style' Judicial Campaigns and the Legitimacy of State High Courts." *The Journal of Politics* 71: 1285–304.

Gibson, James L., and Gregory A. Caldeira. 2011. "Has Legal Realism Damaged the Legitimacy of the U.S. Supreme Court?" *Law & Society Review* 45: 195–219.

Gibson, James L., Gregory A. Caldeira, and Vanessa A. Baird. 1998. "On the Legitimacy of National High Courts." *The American Political Science Review* 92: 343–56.

Gibson, James L., Gregory A. Caldeira, and Lester K. Spence. 2003a. "Measuring Attitudes toward the United States Supreme Court." *American Journal of Political Science* 47: 354–67.

——. 2003b. "The Supreme Court and the U.S. Presidential Election of 2000: Wounds, Self-Inflicted or Otherwise?" *British Journal of Political Science* 58: 187–201.

——. 2005. "Why Do People Accept Public Policies They Oppose? Testing Legitimacy Theory with a Survey-Based Experiment." *Political Research Quarterly* 58: 187–201.

Gibson, James L., Jeffrey A. Gottfried, Michael X. Delli Carpini, and Kathleen Hall Jamieson. 2011. "The Effects of Judicial Campaign Activity on the Legitimacy of Courts: A Survey-Based Experiment." *Political Research Quarterly* 64: 545–58.

Giles, Michael W., Virginia A. Hettinger, and Todd Peppers. 2001. "Picking Federal Judges: A Note on Policy and Partisan Selection Agendas." *Political Research Quarterly* 54: 623–41.

Gladstone, Leslie W. 2004. "Equal Rights Amendments: State Provisions." The Library of Congress: Congressional Research Service. *Available at* http://www.policyarchive.org/handle/10207/bitstreams/3292.pdf.

Gledhill, Lynda. 2005. "Governor's Gay-Rights Moves Please No One; Marriage Bill Vetoed, Partner Benefits Preserved." *San Francisco Chronicle*. September 30: A1.

Glick, Henry R. 1981. "Innovation in State Judicial Administration: Effects on Court Management and Organization." *American Politics Quarterly* 9: 49–69.

Glick, Henry R., and Scott P. Hays. 1991. "Innovation and Reinvention in State Policymaking: Theory and the Evolution of Living Will Laws." *Journal of Politics* 53: 835–50.

Glick, Henry R., and George W. Pruet, Jr. 1986. "Dissent in State Supreme Courts: Patterns and Correlates of Conflict." In *Judicial Conflicts and Consensus: Behavioral Studies of American Appellate Courts*. Sheldon Goldman and Charles M. Lamb, eds. Lexington: University Press of Kansas.

Glick, Henry R., and Kenneth N. Vines. 1973. *State Court Systems*. Englewood Cliffs, NJ: Prentice-Hall.

Goodnough, Abby. 2009. "Rejecting Veto, Vermont Backs Gay Marriage." *The New York Times*. April 8: A1.

Gormley, Ken. 2003. "The Silver Anniversary of New Judicial Federalism." *Albany Law Review* 66: 797–808.

Gormley, William T., Jr. 1986. "Regulatory Issue Networks in a Federal System." *Polity* 18: 595–620.

Gray, Virginia. 1973. "Innovation in the States: A Diffusion Study." *American Political Science Review* 67: 1174–85.

Green, Don, and Alan Gerber. "Web Software for Analyzing Experimental Data." Yale Institution for Social and Policy Studies (http://research.yale.edu/).

Greenhouse, Linda. 2006. "2 Justices Indicate Supreme Court Is Unlikely to Televise Sessions." *The New York Times*. April 5: A16.

Griffin, Stephen M. 2009. "Trust in Government and Direct Democracy." *University of Pennsylvania Journal of Constitutional Law* 11: 551–95.

Grigsby, Jared. 2009. "Jubilation Muted on Calif Gay Marriage Anniversary." *The Associated Press*. June 17.

Grosskopf, Anke, and Jeffrey J. Mondak. 1998. "Do Attitudes toward Specific Supreme Court Decisions Matter? The Impact of *Webster* and *Texas v. Johnson* on Public Confidence in the Supreme Court." *Political Research Quarterly* 51: 633–54.

Haider-Markel, Donald P. 2001. "Policy Diffusion as a Geographic Expansion of the Scope of Political Conflict: Same-Sex Marriage Bans in the 1990s." *State Politics and Policy Quarterly* 1: 5–26.

Haider-Markel, Donald P., and Kenneth J. Meier. 1996. "The Politics of Gay and Lesbian Rights: Expanding the Scope of the Conflict." *The Journal of Politics* 58: 332–49.

Haider-Markel, Donald P. Alana Querze, and Kara Lindaman. 2007. "Lose, Win, or Draw? A Reexamination of Direct Democracy and Minority Rights." *Political Research Quarterly* 60: 304–14.

Hall, Kermit L. 1984. "Progressive Reform and the Decline of Democratic Accountability: The Popular Election of State Supreme Court Judges, 1850–1920." *American Bar Foundation Research Journal* 9: 345–69.

Hall, Melinda Gann. 1987. "Constituent Influence in State Supreme Courts: Conceptual Notes and a Case Study." *The Journal of Politics* 49: 1117–24.

——. 1992. "Electoral Politics and Strategic Voting in State Supreme Courts." *The Journal of Politics* 54: 427–46.

——. 2001. "State Supreme Courts in American Democracy: Probing the Myths of Judicial Reform." *The American Political Science Review* 95: 315–30.

——. 2007. "Voting in State Supreme Court Elections: Competition and Context as Democratic Incentives." *The Journal of Politics* 69: 1147–59.

Hall, Melinda Gann, and Chris W. Bonneau. 2006. "Does Quality Matter? Challengers in State Supreme Court Elections." *American Journal of Political Science* 50: 20–33.

——. 2008. "Mobilizing Interest: The Effects of Money on Citizen Participation in State Supreme Court Elections." *American Journal of Political Science* 52: 457–70.

Hall, Melinda Gann, and Paul Brace. 1989. "Order in the Courts: A Neo-Institutional Approach to Judicial Consensus." *The Western Political Quarterly* 42: 391–407.

Hasen, Richard L. 2012. "End of the Dialogue? Political Polarization, the Supreme Court, and Congress." *Southern California Law Review* (forthcoming). UC Irvine School of Law Research Paper No. 2012–65. *Available at* SSRN: http://ssrn.com/abstract=2130190.

Heagarty, J. Christopher. 2003. "Public Opinion and an Elected Judiciary: New Avenues for Reform." *Willamette Law Review* 39: 1287–311.

Hibbing, John R., and Elizabeth Theiss-Morse. 1995. *Congress as Public Enemy: Public Attitudes toward American Political Institutions*. New York: Cambridge University Press.

——. 2002. *Stealth Democracy: Americans' Beliefs about How Government Should Work*. New York: Cambridge University Press.

Hoekstra, Valerie J. 2003. *Public Reaction to Supreme Court Decisions*. New York: Cambridge University Press.

——. 1995. "The Supreme Court and Opinion Change: An Experimental Study of the Court's Ability to Change Opinion." *American Politics Quarterly*. 23: 109–29.

Hoekstra, Valerie J., and Jeffrey A. Segal. 1996. "The Shepherding of Local Public Opinion: The Supreme Court and Lamb's Chapel." *The Journal of Politics* 58: 1079–102.

Hojnacki, Marie, and Lawrence Baum. 1992. "Choosing Judicial Candidates: How Voters Explain Their Decisions." *Judicature* 75: 300–09.

Holbrook, Thomas, and Emily Van Dunk. 1993. "Electoral Competition in the American States." *American Political Science Review* 87: 955–62.

Howard, S. Kenneth, and David B. Walker. 1985. *The Question of State Government Capability*. Washington, DC: Advisory Commission on Intergovernmental Relations.

Hull, Kathleen. 2006. *Same-Sex Marriage: The Cultural Politics of Love and Law*. New York: Cambridge University Press.

Hume, Robert J. 2009. *How Courts Impact Federal Administrative Behavior*. New York: Routledge Press.

Hwang, Sung-Do, and Virginia Gray. 1991. "External Limits and Internal Determinants of State Public Policy." *Western Political Quarterly* 44: 277–99.

Johnson, Kirk. 2009. "G.O.P. Governor Challenges Utah's Conservative Verities." *The New York Times*. March 14: A12.

Jones, Dale E., Sherry Doty, Clifford Grammich, James E. Horsch, Richard Houseal, Mac Lynn, John P. Marcum, Kenneth M. Sanchagrin, and Richard H. Taylor. 2002. *Religious*

Congregations and Membership in the United States 2000: An Enumeration by Region, State and County Based on Data Reported for 149 Religious Bodies. Nashville, TN: Glenmary Research Center.

Kaiser Family Foundation. 2001. *Inside Out: A Report on the Experiences of Lesbians, Gays and Bisexuals in America and the Public's View on Issues and Policies Related to Sexual Orientation.* Menlo Park, CA: Henry J. Kaiser Family Foundation.

Kaplan, Thomas. 2011. "Rights Collide as Town Clerk Sidesteps Role in Gay Marriages." *The New York Times.* September 27: A1.

Keating, Christopher. 2008. "A Majority Backs Gay Marriage Ruling; Overall, 53 Percent Endorse Decision, but Poll Finds Sharp Differences among Democrats, Republicans." *The Hartford Courant.* October 14: A9.

——. 2008. "A Powerful Question for Voters; Should State Constitution Be Opened Up for Change?; On the Ballot." *The Hartford Courant.* October 18: A1.

Keck, Thomas M. 2009. "Beyond Backlash: Assessing the Impact of Judicial Decisions on LGBT Rights." *Law & Society Review* 43: 151–86.

Kelleher, Christine A., and Jennifer Wolak. 2007. "Explaining Public Confidence in the Branches of State Government." *Political Research Quarterly* 60: 707–21.

Kershaw, Sarah. 2004. "Constitutional Bans on Same-Sex Marriage Gain Widespread Support in 10 States." *The New York Times.* November 3: P9.

Klarman, Michael J. 2005. "*Brown* and *Lawrence* (and *Goodridge*)." *Michigan Law Review* 104: 431–89.

——. 2012. *From the Closet to the Altar: Courts, Backlash, and the Struggle for Same-Sex Marriage.* New York: Oxford University Press.

——. 1994. "How *Brown* Changed Race Relations: The Backlash Thesis." *Journal of American History* 81: 81–118.

Klawitter, Marieka, and Brian Hammer. 1999. "Spatial and Temporal Diffusion of Local Antidiscrimination Policies for Sexual Orientation." In *Gays and Lesbians in the Democratic Process.* Ellen D.B. Riggle and Barry L. Tadlock, eds. Second Edition. New York: Columbia University Press.

Klein, David, and Darby Morrisroe. 1999. "The Prestige and Influence of Individual Judges on the U.S. Courts of Appeals." *Journal of Legal Studies* 28: 371–91.

Knight, Jack, and Lee Epstein. 1996. "The Norm of Stare Decisis." *American Journal of Political Science* 40: 1018–35.

Kozinski, Alex. 2004. "What I Ate for Breakfast and Other Mysteries of Judicial Decision-Making." In *Judges on Judging: Views from the Bench.* David M. O'Brien, ed. Second Edition. Washington, DC: CQ Press.

Kranish, Michael. 2004. "Gay Marriage Bans Passed. Measures OK'D in All 11 States Where Eyed." *The Boston Globe.* November 3: A22.

Kritzer, Herbert H., and Mark J. Richards. 2003. "Jurisprudential Regimes and Supreme Court Decisionmaking: The Lemon Regime and Establishment Clause Cases." *Law & Society Review* 37: 827–40.

——. 2002. "Jurisprudential Regimes in Supreme Court Decision Making." *American Political Science Review* 96: 305–20.

Larkin, Elizabeth A. 2001. "Judicial Selection Methods: Judicial Independence and Popular Democracy." *Denver University Law Review* 79: 65–89.

Lawrence, Susan. 1992. Review of *The Hollow Hope: Can Courts Bring about Social Change?.* *American Political Science Review* 86: 812.

Lax, Jeffrey R., and Justin Phillips. 2009. "Gay Rights in the States: Public Opinion and Policy Responsiveness." *American Political Science Review* 103: 367–86.

Lax, Jeffrey R., and Kelly T. Rader. 2010. "Legal Constraints on Supreme Court Decision Making: Do Jurisprudential Regimes Exist?" *The Journal of Politics* 72: 273–84.

Lewis, Daniel. 2011. "Direct Democracy and Minority Rights: Same-Sex Marriage Bans in the U.S. States." *Social Science Quarterly* 92: 364–83.

Lewis, Raphael. 2005. "After Vote, Both Sides in Debate Energized." *The Boston Globe*. September 15: A1.

Lienesch, Michael. 1993. *Redeeming America: Piety and Politics in the New Christian Right*. Chapel Hill: University of North Carolina Press.

Lindquist, Stefanie A. 2007. "State Politics and the Judiciary." Database assembled thanks to National Science Foundation Grant SES #0550618.

Liptak, Adam. 2012. "In Congress's Paralysis, a Mightier Supreme Court." *The New York Times*. August 21: A10.

Long, J. Scott. 1997. *Regression Models for Categorical or Limited Dependent Variables*. Thousand Oaks, CA: Sage.

Lorentzen, Amy. 2009. "In Iowa, Same-Sex Couples Rush to Tie the Knot." *The Washington Post*. April 28: A4.

Lovrich, Nicholas P., Jr., and Charles H. Sheldon. 1983. "Voters in Contested, Nonpartisan Judicial Elections: A Responsible Electorate or a Problematic Public?" *Western Political Quarterly* 36: 241–56.

Lowi, Theodore J. 1964. "American Business, Public Policy, Case-Studies, and Political Theory." *World Politics* 16: 677–715.

——. 1972. "Four Systems of Policy, Politics, and Choice." *Public Administration Review* 32: 298–310.

——. 1988. "Forward: New Dimensions in Policy and Politics." In *Social Regulatory Policy: Moral Controversies in American Politics*, ed. Raymond Tatlovich and Byron W. Daynes. Boulder, CO: Westview Press.

Luks, Samantha, and Michael Salamone. 2008. "Abortion." In *Public Opinion and Constitutional Controversy*. Nathaniel Persily, Jack Citrin, and Patrick J. Egan, eds. New York: Oxford University Press.

Lupia, Arthur, Yanna Krupnikov, Adam Seth Levine, Spencer Piston, and Alexander Von Hagen-Jamar. 2010. "Why State Constitutions Differ in Their Treatment of Same-Sex Marriage." *Journal of Politics* 72: 1222–35.

Lutz, Donald S. 1994. "Toward a Theory of Constitutional Amendment." *The American Political Science Review* 88: 355–70.

Mann, Thomas E. 1978. *Unsafe at Any Margin: Interpreting Congressional Elections*. Washington, DC: American Enterprise Institute for Public Policy Research.

Manweller, Mathew. 2005. *The People vs. the Courts: Judicial Review and Direct Democracy in the American Legal System*. Bethesda, MD: Academica Press, LLC.

Marshall, Margaret H. 2011. "Remarks." *Albany Law Review* 74: 1595–603.

Martin, Andrew D., and Kevin M. Quinn. 2002. "Dynamic Ideal Point Estimation via Markov Chain Monte Carlo for the U.S. Supreme Court." *Political Analysis* 10: 134–53.

May, Janice C. 1987. "Constitutional Amendment and Revision Revisited." *Publius* 17: 153–79.

Mayhew, David R. 1974. *Congress: The Electoral Connection*. New Haven, CT: Yale University Press.

McCann, Michael W. 1996. "Causal versus Constitutive Explanations (or, On the Difficulty of Being so Positive. …)" *Law & Social Inquiry* 21: 457–82.

——. 1992. "Reform Litigation on Trial." [Review of *The Hollow Hope: Can Courts Bring about Social Change?*] *Law & Social Inquiry* 17: 715–43.

——. 1994. *Rights at Work: Pay Equity Reform and the Politics of Legal Mobilization*. (Chicago: University of Chicago Press).

Mezey, Susan Gluck. 2009. *Gay Families and the Courts: The Quest for Equal Rights*. New York: Rowman & Littlefield.

——. 2007. *Queers in Court: Gay Rights Law and Public Policy*. New York: Rowman & Littlefield.

Mintrom, Michael. 1997. "Policy Entrepreneurs and the Diffusion of Innovation." *American Journal of Political Science* 41: 738–70.

Mondak, Jeffery J. 1992. "Institutional Legitimacy, Policy Legitimacy, and the Supreme Court." *American Politics Quarterly* 20: 457–77.

———. 1990. "Perceived Legitimacy of Supreme Court Decisions: Three Functions of Source Credibility." *Political Behavior* 12: 363–84.

Mooney, Christopher Z. 2001. "Modeling Regional Effects on State Policy Diffusion." *Political Research Quarterly* 54: 103–24.

Mooney, Christopher Z., and Mei-Hsien Lee. 1995. "Legislative Morality in the American States: The Case of Pre-*Roe* Abortion Regulation Reform." *American Journal of Political Science* 39: 599–627.

Moore, Robert G. 2007. "Political Participation and Tolerance: American Evangelicals in Transition." Paper presented at the Annual Meeting of the Midwest Political Science Association. Chicago, IL. April 2007.

Mucciaroni, Gary. 2008. *Same-Sex, Different Politics: Success and Failure in the Struggles over Gay Rights.* Chicago: University of Chicago Press.

Murphy, Walter F., and Joseph Tanenhaus. 1968. "Public Opinion and the United States Supreme Court." *Law & Society Review* 2: 357–82.

Murphy, Walter F., Joseph Tanenhaus, and Daniel Kastner. 1973. *Public Evaluations of Constitutional Courts: Alternative Explanations.* Beverly Hills, CA: Sage.

Newport, Frank. 2006. "Church Attendance Lowest in New England, Highest in South." Gallup Organization. April 27, 2006.

Newport, Frank. 2011. "For First Time, Majority of Americans Favor Legal Gay Marriage." Gallup Organization. May 20, 2011. *Available at* http://www.gallup.com/poll/147662/first-time-majority-americans-favor-legal-gay-marriage.aspx.

Nichols, David A. 2007. *A Matter of Justice: Eisenhower and the Beginning of the Civil Rights Revolution.* New York: Simon & Schuster.

Norton, Edward C., Hua Wang, and Chunrong Ai. 2004. "Computing Interaction Effects and Standard Errors in Logit and Probit Models." *The Stata Journal* 4: 154–67.

O'Connell, Martin, and Gretchen Gooding. 2007. "Editing Unmarried Couples in Census Bureau Data." U.S. Census Bureau. *Available at* http://www.census.gov/population/www/documentation/twps07/twps07.html.

O'Connell, Martin, and Daphne Lofquist. 2009. "Counting Same-Sex Couples: Official Estimates and Unofficial Guesses." Paper presented at the Annual Meeting of the Population Association of America, Detroit, MI. April 30–May 2, 2009.

Overby, L. Marvin, and Jay Barth. 2002. "Contact, Community Context, and Public Attitudes toward Gay Men and Lesbians." *Polity* 34: 433–56.

Overton, Ben F. 1984. "A Prescription for the Appellate Caseload Explosion." *Florida State University Law Review* 12: 205–37.

Patton, Dana. 2007. "The Supreme Court and Morality Policy Adoption in the American States: The Impact of Constitutional Context." *Political Research Quarterly* 60: 468–88.

Patterson, Samuel C., and Gregory A. Caldeira. 1985. "The Mobilization of Voters in Congressional Elections." *The Journal of Politics* 47: 490–509.

Penning, James M., and Corwin Smidt. 2002. *Evangelicalism: the Next Generation.* Grand Rapids, MI: Baker Academic.

Perry, H.W. 1991. *Deciding to Decide: Agenda Setting in the United States Supreme Court.* Cambridge, MA: Harvard University Press.

Petrick, Michael J. 1968. "The Supreme Court and Authority Acceptance." *The Western Political Quarterly* 21: 5–19.

Phillips, Frank, and Lisa Wangsness. 2007. "Same-Sex Marriage Ban Advances. Lawmakers OK Item for Ballot, but Hurdle Remains." *The Boston Globe.* January 3: A1.

Phillips, Thomas R. 2003. "Speech: The Constitutional Right to a Remedy." *New York University Law Review* 78: 1309–45.

Pinello, Daniel R. 2006. *America's Struggle for Same-Sex Marriage.* New York: Cambridge University Press.

———. 2003. *Gay Rights and American Law.* New York: Cambridge University Press.

Posner, Richard. 1992. *Sex and Reason.* Cambridge, MA: Harvard University Press.

Quinn, B., Herman Anderson, Martin Bradley, Paul Goetting, and Peggy Shriver. 1982. *Churches and Church Membership in the United States, 1980.* Washington, DC: Glenmary Research Center.

Ranney, Austin. 1976. "Parties in State Politics." In *Politics in the American States.* Herbert Jacob and Kenneth Vines, eds. Third Edition. Boston: Little, Brown.

Redfield-Ortiz, Kaitlyn. 2011. "Government by the People for the People? Representative Democracy, Direct Democracy, and the Unfinished Struggle for Gay Civil Rights." *Arizona State Law Journal* 43: 1367–414.

Riley, Lisa. 2009. "Guv Calls Self 'Moderating Voice' on Many Issues." *The Deseret Morning News,* February 11.

Rosenberg, Gerald N. 2008. *The Hollow Hope: Can Courts Bring about Social Change?* Second Edition. Chicago: The University of Chicago Press.

Rosenberg, Debra, and Karen Breslau. 2004. "Winning the 'Values' Vote." *Newsweek.* November 15: 23.

Rothfeld, Michael, and Tony Barboza. 2008. "Governor Backs Gay Marriage; Schwarzenegger Voices Hope That Proposition 8 Will Be Overturned by Courts as Crowds Continue to Protest." *The Los Angeles Times.* November 10: B1.

Rutherford, Emelie. 2005. "Lawmakers Nix Measure to Prohibit Gay Marriage." *The Boston Herald.* September 15: 16.

Saad, Lydia. 2012. "U.S. Acceptance of Gay/Lesbian Relations Is the New Normal." Gallup Organization. May 14. *Available at* http://www.gallup.com/poll/154634/acceptance-gay-lesbian-relations-new-normal.aspx.

Saphire, Richard B., and Paul Moke. 2008. "The Ideologies of Judicial Selection: Empiricism and the Transformation of the Judicial Selection Debate." *The University of Toledo Law Review* 39: 551–90.

Sasieni, Peter. 1994. "Natural Cubic Splines." *Stata Technical Bulletin* 4(22): 19–22.

Satcher, David. 2001. "The Surgeon General's Call to Action to Promote Sexual Health and Responsible Sexual Behavior." United States Department of Health and Human Services. *Available at* http://www.surgeongeneral.gov/library/calls/sexualhealth/call.pdf.

Scheb, John M. II, and William Lyons. 2001. "Judicial Behavior and Public Opinion: Popular Expectations Regarding the Factors That Influence Supreme Court Decisions." *Political Behavior* 23: 181–93.

——. 2000. "The Myth of Legality and Public Evaluation of the Supreme Court." *Social Science Quarterly* 81: 928–40.

Schulte, Grant. 2010. "Remaining Four Justices Could Face Ouster Efforts." *Des Moines Register.* November 6: A1.

Scott, Jaqueline, and Howard Schuman. 1988. "Attitude Strength and Social Action in the Abortion Dispute." *American Sociological Review* 53: 785–93.

Segal, Jeffrey A., and Harold J. Spaeth. 2002. *The Supreme Court and the Attitudinal Model Revisited.* New York: Cambridge University Press.

Simon, Jonathan. 1992. "'The Long Walk Home' to Politics." [Review of *The Hollow Hope: Can Courts Bring about Social Change?*] *Law & Society Review* 26: 923.

Simon, Matthew G. 2003. "Revisiting *Michigan v. Long* after Twenty Years." *Albany Law Review* 66: 969–91.

Smith, Christian. 1998. *American Evangelicalism: Embattled and Thriving.* Chicago: University of Chicago Press.

Smith, Daniel A., Matthew DeSantis, and Jason Kessel. 2006. "Same-Sex Marriage Ballot Measures and the 2004 Presidential Election." *State and Local Government Review* 38: 78–91.

Smith, Miriam. 2008. *Political Institutions and Lesbian and Gay Rights in the United States and Canada.* New York: Routledge Press.

Spaeth, Harold J., and Jeffrey A. Segal. 1999. *Majority Rule or Minority Will: Adherence to Precedent on the U.S. Supreme Court.* New York: Cambridge University Press.

Squire, Peverill. 2007. "Measuring Legislative Professionalism: The Squire Index Revisited." *State Politics and Policy Quarterly* 7: 211–27.

———. 2008. "Measuring the Professionalization of State Courts of Last Resort." *State Politics and Policy Quarterly* 8: 223–38.

———. 1993. "Professionalization and Public Opinion of State Legislatures." *Journal of Politics* 55: 479–91.

Stein, Marc. 2012. *Rethinking the Gay and Lesbian Movement.* New York: Routledge Press.

Stith, Richard. 1996. "Unconstitutional Constitutional Amendments: The Extraordinary Power of Nepal's Supreme Court." *The American University Journal of International Law & Policy* 11: 47–77.

Strasser, Mark. 2011. *Same-Sex Unions across the United States.* Durham, NC: Carolina Academic Press.

Tarr, G. Alan. 2009. "Balancing the Will of the Public with the Need for Judicial Independence and Accountability: Do Retention Elections Work?" *Missouri Law Review* 74: 605–33.

———. 1998. *Understanding State Constitutions.* Princeton, NJ: Princeton University Press.

Tavernise, Sabrina. 2005. "Judge's Ruling Opens Window for Gay Marriage in New York City." *The New York Times.* February 5: A1.

Ternus, Marsha. 2011. "Remarks." *Albany Law Review* 74: 1569–77.

Thomas, Cal, and Ed Dobson. 1999. *Blinded by Might: Why the Religious Right Can't Save America.* Grand Rapids, MI: Zondervan.

Tyler, Tom R. 1990. *Why People Obey the Law.* New Haven, CT: Yale University Press.

U.S. Census Bureau. 2001. "Households and Families: 2000." *Available at* http://www.census.gov/prod/2001pubs/c2kbr01–8.pdf.

———. 2003. "Married-Couple and Unmarried Partner Households: 2000." *Available at* http://www.census.gov/prod/2003pubs/censr-5.pdf.

Vining, Richard L., Jr., and Teena Wilhelm. 2011. "Measuring Case Salience in State Courts of Last Resort." *Political Research Quarterly* 64: 559–72.

Vogel, Nancy, and Jordan Rau. 2005. "Gov. Vetoes Same-Sex Marriage Bill; Schwarzenegger Rejects 52 Bills, Including Ones to Raise the Minimum Wage and Give Residents Access to Cheaper Prescriptions in Canada." *The Los Angeles Times.* September 30: B3.

Wald, Kenneth D., James W. Button, and Barbara A. Rienzo. 1996. "The Politics of Gay Rights in American Communities: Explaining Antidiscrimination Ordinances and Policies." *American Journal of Political Science* 40: 1152–78.

Walker, Jack L. 1973. "Comment: Problems in Research on the Diffusion of Policy Innovations." *The American Political Science Review* 67: 1186–91.

———. 1969. "The Diffusion of Innovations among the American States." *The American Political Science Review* 63: 880–99.

Warren, Earl. 1977. *The Memoirs of Earl Warren.* New York: Doubleday.

Wasby, Stephen L. 1970. *The Impact of the United States Supreme Court: Some Perspectives.* Homewood, IL: Dorsey Press.

Webster, Peter D. 1995. "Selection and Retention of Judges: Is There One 'Best' Method?" *Florida State University Law Review* 23: 1–34.

Weinberg, Louise. 2003. "Our Marbury." *Virginia Law Review* 89: 1235–412.

Wels, Robert C. 1984. "Reconsidering the Constitutional Relationship between State and Federal Courts: A Critique of *Michigan v. Long.*" *Notre Dame Law Review* 59: 1118–44.

Wenzel, James P., Shaun Bowler, and David J. Lanoue. 2003. "The Sources of Public Confidence in State Courts: Experience and Institutions." *American Politics Research* 31: 191–211.

Williams, Robert F. 1994. "The New Jersey Equal Rights Amendment: A Documentary Sourcebook." *Women's Rights Law Reporter* 16: 69–125.

Winn, James Andrew, Jr., and Eli Paul Mazur. 2004. "Judicial Diversity: Where Independence and Accountability Meet." *Albany Law Review* 67: 775–91.

Winters, Rosemary. 2009. "Guv, at Odds with Most Utahns, Backs Civil Unions for Gays." *The Salt Lake Tribune,* February 9.

Wolfson, Evan. 2004. *Why Marriage Matters: America, Equality, and Gay People's Right to Marry.* New York: Simon & Schuster.

Wright, R. George. 1991. "Could a Constitutional Amendment Be Unconstitutional?" *Loyola University of Chicago Law Review* 22: 741–64.

Zaller, John R. 1992. *The Nature and Origins of Mass Opinion*. New York: Cambridge University Press.

Zeidman, Steven. 2004. "To Elect or Not to Elect: A Case Study of Judicial Selection in New York City, 1977–2002." *University of Michigan Journal of Law Reform* 37: 791–836.

Zorn, Christopher. 2006. "Comparing GEE and Robust Standard Errors for Conditionally Dependent Data." *Political Research Quarterly* 59: 2006: 329–41.

——. 2001. "Generalized Estimation Equation Models for Correlated Data: A Review with Applications." *American Journal of Political Science* 45: 470–90.

TABLE OF AUTHORITIES

Anderson v. King County, 138 P.3d 963 (Wash. 2006), 8n17, 57n3, 101t

Anonymous v. Anonymous, 67 Misc.2d 982 (N.Y. Sup. Ct. 1971), 61n22

Baehr v. Lewin, 852 P.2d 44 (Haw. 1993), 3n2, 11, 20, 25, 50, 57, 66–70, 72, 101t, 114, 136, 145

Baehr v. Miike, No. 91–1394 (Haw. Cir. Ct. 1996), 69–70

Baehr v. Miike, No. 20371, 1999 Haw. LEXIS 391 (1999), 70n

Baker v. Nelson, 191 N.W.2d 185 (Minn. 1971), 8n17, 57, 61–65, 101t

Baker v. Vermont, 744 A.2d 864 (Vt. 1999), 51, 57n4, 72–75, 76, 101t

Batch v. Town of Chapel Hill, 387 S.E.2d 655 (N.C. 1990), 49n68

Bowen v. Gilliard, 483 U.S. 587 (1987), 90n70

Bowers v. Hardwick, 478 U.S. 186 (1986), 67, 78, 191

Bradwell v. Illinois, 83 U.S. 130 (1873), 140n67

Brause v. Bureau of Vital Statistics, No. 3 AN-95–6562 CI (Alaska Super. Ct. 1998), 11, 71–72

Brown v. Board of Education, 347 U.S. 483 (1954), 4, 6n11, 29–30, 32, 34, 38, 139, 140n66, 191

Bush v. Gore, 531 U.S. 98 (2000), 36

Chambers v. Ormiston, 935 A.2d 956 (R.I. 2007), 57n3, 83, 101t

City of Cleburne v. Cleburne Living Center, 473 U.S. 432 (1985), 14, 90n70

Church of Lukumi Babalu Aye v. City of Hialeah, 508 U.S. 520 (1993), 6n11

Clark v. Board of Directors, 24 Iowa 266 (1868), 140n66

Coger v. North Western Union Packet Co ., 37 Iowa 145 (1873), 140n66

Conaway v. Deane, 932 A.2d 571 (Md. 2007), 57n3, 84, 101t, 108n19

De Santo v. Barnsley, 476 A.2d 952 (Pa. Super. 1984), 65n42

Dred Scott v. Sandford, 60 U.S. 393 (1856), 29, 139

Dudgeon v. United Kingdom, 45 Eur. Ct. H.R. 52 (1981), 78n11

Elden v. Sheldon, 46 Cal. 3d 267 (1988), 13n38

Engel v. Vitale, 370 U.S. 421 (1962), 6n11

Florida Wildlife Federation v. State Department of Environmental Regulation, 390 So. 2d 64 (Fla.1980), 88n62

Frontiero v. Richardson, 411 U.S. 677 (1973), 60n19, 89n70

Gajovski v. Gajovski, 610 N.E.2d 431 (Ohio App. 1991), 65n42

Gay Law Students Association v. Pacific Telephone and Telegraph Co., 24 Cal. 3d 458 (1979), 14n43

Gerst v. Marshall, 549 N.W.2d 810 (Iowa 1996), 88n62

Gomillion v. Lightfoot, 364 U.S. 339 (1960), 6n11

Goodridge v. Department of Public Health, 798 N.E.2d 941 (Mass. 2003), 3n2, 9, 11, 22, 47, 57n2, 77, 79–82, 84, 86, 87, 101t, 114, 140, 146, 171, 187, 191, 192, 193, 196

Green v. County School Board of New Kent County, 391 U.S. 430 (1968), 32n21

Griswold v. Connecticut, 381 U.S. 479 (1965), 6n11, 61

Grutter v. Bollinger, 539 U.S. 306 (2003), 6n11

Hardware Mutual Casualty Company v. Premo, 153 Conn. 465 (1966), 88n62

Hernandez v. Robles, 855 N.E.2d 1 (N.Y. 2006), 16,57n3, 84–85, 101t

Hicks v. Miranda, 422 U.S. 332 (1975), 64n59

Hill v. National Collegiate Athletic Association, 7 Cal. 4th 1 (1994), 92n81

In re Marriage Cases, 43 Cal. 4th 757 (2008), 3n1, 10, 13, 16, 57n2, 91–93, 101t, 118, 140, 165n1, 166, 188

In re Ralph, 1 Morris 1 (Iowa 1839), 139

In re Succession of Bacot, 502 So.2d 1118 (La. App. 4th Cir. 1987), 65n42

Jones v. Hallahan, 501 S.W.2d 588 (Ky. Ct. App. 1973), 62–63

Kerrigan v. Commissioner of Public Health, 49 Conn. Sup. 644 (Conn. Super. Ct. 2006), 89

Kerrigan v. Commissioner of Public Health, 289 Conn. 135 (Conn. 2008), 3n1, 10, 14–16, 48n62, 57n2, 88–91, 92, 101t, 117n40, 141, 146

Lawrence v. Texas, 539 U.S. 558 (2003), 4, 16, 77–80, 191

Lewis v. Harris, 908 A.2d 196 (N.J. 2006), 57n4, 86–87, 101t

Loving v. Virginia, 388 U.S. 1 (1967), 12, 59, 60n18, 61, 118

Lujan v. Defenders of Wildlife, 504 U.S. 555 (1992), 88n61

Lyng v. Castillo, 477 U.S. 635 (1986), 90n70

Mandel v. Bradley, 432 U.S. 173 (1977), 64n39

Marbury v. Madison, 5 U.S. 137 (1803), 31n17, 36

Massachusetts Board of Retirement v. Murgia, 427 U.S. 307 (1976), 89n70

McConnell v. Nooner, 547 F.2d 54 (8th Cir. 1976), 65

Michigan v. Long, 463 U.S. 1032 (1983), 48–49

Morrison v. Sadler, 821 N.E.2d 15 (Ind. Ct. App. 2005), 57n3, 83

Opinion of the Justices to the Senate, 802 N.E.2d 565 (Mass. 2004), 3n2, 9, 11, 57n2, 81, 93, 146, 171

Palko v. Connecticut, 302 U.S. 319 (1937), 58, 68n49

Perez v. Sharp, 32 Cal.2d 711 (1948), 6, 12, 14, 59n14, 91, 118

Perry v. Brown, Nos. 10–16696 and 11–16577 (9th Cir. Feb. 7, 2012), 95n95

Perry v. Schwarzenegger, 704 F. Supp. 2d 921 (N.D. Cal. 2010), 95n95

Plessy v. Ferguson, 163 U.S. 537 (1896), 191

Roe v. Wade, 410 U.S. 113 (1973), 4, 6, 29, 30, 38

Romer v. Evans, 517 U.S. 620 (1996), 15, 16

Sail'er Inn v. Kirby, 5 Cal. 3d 1 (1971), 13–14

San Antonio Independent School District v. Rodriguez, 411 U.S. 1 (1973), 90n70

Singer v. Hara, 522 P.2d 1187 (Wash. App. 1974), 63

Sojourner v. New Jersey Department of Human Services, 828 A.2d 306 (N.J. 2003), 86n52

Standhardt v. Superior Court, 77 P. 3d 451 (Ariz. App. 2003), 57n3, 83

State v. Lynch, 796 P.2d 1150 (Okla. 1990), 49n68

Strauss v. Horton, 46 Cal.4th 364 (2009), 165n1, 166, 197

Texas v. Johnson, 491 U.S. 397 (1989), 36n39

Tumeo v. University of Alaska, No. 4FA-94-43 Civil (Alaska Super. Ct., Jan. 11, 1995), 71

United States v. Virginia, 518 U.S. 515 (1996), 6n11, 89n70

Varnum v. Brien, 763 N.W.2d 862 (Iowa 2009), 3n2, 7, 10, 57n2, 93–94, 100–103, 118, 133, 139–141, 191

Warfield v. Peninsula Golf & Country Club, 10 Cal. 4th 594 (1995), 13n38

Webster v. Reproductive Health Services, 492 U.S. 490 (1989), 6n12, 36n39

Williams v. Garcetti, 5 Cal. 4th 561 (1993), 13n38

Worcester v. Georgia, 31 U.S. 515 (1832), 36

INDEX

Abortion, 138, 153
Alaska, 11
    Brause v. Bureau of Vital Statistics, 11, 70–72
    Constitution of, 70–72
Alaska Ballot Measure 2 of 1998, 72
Albin, Barry T., 86
Amendment procedures. *See* State constitutional
    amendment procedures
Amendments prohibiting SSM. *See* State
    constitutional amendments prohibiting SSM
Amestoy, Jeffrey L., 73–75

Baehr, Nina, 67, 68
Baehr v. Lewin, 66–70
    backlash to, 50, 72–73
    cited by other state courts, 70, 140
    equal rights amendment and, 20
    impact of, 11
    and public opinion, 145
    sex discrimination and, 20, 50, 114
Baehr v. Miike, 69. *See also Baehr v. Lewin*
Baker, Richard, 61
Baldacci, John, 94
Barnes, Michael P., 83
Barwick, Paul, 63
Baum, Lawrence, 99, 110–11, 121
Boies, David, 95
Bonauto, Mary, 25, 77
Bonneau, Chris W., 43
Brace, Paul, 26, 109, 113, 173
Brause, Jay, 70, 71
Brennan, William J., Jr., 7n14
Bush, George W., 193–94

Cady, Mark S., 94, 103, 139–41
Caldeira, Gregory A., 149
California
    Domestic Partner Rights and Responsibilities
        Act (Assembly Bill 205) of 2003, 8–10,
        12–14, 16–17, 92

Proposition 8, 7, 10, 44, 95, 165–66, 187, 188,
    197
    recent developments in, 87–89, 91–93
California Supreme Court, 118
    Perez v. Sharp, 6, 12, 14, 91, 118
    In re Marriage Cases, 3, 10, 16, 92n85, 93, 118,
        166, 188
    Strauss v. Horton, 166, 196
Cann, Damon M., 109, 149–50
Canon, Bradley C., 99, 110–11, 121
Chang, Kevin S.C., 69
Choi, Stephen J., 137, 176, 177
Civil union law, 100–101, 101t
    in California, 165, 166
    in Connecticut, 8–10, 12, 14–17, 88–91, 93
    in Massachusetts, 9, 10, 81
    in Vermont, 75, 76, 117, 135, 156
Civil unions
    amendments banning, 45–46t
    public support for, 193–95, 194t
Cloglog model of SSM decisions, 135–37, 136t
Complementary log-log model of SSM decisions.
    See Cloglog model of SSM decisions
Connecticut, 14
    civil union law in, 8–10, 12, 14–17, 88–91, 93
    Kerrigan v. Commissioner of Public Health, 3, 10,
        15–16, 89–91, 141, 146
    recent developments in, 87–93
Constitutions, state. *See also specific states*
    ages of, 118, 119–20t, 120–21
    design of, 20–21
    features of, 177–78
    procedures for amending, 44, 45–46t, 46–47
Courthouse democracy, 7, 163, 164, 185, 190
Courts, state. *See also specific topics*
    attributes of, 176
    decisions in 1970s, 60–65
    differences between various
        constitutional, 114–21
        environmental/ideological, 121–33

Courts, state. *See also specific topics (Cont.)*
  in institutional design, 4–5, 108–14
  in judicial ideology, 104–8
  factors that influence their impact on
      government policy. *See* Judicial policy
      development
  federal courts contrasted with, 38–39, 47–51
    constitutional amendment procedures, 44,
        45–46t, 46–47
    selection and retention of judges, 39–44. *See
        also under* Judges
    social and political environment, 51–53
  impact depends on contexts in which judges
      are operating, 17
  public trust in their decisions on morality
      policy issues, 150–55
Cuomo, Andrew, 86

Dahl, Robert A., 29
Dancel, Genora, 67, 68
Defense of Marriage Act, 76
Democratization of state courts and constitutional
      systems, 27. *See also* Elections, Initiatives
Desegregation. *See* Racial discrimination
Direct initiatives, 44–46
Douglas, Jim, 94
Due Process Clause (U.S. Constitution)
  Baehr v. Lewin and, 69
  Baker v. Nelson and, 61, 65
  Bowers v. Hardwick and, 67, 78
  consensual sodomy and, 67
  Equal Protection Clause and, 59
  Lawrence v. Texas and, 16, 78, 79
  Loving v. Virginia and, 59, 61
  nature of, 49, 58, 79, 85
Due process clauses, state, 58
  of Alaska Constitution, 71
  of California Constitution, 91
  of Connecticut Constitution, 58, 89
  of Hawaii Constitution, 67, 69
  of Massachusetts Constitution, 77, 80
  of New York Constitution, 84, 85
Dugan, Gene, 70, 71
Dworkin, Ronald, 15

Elections, judicial, 7–8. *See also* Electoral
      incentives; Judges: methods of initial
      selection and retention of; Public
      support: for decisions of state institutions
  and the impact of state supreme courts, 39,
      41–44
Electoral incentives, 7–8, 104, 109–10, 172, 174,
      176. *See also* Judges: methods of initial
      selection and retention of
Endurance stage (judicial policy development),
      18, 18f, 21. *See also under* Policy
      endurance

Environmental differences across states, social and
      political, 51–52
  activity of interest groups influencing supreme
      courts, 53
  ideology of citizenry, 52, 122. *See also* Public
      attitudes about SSM
  ideology of political institutions, 52–53. *See
      also* Institutional ideology
Environmental explanations for the adoption of
      amendments, 178–80
Equal Protection Clause (14th Amendment to
      U.S. Constitution), 15, 16, 49, 51, 59, 61,
      65, 74
Equal protection clauses, state, 9, 60
  in Alaska Constitution, 11, 70, 71
  in California Constitution, 12, 13, 91, 92
  in Connecticut Constitution, 12,
      89–91, 117
  in Hawaii Constitution, 11, 67–70
  in Iowa Constitution, 94, 103, 139–40
  in Massachusetts Constitution, 80
  in New Jersey Constitution, 86
  in New York Constitution, 84, 85
Equal Rights Amendment (ERA), federal, 61
Equal rights amendments (ERAs), state, 117
  in Connecticut Constitution, 117
  court decisions and, 20–21, 27, 114, 116–17,
      139
  in Hawaii Constitution, 20
  in Iowa Constitution, 103, 140
  in Massachusetts Constitution, 77, 114,
      134–35
  permissive institutions and, 117, 133–34
  states with and without, 49–50, 114, 115–16t,
      117–18
  in Washington State Constitution, 63, 117
Evangelical population of various states, 127,
      128–29t, 129–30

Faubus, Orval, 32
Federalism, judicial, 47–51
Felkner, Tom, 188
Foley, Dan, 66, 69
Fourteenth Amendment to the U.S. Constitution,
      49. *See also* Due Process Clause; Equal
      Protection Clause

Gay & Lesbian Advocates & Defenders (GLAD),
      ix, 25, 77
Gay population in various states, 130, 131–32t,
      132–33
Gender discrimination. *See* Sex discrimination
George, Ronald M., 12–13, 92*n*85, 93, 104*n*85,
      166
Gibson, James L., 149
GLAD (Gay & Lesbian Advocates & Defenders),
      ix, 25, 77

Goodridge, Hillary, 77
Goodridge, Julie, 77
Graffeo, Victoria A., 84, 85
Greaney, John M., 77, 114, 116
Green, Mary E., 71

Hall, Kermit L., 6n10
Hall, Melinda Gann, 26, 43, 109, 113, 149, 173
Hamilton, Alexander, 28–29
Hawaii Constitution, 59, 68, 134
Hawaii Constitutional Amendment 2 of 1998, 70
Hawaii Supreme Court, 20, 68–70. *See also Baehr v. Lewin*
Hibbing, John R., 173
High court professionalization. *See* Professionalization
Huntsman, Jon, Jr., 194–95

Indirect initiatives, 44–46
Initiation stage. *See* Policy initiation
Initiatives, 7. *See also* California: Proposition 8
    direct vs. indirect, 44–46
Institutional ideology, 122, 124, 125–26t, 126–27, 136t, 137. *See also under* Courts, state: differences between various
Interest groups, 21, 36–37, 53
    conservative, 53, 184
    LGBT, 17, 35, 53, 66, 72–73, 76, 122
    liberal, 7
Interpretivivism vs. noninterpretivism, 49–51
Iowa, 133, 139
    liberalism vs. conservatism, 100–101, 103, 117, 133, 139
Iowa Constitution, 94, 117, 140
    equal protection clause, 94, 103, 139–40
    equal rights amendment, 103, 140
    history, 103, 139, 140
    Marriage Amendment, 102
Iowa Supreme Court, 93–94, 100, 103, 139–40
    history, 139–40
    justices voted out of office after requiring marriage equality, 7, 10–11, 191
    liberalism vs. conservatism, 139–41
    retention elections, 7–8, 102
    Varnum v. Brien, 7, 10–11, 93–94, 100–103, 118, 139–41, 191

Jackson, Andrew, 36
Jefferson, Thomas, 36
Judges. *See also specific topics*
    judicial ideology, 104–8
    methods of initial selection and retention of, 27, 39–44, 40–41t, 102, 109–12t, 149–50, 153, 174, 189. *See also* Electoral incentives; Public support for decisions of state institutions
Judicial elections. *See* Elections

Judicial policy development
    factors influencing, 188t, 188–89
    stages of, 18f, 18–21
Judicial power. *See also* Policy legitimation
    constitutional amendments as effort to curb, 170–72
    constraints on, 28–35
    overcoming the, 35–38
Judicial professionalization. *See* Professionalization
Judicial selection and retention methods. *See* Electoral incentives; Judges: methods of initial selection and retention of

Keck, Thomas, 11, 72n71, 145
Kennedy, Anthony, 78–80
Kentucky Court of Appeals, 62, 67
Kerrigan, Elizabeth, 89
Klarman, Michael J., 34n31

Lambda Legal, 66, 69, 76n1
Legislatures, state, 178. *See also* Professionalization: state legislative
    legislative attributes and behavior, 178. *See also* Professionalization: state legislative
    public trust in their decisions on morality policy issues, 150–55
Legitimacy theory, 36, 147–51, 163. *See also* Policy legitimation
Legitimation stage (judicial policy development), 18f, 18–21. *See also* Policy legitimation
Levinson, Steven H., 68, 69
Ling-Cohan, Doris, 84

Marriage. *See also* Same-sex marriage (SSM) decisions
    definitions of, 61–62, 73
    interracial, 12, 59–62, 118
Marshall, John, 36, 79, 80
Marshall, Margaret H., 192
Maryland Court of Appeals, 84
Massachusetts, 76–77, 79–82
    civil union law in, 9, 10, 81
Massachusetts General Court, 81–82
Massachusetts Supreme Judicial Court, 9
    Goodridge v. Department of Public Health, 11, 47, 77, 79–82, 87, 114, 116, 146, 187, 191–93, 196
McCann, Michael W., 34–35
McConnell, James, 61
Merit system. *See* Judges: methods of initial selection and retention of
Michalski, Peter A., 71
Miike, Lawrence H., 69
Minnesota, 133–35

Minnesota Supreme Court, 62, 113, 136
  Baker v. Nelson, 57, 61–65
Murray, Susan, 72

Neo-institutional approach, 26
New Jersey
  Domestic Partnership Act of 2004, 86
  Law Against Discrimination of 1991, 86
  Supreme Court, 86–87
New York Court of Appeals, 84–87
Noninterpretivism, 50–51

O'Connor, Sandra Day, 16, 48
Olson, Theodore, 95

Palmer, Richard N., 15, 16, 48, 91, 117
Paterson, David, 85
Peterson, C. Donald, 61, 62
Pinello, Daniel R., 25, 104–5, 113n35, 146
Pittman, Patty Jenkins, 89
Policy endurance, 166, 186–87, 188t, 189. *See
    also* Endurance stage; State constitutional
    amendments prohibiting SSM:
    explanations for the adoption of
  biggest obstacle to, 166
  defined, 166
  endurance stage (judicial policy development),
    18, 18f, 21
Policy initiation, 99–104, 138, 175
  defined, 99
  initiation stage (judicial policy development),
    18f, 18–19
Policy innovation. *See also* Policy initiation
  environmental and institutional barriers to,
    138–39. *See also specific barriers*
Policy legitimation, 142–43, 145–47, 163–64.
    See also Legitimacy theory; Legitimation
    stage; Public support for decisions of state
    institutions
  state courts and, 147–50
Poritz, Deborah T., 87
Posner, Richard, 15
Precedents from out-of-state courts, following,
    14–16, 136t, 136–37. *See also* Public
    attitudes about SSM: and recognition of
    SSMs from other states
Professionalization
  judicial/high court, 104, 172, 173, 186
    defined, 110, 172
    and impact of court decisions, 181–82t,
      183–86, 189
    impact on court decisions, 19, 112–13, 133,
      139, 169, 173–74, 183–84,
      186, 188t
    institutional differences across states and,
      110, 111–12t, 112–14, 133
    measures of, 173

movement toward, 173
  public opinion and, 173, 176
state legislative, 173, 178, 184
Proposition 8. *See* California: Proposition 8
Public attitudes about SSM, 122, 123–24t, 124,
    126, 193, 194f
  and recognition of SSMs from other states, 143,
    144–45t, 145–47
Public support
  for civil unions, 193–95, 194t
  for decisions of state institutions,
    155–64
Public trust in state institutions to decide morality
    policy issues, 150–55

Quasi-suspect class, 15
  sexual orientation as, 9, 14–16, 89–92, 117

Racial discrimination, 139–40. *See also* Marriage:
    interracial
  Brown v. Board of Education, 29–30, 32, 34, 38
Ramil, Mario R., 70
Rational basis test, 15, 16, 59–60, 67, 80, 84, 86
Regional effects on policy diffusion, 180–81
Religiosity of citizenry
  and support for decisions of state institutions,
    159
  of various states, 127, 128–29t, 129–30
Rhode Island Supreme Court, 83
Robinson, Beth, 72, 76n1
Rosenberg, Debra, 192
Rosenberg, Gerald N., 29–35

Same-sex households in various states, percentage
    of, 130, 131–32t, 132–33
Same-sex marriage (SSM) decisions. *See also*
    Courts, state: decisions in 1970s; *specific
    topics*
  a descriptive typology of, 133–35, 134t
  early, 57–58. *See also* Alaska: Constitution of;
      Hawaii Supreme Court
  legal challenges to SSM bans, 58–60
  modeling the timing of, 135–38
Satcher, David, 15
Scalia, Antonin, 79
Schwarzenegger, Arnold, 171n15, 187
Segregation. *See* Racial discrimination
Sex discrimination
  Baehr v. Lewin and, 11, 20, 50, 68
  Conaway v. Deane and, 84
  ERAs and, 20
  federal vs. state constitutional protection
      against, 49
  Goodridge v. Department of Public Health and,
      114
  Sail'er Inn v. Kirby and, 13
  Singer v. Hara and, 63

variation in levels of state constitutional
    protection against, 20, 57, 114, 115–16t
Singer, John F., 63
Smith, Miriam, 118, 120
Smith, Robert S., 84
Squire, Peverill, 171–72
SSM decisions. *See* Same-sex marriage (SSM)
    decisions
State constitutional amendment procedures, 44,
    45–46t, 46–47
State constitutional amendments prohibiting
    SSM, 165–66, 168–69
  dates of initial consideration and adoption of,
    166, 167–68t
  explanations for the adoption of, 174–75, 181–87
    constitutional features, 177–78
    court attributes, 176
    court-curbing, 170–72
    environmental, 178–80
    judicial behavior, 176–77
    judicial selection and retention methods,
      174. *See also under* Judges
    legislative attributes, 178
    .professionalization of state supreme courts,
      172–74
    regional effects, 180–81
  politics of, 169–70
State constitutions. *See* Constitutions
State courts. *See* Courts
State legislatures. *See* Legislatures
Stevens, John Paul, 48
Supreme Court, U.S. *See also* Courts, state: federal
    courts contrasted with
  lack of formal implementation powers, 31–32
  lack of judicial independence, 30–31
  structural limitations that constrain the power
    of, 30–32
Supreme courts, state. *See also* Courts, state
  as key government institutions driving SSM
    policy, 3
  professionalization of, 172–74
  understanding the impact of, 17–21
Suspect classification/suspect class, 13, 15, 60, 74.
    See also Quasi-suspect class
  gender as, 94
  sexual orientation as, 9, 13, 15, 16, 67–69,
    85, 92

Tarr, G. Alan, 169
Ternus, Marsha K., 102–3, 191–92
Theiss-Morse, Elizabeth, 173
Traynor, Roger J., 91
Tumeo v. University of Alaska, 71

University of Alaska, 71

Vermont, 50–51
  civil union law in, 75, 76, 117, 135, 156
Vermont Constitution, Common Benefits Clause
    of, 51, 59, 73–75
Vermont Supreme Court, *Baker v. Vermont*, 51,
    72–75
  reactions to, 76n1

Washington Court of Appeals, 63–64, 117
White, Byron, 67–68
Wilhelm, Teena, 109, 149–50
Wolfson, Evan, 66n43, 69, 72

Printed in the USA/Agawam, MA
January 29, 2014

584721.064